THE EPISTLES OF JOHN

THE
EPISTLES
OF
JOHN

James Montgomery Boice

Ministry
Resources
Library

Zondervan Publishing House • Grand Rapids, MI

TO HIM
*who has come
and has given us understanding,
to know Him who is true*

THE EPISTLES OF JOHN: AN EXPOSITIONAL COMMENTARY
Copyright © 1979 by The Zondervan Corporation
Grand Rapids, Michigan

MINISTRY RESOURCES LIBRARY is an imprint of Zondervan
Publishing House, 1415 Lake Drive, S.E.,
Grand Rapids, Michigan 49506

Library of Congress Cataloging in Publication Data

Boice, James Montgomery, 1938–
    Epistles of John.

    Bibliography: p.
    Includes indexes.
    1. Bible. N.T. Epistles of John—Commentaries. I. Title
BS2805.3.B64   227'.94'07   79-16214
ISBN 0-310-21531-5

All scripture quotations, unless otherwise noted, are taken from the HOLY BIBLE: NEW INTERNATIONAL VERSION (North American Edition). Copyright © 1978 by The International Bible Society. Used by permission of Zondervan Bible Publishers.

Printed in the United States of America

85 86 87 88 89 90 91 92 / 14 13 12 11 10 9 8 7 6 5 4

Contents

Preface

The dominant theme of 1 John is "Christian Assurance," as anyone who has studied the book knows. But it is a unique kind of assurance, and it has far more bearing upon how we live our lives than the words themselves would indicate.

I must admit that when I first began a study of 1, 2, and 3 John, I thought of assurance mostly in abstract terms. That is, I believed that we should be assured of salvation primarily because God declares that those who believe on the Lord Jesus Christ possess it. "We accept man's testimony, but God's testimony is greater" (1 John 5:9). As I studied the book, however, I began to see that while this is undoubtedly true, nevertheless, the apostle John also works on a more practical level, showing that the Christian can be assured of his salvation in that God has brought about fundamental changes in his life. He has given him a sure knowledge of himself in Jesus Christ. This involves *truth*. He has given him a desire to pursue and obey the commandments of Christ. This involves *righteousness*. He has given him a new relationship with other believers. This involves *love*.

Moreover, as I continued my studies, I saw that it is impossible to overestimate the importance of these three elements in the Christian life. Truth! Righteousness! Love! We need them all. Indeed, it is only when all three are present that any of us can claim to have entered into a well-rounded, vital, and growing Christian experience.

Love without righteousness is immorality, though today in

9

Preface

some religious circles it is called the "new morality." Righteousness without doctrine is legalism. This is the kind of religion that existed in Christ's day in Judaism and against which He was so outspoken. Doctrine without love is a bitter orthodoxy. It is the kind of truth that is rigorously perfect, in a sense, but which does not win anyone. All three of these elements must be present in the life of any true and growing Christian. Consequently, it is my earnest wish that this study might be used of the Holy Spirit to contribute to such growth in the lives of many persons.

The chapters that appear here were presented in somewhat similar form to the evening congregations of Tenth Presbyterian Church in Philadelphia from September, 1974, to May, 1975. The following summer they were aired in a more popular form over the nationally heard radio program *The Bible Study Hour*, upon which I have been privileged to be the speaker for the past eleven years.

I am deeply grateful to the officers and congregation of Tenth Presbyterian Church for allowing me to spend much of my time in this kind of research and writing. I trust that they also profit from it. I am thankful to my secretary, Miss Caecilie M. Foelster, who has laboriously typed the manuscript, assisted in the editing, and carefully speeded the book through several stages of production. May the Lord Himself, who is the only source of all true knowledge, bless this study of this important portion of His Word to all who use it.

James Montgomery Boice

Introduction to 1 John

It is possible to read a book without understanding the purpose for which it was written. Indeed, much reading is done on this level by many persons. But it is not possible to *study* a book without dealing with this primary question.

This is true of any document. If an article has been written to argue a legal point, we would not turn to it to find religious inspiration. It was just not written for that purpose. Again, if a verse was composed as love poetry, we would not turn to it for its narrative value, as we would to a novel, for instance. Instead, we would turn to it to discover and in some sense experience the emotions that love poetry conveys. It is the same in approaching the Bible. Each book of the Bible has a purpose, in most cases a distinct purpose. So it is of value, in fact it is essential, to determine what that purpose is in the case of the book to be studied. In the case of John's first letter this is also extremely rewarding. For the problems which John faced in his day are strikingly the problems of our own time, and the objectives which he sets before himself are objectives which Christians today must also have if they are to grow in grace and are to continue to present the authentic message of the Word of God to their contemporaries.

Christian Assurance

So why was 1 John written? The first answer to this question (and the clearest) is that which John himself gives toward the end of his letter. It is expressed in 5:13. "I write these things to you who

11

believe in the name of the Son of God so that you may know that you have eternal life." The emphasis is upon the word "know." Those to whom it is addressed are Christians. Thus, John's first purpose is to bring Christians to the absolute assurance of their salvation.

The nature of this purpose is seen in sharp relief when it is contrasted with the equally explicit statement of John's purpose in writing his Gospel. Toward the end of the Gospel John says that there were many other things that Jesus did which he has not recorded but that "these are written that you may believe that Jesus is the Christ, the Son of God, and that by believing you may have life in his name" (John 20:31). Those to whom he was writing were not yet Christians (though we are not to suppose by this that Christians did not use the Gospel), and his purpose was to lead these to faith. In his first Epistle, his purpose is to lead those who already believe to a deeper understanding of the faith and to confidence in that which they already possess. Of these distinct purposes Plummer notes, "The one is an historical, the other an ethical statement of the truth. The one sets forth the acts and words which prove that Jesus is the Christ, the Son of God; the other sets forth the acts and words which are obligatory upon those who believe this great truth."[1]

That believers can know and should know that they are children of God is not a teaching that is unique to John, of course. But it is clearly one that needed to be stated forcefully in his day. Earlier, Paul had written of the Christian's assurance to those at Thessalonica, "because our gospel came to you not simply with words, but also with power, with the Holy Spirit and with *deep conviction*" (1 Thess. 1:5). The author of Hebrews wrote, "since we have a great priest over the house of God, let us draw near to God with a sincere heart in *full assurance* of faith, having our hearts sprinkled to cleanse us from a guilty conscience and having our bodies washed with pure water" (Heb. 10:21, 22). Colossians says that we should be "encouraged in heart and united in love, so that [we] may have the full riches of *complete understanding,* in order that [we] may know the mystery of God, namely, Christ" (Col. 2:2). Isaiah wrote that "the fruit of righteousness will be peace; the effect of righteousness will be quiet-

---

[1] A. Plummer, *The Epistles of S. John* (New York: Cambridge University Press, 1954), p. 35.

ness and *confidence forever*" (Isa. 32:17). When we put these phrases together we find that God intends for Christians to have a full conviction and assurance of faith, that they are to have a settled understanding, and that this is to be true forever. Yet when we have said this, we must admit that it is only in John's letter (and not in the others) that this becomes a major and not merely an incidental reason for writing.

What caused John to write in this fashion, elaborating upon what other biblical writers seem almost to assume? As we read the Epistle we discover that it was due to a situation in the church to which he was writing, produced by the fact that shortly before this some of the more talented or intellectual members had withdrawn from the fellowship to found a new one (2:19ff.) They claimed that it represented an improvement on what had been taught before. Naturally many of the other members of the church were confused. Were the new teachers right? Was the old teaching to be abandoned? Where did the truth lie? Had they been Christians all along, or were their former beliefs only a preparation for this higher and only authentic form of Christianity? In short, how could one know when he was truly a child of God? How could a believer know when he was born again?

To these questions John replies, first, with the categorical statement that a Christian can know and should know that he has eternal life and, second, with three practical tests by which an individual can settle the matter.

The statement

The statement that a Christian can know he has eternal life is that already quoted: "I write these things to you who believe in the name of the Son of God so that you may know that you have eternal life" (5:13). But to this many similar statements found throughout the letter may be added: "This is how we know we are in him" (2:5); "I write to you, dear children, because you have known the Father" (2:13); "But you have an anointing from the Holy One, and all of you know the truth" (2:20); "I do not write to you because you do not know the truth, but because you do know it" (2:21); "Dear friends, now we are children of God" (3:2); "We know that we have passed from death to life" (3:14); "We belong to the truth" (3:19); "We know that he lives in us" (3:24); "You, dear children, are from God" (4:4); "We

13

know that we live in him and he in us" (4:13); "This is how we know that we love the children of God" (5:2); "We know. . . . We know. . . . We know" (5:18-20).

If these are true statements and if they apply to Christians living at all periods of history, as John obviously implies, then they are of great importance today, for there has hardly been an age in which confusion and uncertainty have been more dominant. Today's world puts a high premium on knowledge and on the confidence it is supposed to bring. But knowledge has outstripped the ability of most persons to absorb it, except in one or more highly specialized areas; and even in the area of a person's specialty change comes so rapidly that what was apparently true during the years of the student's preparation is often outmoded before he enters middle age. Can a person really know anything for certain in such circumstances? Are there any absolutes? Is there anything that will be true, not only today, but tomorrow and the day after that as well? John replies that in spiritual matters, which are the most important anyway, there can be certainty. And if this is true, then this is obviously a message that our age (as well as every other age) needs to hear.

The tests

It is obvious that such a statement can easily lead to presumption, however. That is, a person can claim a certainty which is in fact unfounded. Or, to put it in John's words, he can claim to be a child of God when actually he is not or, which is worse, when he is a child of the devil. How can a person who claims to be a believer guard against such presumption?

In answer to this problem John offers three tests which in one form or another are repeated again and again throughout the letter. They are, as distinguished by Law and subsequently restated by Stott: the *moral* test (the test of righteousness or obedience), the *social* test (the test of love), and the *doctrinal* test (the test of belief in Jesus Christ). The first is the test of practical righteousness in the believer's life. It does not mean that the Christian must be without sin—indeed, John says that the one professing to be without sin deceives himself and makes God a liar (1:8, 10)—but it does mean that he must be progressing in righteousness so that his profession is increasingly matched by his conduct. Any claim to a higher experience of Christianity that is not

14

matched by superior moral conduct is to be rejected (1:6). The second test is the test of the Christian's relationship to other Christians. Does he love them? Since God is love and since love comes from Him, anyone claiming to know God but failing to show love for others is either self-deceived or is attempting to deceive. The third test is theological, for it is John's claim that no one who fails to believe that the preexistent Son of God, the Second Person of the Trinity, became flesh at a fixed point in time and history and died for our sin can be a Christian.

On the one hand, these tests challenge presumption. They are tests by which anyone who claims to be a Christian may examine himself to determine whether he is actually a child of God or not. On the other hand, these tests can also (and should also) lead a Christian into that holy boldness in his approach to God which is his privilege and right as a Christian and can endow his speech with that note of authority which he needs as he attempts to bear witness to other persons.

A HISTORICAL FAITH

The second purpose John had in writing his letter is related to the first one, but it is rightly considered a distinct purpose in that by it John was dealing with a new and dangerous movement in his day and was warning Christians about it. The movement was what today we would call an early form of Gnosticism, and John's objective in writing against it is to stress the historical origins of Christianity.

It is hard to speak of the precise nature of Gnosticism in John's day, because Gnosticism was always a hydra-headed faith, difficult to describe, and because the only documents which we have concerning Gnosticism date from a much later period in church history. Nevertheless, from the statements in the letter and from traditions which relate to this period, several characteristics of the movement seem certain. First, there was the principle which Ross calls "the supremacy of the intellect and the superiority of mental enlightenment to faith and conduct."[2] The Gnostics put themselves forward as being "the knowing ones," which is the essential meaning of the word "Gnostic," while at the same time insisting that salvation was primarily by knowledge, that is,

---

[2]Alexander Ross, *The Epistles of James and John, NIC* (Grand Rapids: Eerdmans, 1954), p. 115.

by an initiation into the mystical and allegedly superior knowledge they possessed. In most forms of Gnosticism this meant that the importance of moral conduct was denied. The Gnostic might say that he had no sin, or that what he did was not sin, or that he could have fellowship with God even though he continued sinning. In view of this characteristic John's insistence that Christians are the true "knowing ones" and that their lives must be marked by righteous conduct is understandable.

The second characteristic of the Gnostic system was its belief in the radical and unbridgable distinction between spirit and matter coupled with the conviction that matter was inherently evil and that spirit alone was good. This view was held in common by most other systems of thought at this period. On the one hand, it clearly accounted for the denial of the importance of the moral life, as already noted, for salvation was in the realm of the spirit or mind, which alone was good. On the other hand, it produced a type of philosophical religion which was divorced from concrete history. Here, obviously, Gnosticism came into conflict with authentic Christianity, for, given this system, any real incarnation of the Son of God was impossible. If matter is evil, then God could not have taken a human body upon Himself. And if this is so, then the incarnation of God in Christ must have been in appearance only. In some forms of allegedly Christian Gnosticism the Incarnation was therefore expressed by saying that the spirit of God merely came upon the man Jesus at the time of His baptism, remained with Him during the years of His ministry, and then deserted Him just before His crucifixion. In Asia these views were associated with a Gnostic named Cerinthus who is said to have been both a contemporary and an opponent of the apostle John.[3]

To have adopted this view would have made Christianity popular in the Greek world of the first century no doubt, but John correctly saw that to do so would have destroyed the essential content of the faith. If Christianity is no more than a set of

---

[3]We learn about Cerinthus from the historian Eusebius (*Ecclesiastical History*, iii. 28, 6; iv. 14. 6) and from Irenaeus, who quotes Polycarp as having said that "John, the disciple of the Lord, going to bathe at Ephesus, and perceiving Cerinthus within, rushed out of the bath-house without bathing, exclaiming " 'Let us fly, lest even the bath-house fall down, because Cerinthus, the enemy of the truth is within'" (*Adversus Haereses*, iii. 3. 4).

ideas, then it is no more valid than any other philosophy. Its truths are relative (true now or true for some people, but not true in any absolute sense); and its values are pragmatic (good only if they help). Such a system can obviously be phased out. On the other hand, if, as John teaches, Christianity is more than ideas—if it is something unique which God has done in history—then it has a claim to being true for everyone and true for all time. Moveover, it requires that a person become conformed to the revelation of God which it embodies rather than that the faith constantly be readjusted to the individual or to "modern" thinking.

This concern is uppermost in John's mind at many points throughout the Epistle but nowhere more than in the opening verses in which he stresses faith's historical character. "That which was from the beginning, which we have heard, which we have seen with our eyes, which we have looked at and our hands have touched—this we proclaim concerning the Word of life. The life appeared; we have seen it and testify to it, and we proclaim to you the eternal life, which was with the Father and has appeared to us. We proclaim to you what we have seen and heard, so that you also may have fellowship with us" (1:1-3).

This same note needs to be sounded today, whenever the historical basis of the faith is questioned or salvation is imagined to consist in anything other than that which God has done in Jesus for the redemption and sanctification of those who believe on Christ and follow Him.

THE NEW COMMANDMENT

A third purpose for the writing of 1 John is to elaborate upon Christ's new commandment: "A new commandment I give you: Love one another" (John 13:34).

This verse from John 13 is in the midst of a narrative of the events that took place at the Last Supper, and it is this narrative that throws light on the third reason why 1 John needed to be written. The chapter is a record of Christ's farewell words to the disciples and of their puzzled and almost unbelieving reaction to His disclosure of His departure from them. The disciples had been with the Lord for three years. During this time they had grown to love Him and to know of His love for them. They had left everything to follow Him. He was their life. Now, suddenly

17

(although He had tried to tell them of it before), they are told that He is leaving: "My children, I will be with you only a little longer. You will look for me, and just as I told the Jews, so I tell you now: Where I am going, you cannot come" (13:33). This statement must have hit them like a thunderbolt, for they became entirely wrapped up in it and heard little He said from that point on. We know this because, in the narrative which follows, their questions always come back to this point and do not relate to what Christ has said in the meantime.

Following the announcement of His departure, Jesus went on to give the "new commandment." But when He paused for breath, Peter immediately returned to the earlier topic—"Lord, where are you going?" (v. 36). Jesus interrupted His instructions about the new commandment and went back to explain what was happening.

A little while later Thomas, who was quieter than Peter but who was thinking exactly the same thing, blurted out, "Lord, we don't know where you are going; so how can we know the way?" (John 14:5). Philip added, "Lord, show us the Father and that will be enough for us" (v. 8); that is, "You do not need to go away; just give us a theophany." These statements indicate how the minds of the disciples were working at this time and show that not one of the disciples really heard and understood this new and great commandment of the Lord Jesus.

Jesus went to the cross, rose from the dead, ascended into heaven, and then, years later, spoke again to the apostle John through the Holy Spirit to explain, in a manner that was to be recorded for the church in all ages, what this commandment is all about. Thus, in his first Epistle John writes that Christians are to love one another. He writes: "But if anyone obeys his word, God's love is truly made complete in him" (2:5); "Do not love the world" (2:15); "Anyone who does not do what is right is not a child of God; neither is anyone who does not love his brother" (3:10); "This is the message you heard from the beginning: We should love one another" (3:11); "We know that we have passed from death to life, because we love our brothers" (3:14); "Dear children, let us not love with words or tongue but with actions and in truth" (3:18); "Dear friends, let us love one another, for love comes from God" (4:7); "Since God so loved us, we also ought to love one another" (4:11); "And he has given us this

command: Whoever loves God must also love his brother"
(4:21).

To judge from fighting among Christians and in the
churches, this, no less than the first two goals of the letter, is
needed today.

CONCLUSION

What, then, are the major emphases of John's first letter for ourselves and our contemporaries? There are five of them.

The old gospel

The first message of John is his insistence upon the truth and
value of the old message of the gospel as opposed to new or
modern alterations of it, such as would change its character.
Clearly John is not against a new statement of the gospel in and
of itself. There can be a true restatement of the gospel just as
there can be a false one. Indeed, it can be claimed that John has
given us an example of the first in the fourth Gospel. But John is
opposed to any statement of the gospel which would change it.
Since the message received from the beginning is true, any alter-
ation is obviously false and should be rejected.

The same should be said for our age. It is the old message
that needs to be sounded forth once again from our pulpits and
in our seminaries, a message of the incarnate Son of God, who
for the joy that was set before Him endured the cross, despising
the shame, in order that He might bring many sons into glory. On
this point Charles Haddon Spurgeon, the great Baptist preacher
of the nineteenth century, wrote, "The old truth that Calvin
preached, that Augustine preached, is the truth that I must preach
today, or else be false to my conscience and my God. I cannot
shape the truth; I know of no such thing as paring off the rough
edges of a doctrine. John Knox's gospel is my gospel. That which
thundered through Scotland must thunder through England
again."[4] This should be the desire of God's people in *every*
period of church history.

The historical Christ

The second message is that of the historical Christ, without which

---

[4]*C. H. Spurgeon Autobiography, Volume I: The Early Years, 1834-1859*
(Carlisle, Pa.: The Banner of Truth Trust, 1973) p. 162.

Christianity ceases to be Christianity. What we believe about Christ is not optional. If Jesus did not really come in the flesh, die for sin, rise from the dead, ascend into heaven from which He will come again, then Christianity is stripped of its essential doctrines. There is no sure revelation of God, no atonement for sin, no hope of life beyond the grave, and no future either for the world or the individual. Without the historical Christ and His work there is nothing left. With this message Christianity has a sure and life-shaking message for the world.

Assurance

We live in an uncertain world, in particular a world which today is as confused and unstable as it has ever been. But into this world Christianity breathes a note of certainty. According to John a Christian can know, first, that Christianity is true (this is an objective or historical certainty) and, second, that he is a Christian (this is a subjective or personal certainty). The message of the letter is that this double assurance is right, necessary, and normal for Christian people.

The ethical life

John teaches that righteousness must characterize the life of those who claim to be Christians. "God is light; in him there is no darkness at all" (1:5). Consequently, if a person says that he has fellowship with God but actually continues to live in bondage to sin, he is lying or is self-deceived. Here the first letter of John offers a continuing challenge to all who claim to be Christians. Do their lives show evidence of God's presence?

The need for love

Finally, John stresses the need for Christians to let all that they do be characterized by love. This, indeed, is the "mark of the Christian," as Francis Schaeffer calls it. There may be right doctrine, but without love it will be but a bitter orthodoxy. There may be a sharp and well-reasoned apologetic, but without love no one will be converted.

Are our churches today characterized by love? Are the lives of Christians? If we answer honestly, what Christian will fail to admit that in many areas and at many times the answer is clearly No and that, as a result and as Jesus clearly taught, the believers involved have no right to think that the world should consider them Christians. "All men will know that you are my disciples if you love one another," said Jesus (John 13:35). Do we want others to come to faith in the Lord Jesus Christ? Then we must love.

OUTLINE

Different outlines have been developed for 1 John, but none has impressed scholars as being overwhelmingly superior to the others. The following is the outline adopted for the present work:

Preface (1:1-4)

I. The message (1:5-2:2)

   A. God is light (1:5)

   B. All are sinners (1:6-10)
      1. The first denial (1:6, 7)
      2. The second denial (1:8, 9)
      3. The third denial (1:10)

   C. The call to holiness (2:1, 2)

II. The basis of the Christian's assurance (2:3-27)

   A. The moral test: righteousness (2:3-6)

   B. The social test: love (2:7-11)
      1. Parenthesis on the church (2:12-14)
      2. Parenthesis on the world (2:15-17)

   C. The doctrinal test: truth (2:18-27)

III. An exhortation to righteousness in view of the Lord's return (2:28-3:3)

IV. The church and the world (3:4-4:6)

   A. The first contrast: righteousness and sin (3:4-10)

   B. The second contrast: love and hate (3:11-18)
      Parenthesis dealing with doubt (3:19-24)

   C. The third contrast: truth and error (4:1-6)

V. An exhortation to love in view of the Christian's relationship to God (4:7-21)

21

1 John 1:1-4
What Is Christianity?

> That which was from the beginning, which we have heard, which we have seen with our eyes, which we have looked at and our hands have touched—this we proclaim concerning the Word of life. The life appeared; we have seen it and testify to it, and we proclaim to you the eternal life, which was with the Father and has appeared to us. We proclaim to you what we have seen and heard, so that you also may have fellowship with us. And our fellowship is with the Father and with his Son, Jesus Christ. We write this to make our joy complete.

A number of years ago, in preparation for a discussion period on a Christian radio program, an interviewer went into the streets of Philadelphia to ask people this question: "What is Christianity?" The answers were surprising. Some said that Christianity was "the American way of life." Others called it "an organization." It was "an ethic." One man termed Christianity "a tool used by capitalists to repress the poor." When the interviewer tried to help the people by asking, "And who is Jesus Christ?" the answers were even more outlandish. He was called "pure essence of energy," "a good man," "our leader." Many replied, "I am not sure. . . . I just don't know."

The problem faced by the interviewer in Philadelphia was similar to the problem faced by the apostle John as he wrote to the people in his day, although in John's case those to whom he was writing were Christians.

In the early days of the expansion of the Christian church

there was a large measure of agreement, if not unanimity, as to what the faith was. But in time, as various heretical movements began to appear within the church, this initial agreement broke up in places and many normal Christians found themselves asking: What is Christianity after all? Is belief in Jesus Christ essential to the highest form of Christianity? Is Christianity Christ? If not, what is? Or if Christ is essential to Christianity, then what precisely is one to believe about Him? In the churches to which John wrote, these questions had grown out of a major schism caused by those whom we would today call Gnostics. They were intense and fundamental questions. (Who are we? What is the truth?) Moreover, they obviously involved authority (Who is right?) as well.

In the opening verses of his letter John meets these questions head on. Instead of what would be a customary introduction to any ancient letter (the kind of introduction normally followed by Paul, for instance) John leads off with a preface reminiscent of the prologue of the fourth Gospel. It is his answer to the Gnostics. In it he speaks of the essential core of Christianity, the evidences for Christianity, the Christian proclamation, and finally the twofold objective of the proclamation, namely, the fellowship of an individual with other men and God, and Christian joy.

THE ESSENCE OF CHRISTIANITY (vv. 1, 2)

The most important thing John has to say in his preface is that Christianity is Jesus Christ. Without Christ there would have been no Christianity, for Christianity began by God's revelation of Himself in Jesus and continues by the authoritative testimony of the apostles and others to that revelation. It follows that without Christ there can be no Christianity today. "It is," as Malcolm Muggeridge has recently written, "Christ or nothing."[1]

Here, however, we come to the first of several technical problems in John's letter, for we find ourselves asking, At what points in the preface is John actually speaking of Jesus? At first glance this seems to be easy to answer, for the phrase "the Word of life" immediately makes us think of the "Word [who] became flesh" from the prologue to the Gospel. Since the "Word" in the

---

[1] M. Muggeridge, *Jesus Rediscovered* (Garden City: Doubleday, 1969), p. 58.

prologue is Christ, it seems that "the Word" in the preface should be Christ too. In this case the phrase "of life" should be taken as a descriptive genitive, and the phrase should be understood as "the life-giving Word" or "Christ who gives life."

There are several reasons for questioning this first and easy identification of "the Word of life" with Jesus, however. In the first place, as we read on in the letter we find that it is the word "life" that is actually used of Jesus, rather than "Word." In fact, this occurs in verse 2, for there Christ is portrayed as that "eternal life, which was with the Father and has appeared to us." Second, it is "life" rather than "Word" that is emphasized. This would be strange, granted John's concern for the centrality of the historical Christ, if the "Word" were Jesus. Finally, the phrase "the Word of life" does not stand alone as a subject or even as an object of its sentence, but rather as what may best be taken as an independent adverbial clause introduced by *peri* ("concerning"). In other words, it is not the "Word" that is proclaimed, but Christ, who is the content of it.

For these reasons it seems best to take "Word" as the gospel which is centered in Christ, "beginning" as referring to the beginning of the Christian era, and the other phrases as referring to Jesus, who is proclaimed by those who heard, saw, beheld, and touched Him during the days of His earthly ministry.[2]

There is an important principle here, for while it is true that it is impossible to proclaim Christ without doctrine and while it is equally true that neither John nor any other New Testament writer ever disparages any verbalized statement of God's true revelation, nevertheless it is also true that it is Jesus and not a system of thought which is the essential core of the Christian proclama-

---

[2]There is an interesting variation of this interpretation in Westcott. Westcott takes "Word" somewhat in the sense we have indicated, terming it God's "revelation," but he applies most of the other phrases to it, thereby establishing a historical sequence to God's revelation, beginning in eternity. "That which was" indicates that the gospel existed in the purposes of God from eternity past. "Which we have heard" refers to God's gradual disclosure of His purpose in the Scriptures during the Old Testament period. "Which we have seen . . . looked at . . . and touched" is said of Christ; but this too continues the sequence of revelation from the early days of Christ's ministry through the Resurrection. Westcott also sees a climax of personal experience "from that which was remotest in apprehension to that which was most immediate" (B. F. Westcott, *The Epistles of John* [Grand Rapids: Eerdmans, 1960], pp. 4-6).

tion. The Gnostics had a system, just as many professional religionists have a system today. But a system is not life, nor does it transform a life. A system in and of itself is nothing. What Christianity has and the others do not have is life, in fact, *the* life of Jesus Himself, the One who is the creator and sustainer of all life and who as the life is also the light of men (John 1:4). It is Christ, then, who is proclaimed in Christianity.

THE EVIDENCES FOR CHRISTIANITY (vv. 1, 2)

To proclaim Christ, as John does, is not the same thing as proving that the word proclaimed is true, however. So in the same verses in which John speaks of Jesus as the essence of Christianity he also indicates the grounds of his convictions. These are twofold. On the one hand, there are objective grounds. Confronted with the Gnostic challenge, John gives the greatest place to these. On the other hand, there is that which is subjective. John develops this latter point more fully throughout the letter, although he indicates it here in the phrase that closes verse 2.

The objective evidences

John's objective evidences are centered in the firsthand knowledge of Jesus possessed by himself and the other apostles. The "we" must be taken as this apostolic band, for it is distinct from those Christians to whom John is writing and others ("you," vv. 2, 3). Others, living in a later generation, may not have seen Jesus. But the apostles had seen Him, and John reports with authority that not only had they seen Him, they had also experienced Him in such a way that the impression was permanent. Such seems to be the force of the perfect tenses "have seen" and "have heard" in verses 1 and 3.

There are several channels through which this firsthand knowledge came to the apostles. The first is the ears, for John says that they "have heard" Him. It is possible, as Westcott argues, that this is to be understood of God's written revelation in the Old Testament period. But it is not necessary to take the phrase in this sense. Indeed, if "the Word of life" in verse 1 is to be understood of the gospel and if in verse 5 John immediately stresses "the message we have heard from him," it is more likely that John intends this to be a hearing of the words of Jesus.

And what words they were! The officers who had been sent to arrest Him testified, "No one ever spoke the way this man does" (John 7:46). Those who heard him were privileged. Jesus declared, "Blessed are your eyes because they see, and your ears because they hear. For I tell you the truth, many prophets and righteous men longed to see what you see but did not see it, and to hear what you hear but did not hear it" (Matt. 13:16, 17; cf. Luke 10:23, 24).

The second channel through which John gained knowledge of Christ was the eye, for the apostle says that he and other apostles "have seen" Him. Of all the sense words used by John in this preface—hear, see, look upon, and touch—this one was apparently the most important to John personally, for he repeats it in each of the first three verses.

Why should this be important? The answer may be found in the fact that this is the word used by John in his Gospel to describe the moment of his own conversion, if (as seems natural) we are to take the unnamed disciple of John 20 as the author. The chapter tells of the events of the morning of the Resurrection, beginning with Mary's first arrival at the tomb and continuing with the race of Peter and the unnamed disciple, who is probably John, to the sepulcher. It contains three different Greek words for "see," culminating in the one used here. Peter and John had been told by Mary that the body of Jesus was missing. So they ran to the tomb. John, who was the younger, arrived first. Here, he writes, he stopped at the door and looked in, as the result of which he "saw" the linen bands in which the body of Jesus had been wrapped. This word for "see" is *blepō,* the most common Greek word. It indicates only that the object had impressed itself on John's eyes. From what is known of the circumstances it may even be that John could not see the linen cloths too well, for he was outside in the light and they were in shadow.

In a few moments Peter arrived. He had always been more forceful than John; so, true to character, Peter did not stop at the door but rather pushed John aside and entered. The author tells us at this point that Peter now also "saw" the linen cloths. But he uses a different word for Peter. It is *theōreō,* which means to "behold with intelligence, perceive, or scrutinize." Apparently there was something about the graveclothes that caused Peter to puzzle over them. They were still there, for one thing. That alone was puzzling; for if the body of Jesus had been removed the bands would presumably have been moved with it. Moreover, the bands were in order, lying just where the body had been. If the body had been unwrapped, for whatever inconceivable reason, the cloths would have been scattered about and the spices spilled. Finally, the disciples noticed that the napkin that had been about the head was not with the other graveclothes but was in a place by itself; that is, it was lying precisely where it had been when it was around the head of Jesus, but it was separated from the cloths by the space where in accord with Jewish practices of embalmment the unwrapped face and shoulders of the master had been. What would account for the presence and arrangement of the graveclothes? Nothing but a resurrection in which the transformed body of Jesus would have passed through the linen cloths leaving them undisturbed, just as it was later to pass through closed doors (John 20:19).[3] At this point the significance of the graveclothes got through to John, for he tells us that he "saw" (the third of the words for "see," *oraō,* meaning "to see with understanding") and believed.

It is this last word, *oraō,* that John uses three times in the preface to 1 John, as he thinks (it can hardly be otherwise) of his own experience. Others might doubt, but he at least had heard, scrutinized, and seen Jesus with that insight that led to belief.

The third channel through which John gained knowledge of Christ was touch, for he tells his readers that the apostles had "touched" him, adding "with our hands." This is the most intimate experience of all. Westcott says that "there can be no doubt that the exact word is used with a distinct reference to the invitation of the Lord after his resurrection,"[4] and this is probably true.

At all events it is the word Christ used: "Look at my hands and my feet. It is I myself! Touch me and see; a ghost does not have flesh and bones, as you see I have" (Luke 24:39). It is the expe-

---

[3]The evidence of the graveclothes to the Resurrection is discussed at greater length by H. Latham, *The Risen Master* (New York: Cambridge, 1901); J. R. W. Stott, *Basic Christianity* (Chicago: Inter-Varsity, 1958); and M. C. Tenney, *The Reality of the Resurrection* (Chicago: Moody, 1963).

[4]Westcott, *The Epistles of John,* p. 6.

rience preserved by John's own account of Christ's appearance to Thomas, though the word itself is not used in that narrative (John 20:24-28).

The subjective evidences

As objective and tangible as the revelation of God in Christ was, this would nevertheless have gone unnoticed by John and the others had God not intervened to reveal Christ to them subjectively. This seems to be the meaning of the twofold repetition of the word "appeared" in verse 2. In the first instance it refers merely to the fact of the Incarnation: "the life appeared." It refers to the same point of which John is speaking in the prologue to the Gospel when he says that the true light "was in the world, and though the world was made through him, the world did not recognize him" (John 1:10). In the second instance the reference is to the life having been revealed to John personally: "and has appeared to us." This refers to the point at which the disciples "have seen his glory" or "believed."

No one today can repeat the objective experiences of Christ possessed by the apostles. That is why we need their testimony to Christ as preserved in their writings. Nevertheless, we can and must repeat their subjective experience as, on the basis of the objective revelation, the Holy Spirit makes Christ alive and real both to our minds and hearts.

The historical Jesus and a personal commitment to Him belong together. In John's day this was the antidote to the heresy that would have separated the historical Jesus from the so-called Christ of faith. In our day it is equally valid as an antidote either to any who would, on the one hand, attempt to "demythologize" the faith through science or a mystical experience or who, on the other hand, would substitute a historical but distant Christ for a personal commitment to Him by which He becomes both the Savior and the Lord of life.

THE CHRISTIAN PROCLAMATION (vv. 3, 4)

The message which John and the other apostles received was not only for themselves. Rather it was for the whole world, as Jesus commanded (cf. Matt. 28:19, 20; Mark 16:15; Acts 1:8). Here was a striking contrast with the Gnostics and, by extension, with any other kind of exclusive Christianity. The Gnostics wanted to establish a fellowship of the intellectually elite. The apostles by contrast were attempting to proclaim to the world what they had received.

There are three words which John uses in describing how the gospel is shared. First, he says, we "testify" to what we have seen and heard. This word (*martyrein*, v. 2) is an important word in John's Gospel. Originally it comes from the courts of law and denotes the bearing of testimony to that which one has seen. In the Gospel Jesus is said to have borne witness to the Father because He has seen the Father and is willing to reveal Him (John 3:31, 32; 18:37). In the same way the disciples are called to bear witness of Jesus because they had experienced Him firsthand during His three-year ministry (John 15:27). Second, John says, we "proclaim" what we have seen and heard to you. On the surface this verb seems much like the other, involving a verbalized testimony to what has been seen and heard. But it also suggests something else. It suggests a commission from Christ, authority. Thus, as Stott says, Jesus "not only manifested Himself to the disciples to qualify them as *eyewitnesses*, but gave them an authoritative commission as *apostles* to preach the gospel."[5] Finally, as John says in verse 4, we "write" these things that our joy might be full.

This then is the way in which the gospel has come to us and must be passed on. The apostles bore witness to what they had seen and heard of Jesus, proclaimed it authoritatively on His commission, and finally preserved it in the writings which have since become our New Testament. Today believers are to take their writings and, having through them entered into the experience of the apostles, proclaim the Christ of the apostles to the world.

THE TWOFOLD OBJECTIVE (vv. 3, 4)

But why is this done? Why this enormous effort, beginning in eternity past, prepared for in the Old Testament writings, focused in Christ, seen by the apostles, preached by them, and recorded by them in the New Testament? And why should we be a part of it? John concludes the preface by stating as this objective: "that

---

[5]John R. W. Stott, *The Epistles of John* (Grand Rapids: Eerdmans, 1964), p. 62.

you also may have fellowship with us" and "to make our joy complete."

John speaks of fellowship rather than salvation in these verses, perhaps because the fellowship had been so recently broken by the Gnostic schism. Properly understood, however, the word includes the full meaning of salvation, as the accompanying phrases indicate. There is salvation on the horizontal dimension. It is an overcoming of hostility between man and man. There is also salvation on the vertical dimension, between God and man. Indeed, John indicates that it is only when the latter is established that the first becomes possible. Why is it that human beings experience friction with one another? The answer, as James writes in his Epistle, is sin (James 4:1ff.). And how can sin be conquered? Not by men, certainly, for all are sinners. It can be conquered only by Christ, who died once that fellowship might be restored between man and God and who now lives in order to communicate the power of God in overcoming sin to those who follow Him.

Those who are already Christians must take the words of John seriously. He says that the purpose of this great plan of God for the revelation of Himself to men and for their salvation is fellowship, and that on the horizontal level. How then can believers be content with that which disrupts their fellowship? Or how can they be content with an evangelism that wins men to God but fails to draw them into a vital and visible relationship with one another?

Finally, says John, we have written "to make our joy complete." There is a textual variant at this point in which "your" is substituted for "our" in John's statement. Either would be correct, and in fact there is not much difference. Yet "our" is dramatic; for it is John's way of saying that his joy is their joy—it was also John the Baptist's testimony (John 3:29)—and that the apostle will have full joy only when the Christians to whom he is writing, as well as all who would come after, enjoy fellowship. This is real joy, but it will not be perfected in our or any other lifetime. Therefore, verse 4 may rightly be understood as pointing forward ultimately to heaven.

If believers will ultimately be one in heaven, however, why should they not be one while here on earth? And why should there not be a joy in true Christian fellowship, as there certainly will be later? Clearly Christians are to recognize and work toward a vital fellowship here as well as pray for and anticipate that day in which that which began with the revelation of God in the historical Christ and which was preached and believed on by millions in this world will be consumated.

1 John 1:5-10
The Message of Jesus Christ

This is the message we have heard from him and declare to you: God is light; in him there is no darkness at all. If we claim to have fellowship with him yet walk in the darkness, we lie and do not live by the truth. But if we walk in the light, as he is in the light, we have fellowship with one another, and the blood of Jesus, his Son, purifies us from every sin. If we claim to be without sin, we deceive ourselves and the truth is not in us. If we confess our sins, he is faithful and just and will forgive us our sins and purify us from all unrighteousness. If we claim we have not sinned, we make him out to be a liar and his word has no place in our lives.

"What is God?" asks the fourth question of the Westminster Shorter Catechism. And well it might, for this is a question that has puzzled men and stretched their minds for centuries. Religion has to do with God; and people, as anyone can observe, are religious. But who is the God they worship? What is He like? What are His characteristics? Most important of all perhaps, How can we know Him? The Catechism says that we are made to know God, calling this "man's chief end." It defines Him: "God is a Spirit, infinite, eternal, and unchangeable, in his being, wisdom, power, holiness, justice, goodness, and truth." But one can read this definition and feel that, while it may help us to know *about* God, nevertheless it does not really help us to know *Him*. Besides, it is abstract and complicated. So the questions remain.

John apparently also had to do with people who asked such questions, but he has given us an answer which is at once simpler and more profound. What is God? John answers: "God is light; in him there is no darkness at all."

This statement is John's first great thesis, leading naturally into much of the material that follows. We must notice, however, that it also exhibits a twofold connection with what has gone before. In the preface John wrote of the revelation of God in Christ, which he has seen and heard and has declared to others. But what is that message? It is this that he reports in the verse that immediately follows. In Greek the connection is more obvious even than in English, for the word "message" *(angelia)* is from the same root as the word translated "we proclaim" *(apangello-men)* in verses 2, 3, and 4. Moreover, *angelia* is a rare word in the New Testament, occuring only here and in 3:11, which suggests that John chose it after some thought and in order to make this connection. The second link between verse 5 and the preceding verses is in regard to fellowship. Here, as Brooke summarizes, "Having stated that his object in writing is to enable his readers to enter into fellowship, and that the mutual fellowship of Christians leads onwards to that higher fellowship with God in Christ on which indeed it is based, the writer proceeds to deduce from the nature of God the conditions under which fellowship with him is possible."[1]

In this section of the letter John presents his first thesis (both from a positive and negative perspective), deals with three related denials concerning the nature and consequences of sin, and issues a call to holiness, without which, as the author of Hebrews states, "no one will see the Lord." The outline might also be presented as: the holiness of God, the sinfulness of man, and man's need of a Savior. That is, it is a statement of the whole of the Gospel.

GOD IS LIGHT (v. 5)

None of the other biblical writers tells us so much about what God really is as does the apostle John. All of them tell what He does. Some describe the glory which surrounds Him. But John tells what God is in His true nature. He does this in three striking definitions: God is spirit (John 4:24), God is light (1 John 1:5), and God is love (1 John 4:8). It is a characteristic of these three

---

[1]A. E. Brooke, *A Critical and Exegetical Commentary on the Johannine Epistles* (London: T. and T. Clark, 1912), p. 10.

definitions that the predicates occur without the definite article. We are told, then, not that God is *the* Spirit, *the* light, and *the* love or even, in all probability, *a* spirit, *a* light, and *a* love, but rather spirit, light, and love themselves. In this we have the broadest and most comprehensive definition of God that can probably be devised in human language.

The positive statement

John's definition of God is stated both positively and negatively, but he offers the positive statement first: God is light. This statement carries the reader into a world of imagery that is as old as religion and which would have been quite familiar and agreeable both to John's readers and to his opponents.

It is found in the Old Testament, for instance. David writes in one psalm, "The LORD is my light and my salvation" (Ps. 27:1). Another psalm declares, "For with you is the fountain of life; in your light we see light" (Ps. 36:9). In Psalm 104 we read, "You are clothed with splendor and majesty. He wraps himself in light as with a garment" (vv. 1, 2). Isaiah wrote concerning God's plan for the Messiah, "I will also make you a light for the Gentiles, that you may bring my salvation to the ends of the earth" (Isa. 49:6). In each of these verses light seems strikingly appropriate as an image of God, for it points to God as the true source of revelation, intelligence, stability, ubiquity, excellence, vision, and growth. It is the nature of light that it is visible and that it makes other things visible. So also is it God's nature to make Himself known.

In biblical thought two special ideas are associated with light, however. First, the image generally has ethical overtones. That is, it is a symbol of holiness or purity as well as of intelligence, vision, growth, and other realities. This is apparent several times in John's Gospel, as when John declares Jesus to be "the light of men" (John 1:4) or later, when he says, "This is the verdict: Light has come into the world, but men loved darkness instead of light because their deeds were evil" (John 3:19). Clearly this use of the imagery would not be so agreeable to John's opponents, particularly when he challenges Christians to "walk" or "abide" in the light, as he does later.

These ethical or moral overtones are of great importance. Is God righteous? Then the lives of Christians should be known for

35

being righteous. If He is holy, we should be holy. Indeed, says John, if anyone claims to know God while yet living a sinful life, he is either deceiving himself or lying.

The second unique characteristic of the biblical use of light is in applying it to Jesus; that is, in applying it to the historical Jesus in exactly the same way that it is applied to God. In a much lesser sense those who follow Christ are said to be "children of light" or even "light" itself (John 12:36; Matt. 5:14), but this is not true for them in the same sense that it is true for Jesus. They are kindled lights, as Jesus said John the Baptist was (John 5:35). But Jesus is light in the same sense that God is light. He is holy and the source of all good. In the Gospel John tells us that Jesus is the One who reveals the world's darkness and is victorious over it (John 1:4, 5).

How is it that John received the message that "God is light; in him there is no darkness at all"? Is it not in this: namely, that Jesus is also the light and that He revealed Himself to John? Commentators have pointed out that we do not have any explicit teaching of Jesus in the New Testament to the effect that God is light. But we have very little direct teaching of Jesus about the Father at all. Why? Clearly because He is Himself the revelation of the Father. "Anyone who has seen me has seen the Father," He told Philip. In this as in the other Johannine literature it is, therefore, not simply the revelation of God expressed in propositional statements, but the revelation of God in Christ that is presented to us. Nothing, then, must detract from Christ. Rather, it is He who was seen and heard and touched who must be fully proclaimed.

The negative statement

It is a characteristic of this letter that John frequently accompanies a positive statement of some truth with a negative statement designed to reinforce it, here reinforcing the claim that God is light by the longer phrase "in him there is no darkness at all." This is an important principle in the biblical concept of truth, indeed of any truth properly understood. A statement that does not imply corresponding negations is not a true statement. Rather it is a meaningless one. If "A" is true, then something else must be false; or else, "A" is meaningless. John knew this, of course. Consequently, when he says that God is light he immediately denies that He is darkness. God is good; hence, God is not bad. God is holy; so He is not sinful. Men may mix the two, as in many of the Eastern religions, in which all things, good and bad, unite in the One. But this is not John's teaching, nor that of the Bible as a whole. In this outlook God emerges as that which is totally holy and therefore as that which is totally opposed to all that is sinful and false. It follows from this that men must be holy if they are to have fellowship with Him, as John now shows.

THE FIRST DENIAL (vv. 6, 7)

John's definition of God as light is followed by a denial of three false claims in which the reader is probably right in hearing an echo of the erroneous teachings of the Gnostics. These men claimed to have entered into a higher fellowship with God than was known by most other Christians. They professed great things, but there was a flaw in their profession. They claimed to know God; but even as they made their claims they showed by their actions that they failed to take sin, which is opposed to the nature of God, seriously. Their religion consisted from the ethical standpoint of what Dietrich Bonhoeffer called "easy grace." They claimed fellowship with God, but the fellowship was not costly. They separated religion and ethics. Consequently, they claimed the highest privileges while living precisely as they pleased. In answering their views John denies three of their claims, while on each occasion also pointing to the divine remedy for sin for all who will avail themselves of it.

The outline for this section is apparent from John's threefold repetition of the phrase "If we claim" in verses 6, 8, and 10. In each case it introduces one of the false claims. This is followed by John's denial of the teaching ("we lie," we deceive ourselves," "we make him out to be a liar") and, finally, by a correct affirmation. In the third case the affirmation takes a different and slightly expanded form as a result of which it has been set apart at the beginning of chapter 2. It will be considered by itself in the next section of the present study.

The first false claim is a common one; namely, that a person can have fellowship with God at the same time that his life is characterized by unrighteousness. John expresses it as the claim to have "fellowship with him yet walk in the darkness." Here to "walk in the darkness" means to sin habitually, the contrast being, not a sinless life (for John teaches that everyone sins, v. 8), but a progressive growth in godliness. The present tense indicates a continual practice of that which is opposed to God. Naturally the Gnostic teaching is in view as John denies this erroneous assertion. But we must not miss the fact that his rebuke applies to anyone who claims to know God while at the same time treats either sin or the need for establishing and maintaining a moral life lightly. As Bruce says, "It may well be that the false teachers against whom John puts his readers on their guard were wide open to criticism in this respect, but it is equally necessary for those who adhere to the apostolic teaching and fellowship to be reminded that orthodoxy of doctrine is no substitute for righteousness of life. 'Truth in the inward being' (Ps. 51:6) is what God desires in his people, and where that is present, it will manifest itself in all the ways of life."[2]

The contrast to a claim to fellowship with God while actually walking in darkness is an actual walking in the light, which is of necessity accompanied by the reality of Christian fellowship and continual and repeated cleansing from present sin. The fact that John speaks of cleansing from sin, using the present tense of the verb, indicates that he does not understand "walking in the light" to mean perfection. Rather, he means a genuine and continuous pursuit of holiness out of which increased fellowship with other Christians and confession of sin will come. It is this that must characterize all who know God.

The two results of walking in the light deserve special notice. First, having said that one who claims fellowship with God while actually walking in darkness lies, we might, in verse 7, expect John to reply that the one who walks in the light has fellowship with God. This would be true, of course. But John, in a somewhat condensed form of writing, skips over this to show that it also means that he will have fellowship with other believers. Indeed, it is in fellowship with one another on the horizontal dimension that our fellowship with God on the vertical dimension is demonstrated. Did the Gnostics claim fellowship with God? Then, how did they see their way clear to separate from other believers, as they have done? Why did they not maintain the fellowship? The same critique applies to those who in the name of a better or purer fellowship with God break Christian fellowship today.

[2]F. F. Bruce, *The Epistles of John* (Old Tappan: Revell, 1970), p. 42.

Second, John says that the one walking in the light will find the blood of the Lord Jesus Christ available to him for continued cleansing. At first glance this seems a contradiction. For why does the one who already walks in the light need cleansing? Is he not already cleansed? Or, on the other hand, if he is being cleansed from sin, does this not imply that he was walking in the darkness previously? The contradiction is only superficial; for John is merely saying that one who walks in fellowship with God will find forgiveness for any sin that might enter his life. In fact, such forgiveness is already provided for by the sacrifice of Christ. This is not said to encourage sin, as some might think ("Let us do evil that good may result," Rom. 3:8), but to encourage holiness.[3]

THE SECOND DENIAL (vv. 8, 9)

The second false teaching which John denies is the teaching that, in the case of a particular Christian, sin can have been eradicated. It is the claim that we are "without sin" (v. 8). In itself this statement can have more than one meaning. It can mean that there is no such thing as sin and that, therefore, no one is a sinner. This is a view which has become quite popular in western contemporary thought largely through Freudian psychology, which denies an objective basis for guilt.[4] It can mean that the particular individuals who make the claim have no sin and have never had it, that they are a unique and privileged people. Or, finally, it can mean that they do not have sin now. In view of the fact that there seems to be a progression in the intensity and seriousness of the claims that John denies, it would seem that the third of these

---

[3]The matter is discussed at greater length in the next chapter since the verses with which it deals (2:1, 2) are the summation of the entire discussion and present the case for holiness. The importance of "the blood of Jesus" is also discussed in that chapter. Westcott has an additional note on "The Idea of Christ's Blood in the New Testament" (pp. 34-37). See also: A. M. Stibbs, *The Meaning of the Word "Blood" in Scripture* (London, 1947); L. Morris, "The Biblical Use of the Term Blood" (*Journal of Theological Studies*, n.s. 3, 1952, p. 216ff.) and "The Blood," *The Apostolic Preaching of the Cross* (Grand Rapids: Eerdmans, 1955, pp. 108-124); and J. Behm, *"Haima,"* Theological Dictionary of the New Testament, Vol. 1 (Grand Rapids: Eerdmans, 1964, pp. 172-177).

[4]It is, however, roundly opposed by psychiatrist Karl Menninger, famed founder of the Menninger Clinic, in *Whatever Became of Sin?* (New York: Hawthorn, 1974).

possible interpretations should be preferred. The first false teaching was that it is possible to have fellowship with God and still continue sinning. In this second claim there is the additional error that the individual has, either through the Gnostic process of enlightenment or through spiritual development, ceased to sin at all.

Interestingly enough, in this case John does not say that the person professing such perfection is lying, as he did of the lesser claim in verse 6. He merely says that he has deceived himself. The reason is obvious. In the first case the person is making a claim which he himself, as well as all others, knows to be untrue. But in the second case there is the possibility at least that the person making the claim is deceived. It is far more serious, for it is always better at least to see the facts clearly. Nevertheless, it is error in a different area. The seriousness of the matter emerges in the fact that if a person believes himself not to sin, he therefore excuses his sinful deeds and does not bring them to God for confession and cleansing.

But this is what is needed; indeed, this is what is needed by every Christian. Instead of denying that we sin, we are to admit and confess the sin. Only then can God truly cleanse us from all unrighteousness.

John says that if we confess our sin, God is *faithful* and *just* in forgiving it. But why does John use these two particular words? In what sense is God faithful? In what sense is He just? Here the interpreter must draw upon the full biblical teaching. To understand the word "faithful" he must understand that God has promised to forgive sin when it is confessed to him. Thus, Isaiah wrote of God's promise: "'Come now, let us reason together,' says the LORD. 'Though your sins are like scarlet, they shall be as white as snow; though they are red as crimson, they shall be like wool'" (Isa. 1:18). Jeremiah declared, "I will forgive their wickedness and will remember their sins no more" (Jer. 31:34). Clearly, if God had spoken such promises and then had refused to forgive sin, He would have been unfaithful. But He is not. He is faithful to forgive in that He has promised to do so and does do so.

The answer to the question of the justice of God in forgiving sins is found in Romans 3:20-28, where Paul explains how it is that God is both "just, and the justifier of him who believeth in

Jesus" (v. 26, KJV). It is possible, he says, through Christ, who, being God and therefore having no sin of His own, was able and did die for us. God punished our sin in Christ. Jesus became the "propitiation" for our sins, meaning that by Him God's just wrath against our sin was satisfied. It is interesting in this context that the word "propitiation," used by Paul in Romans, is used by John just three verses farther on as he enters more fully into a discussion of Christ's work.

THE THIRD DENIAL (v. 10)

The third of the false claims is the most serious of all. It is the claim, not merely that the one making it is not sinning now, but that he has never sinned. This is indicated by a change of tense, from the present ("to be," v. 8) to the aorist ("have not sinned," v. 10). This is so blatant an affirmation in view of the evidences of sin which all men have in themselves that John drops the idea of deception and returns to the thought of lying once again. But now even this is strengthened. For John says not that the man himself lies, although this is also true, but that he makes God out to be a liar; for God has declared that all are sinners and in need of His grace (1 Kings 8:46; Ps. 14:2, 3; Isa. 53:6; Rom. 3:23). Who is right? The man who denies the reality of sin in general and in himself in particular, or God, who declares that all have sinned? There is only one answer. "Let God be true, and every man a liar" (Rom. 3:4).

CONCLUSION

The application of this section of John's letter must be to each man or woman individually. John has contrasted the nature of God ("God is light") with the nature of man; and he has begun to show the characteristics of those who walk in the light as opposed to those who walk in darkness. It is not enough that a man should claim to be in the light. He must actually walk in it. He must be a child of the light.

What will be true of the individual if God is actually the light of his life? Obviously, the light of God will be doing for him what light does. For one thing, the light will be exposing the darkness so that the dark places are increasingly cleansed of sin and become bright and fruitful places for God's blessing. This does not mean that the individual will become increasingly conscious of

41

how good he or she is becoming. On the contrary, a growth in holiness will mean a growth in a true sensitivity to sin in one's life and an intense desire to eliminate from life all that displeases God. Instead of boasting in his progress, the person will be increasingly ready to acknowledge sin and seek to have it eliminated.

It will be a genuine acknowledgment. It will not be as it was in the case of a woman who once asked Charles Wesley to pray for her because, as she said, "I am a great sinner." She added, "I am a Christian, but I sometimes fail so dreadfully. Please pray for me."

Wesley looked at her rather sternly and replied, "Yes, Madam, I will pray for you; for truly you are a great sinner."

She answered, "What do you mean? I have never done anything very wrong."

If God's light is really shining on us, we will rather say, as did Isaiah, "Woe to me! I am ruined! For I am a man of unclean lips, and I live among a people of unclean lips, and my eyes have seen the King, the LORD Almighty!" (Isa. 6:5); or with Peter, "Go away from me, Lord; I am a sinful man" (Luke 5:8); or with Paul, "I am the worst [of sinners]" (1 Tim. 1:15).

Second, if God is our light and if we walk in the light, we will be growing spiritually. The Bible will be becoming more precious, for God is revealed in it. We will love godliness. And we will be finding fellowship with God's people more and more delightful and valuable.

Finally, we will also be finding it increasingly desirable to serve the Lord Jesus Christ. Indeed, we will yearn to serve Him, for we will know Him more and more as the One who brought us out of the bondage of our darkness into His marvelous light. Wesley wrote of this desire:

> Long my imprisoned spirit lay,
>   Fast bound in sin and nature's night:
> Thine eye diffused a quickening ray,
>   I woke, the dungeon flamed with light:
> My chains fell off, my heart was free,
>   I rose, went forth, and followed Thee.

To follow Christ is the natural desire of the one whose life has been illuminated by Him.

1 John 2:1, 2
A Call to Holiness

> My dear children, I write this to you so that you will not sin.
> But if anybody does sin, we have one who speaks to the
> Father in our defense—Jesus Christ, the Righteous One. He
> is the atoning sacrifice for our sins, and not only for ours but
> also for the sins of the whole world.

Nothing that John has written thus far can be taken as an endorsement of sin. But it is possible that some might misunderstand his statements and thereby reach that conclusion. Has he not argued that all men sin? "Well," they might argue, "if sin is inevitable, why struggle against it? You will sin, no matter what you do. So resign yourself to the facts." Or again, has John not said that there is forgiveness for sin through what Jesus has done and, indeed, continues to do? "All right," they might add, "why worry about committing sin? If God forgives it, the outcome is assured. As a matter of fact, why not sin more, for God can forgive more and get greater glory in such circumstances."

John's words do not say this, of course, nor do his principles lead in this direction. In fact, they lead to precisely the opposite conclusion. In order to show this, he now interrupts the form he has been following in stating and answering the false views of the Gnostics (there would have been an "if we walk" or "if we confess" clause following 1:10) and instead begins a new sentence in which the problem of sin in the Christian is dealt with directly. The sentence contains a call to holiness, which in turn is based upon two great Christian certainties. The first is the promise of

God to forgive sin, already stated in chapter 1. The second is the work of Christ, upon which he elaborates.

THE PROMISE OF GOD (v. 1)

The thrust of John's message is at once evident, both in the appeal itself and in the tone in which it is made: "My dear children, I write this to you so that you will not sin." It is an endearing appeal and has the effect of reassuring his readers that, whatever may seem to be the implications of his earlier statements, his concern for them is precisely in this, that they might not sin. Nothing he has said should ever be construed as an endorsement of unrighteousness.

A question still remains, however. John obviously wants those to whom he is writing to keep free of sin, but how precisely do the truths about which he has been speaking lead to godliness? What in chapter 1 actually promotes this goal? Or, to put it in different language, to what does "this" refer? It is possible, first, that it refers to nearly everything that comes before it. But it is unlikely that the preface is involved (which narrows the material to vv. 5-10); and, if that is so, then the reference may be even more restricted. It is possible, secondly, that John is referring to the main thesis of the preceding verses; namely, that God is light. If this is so, the logic is obvious. Christians ought not to sin because God is sinless. Third, there is the possibility that John is referring to the statement of verse 9, in which he has said that God will forgive us our sins if we confess them. This reference may be preferred because of the proximity of the two verses and because of the tone and content of 2:1, 2, which speak of forgiveness within a family relationship.

But how does the assurance of forgiveness actually lead to holiness? Is not the opposite the case? If we know that we are forgiven in advance, will we not feel free to sin? The objection sounds logical, but it is not. In fact, it is contradicted by human experience. Actually, the knowledge of such a great love and of such undeserved forgiveness makes the Christian earnestly desirous not to sin against them.

An illustration is necessary to make this point clear. Shortly after World War II, Donald Grey Barnhouse, who was then pastor of the Tenth Presbyterian Church in Philadelphia, was counseling a certain young man. He was a professor in a major

A Call to Holiness

university and had a sad story to recount. He had been a second lieutenant in the American army and had been sent overseas to France where he had fallen in with bad companions. He was not a Christian at the time, and while stationed there he had lived a life of gross sin. Now, however, he had returned home, become a Christian, met a fine Christian girl and wished to marry her. But he had a problem. He remembered his past sin and feared that he might again fall into it. If so, he would wound the girl he loved. What should he do? Because of his uncertainty he had hesitated to speak of his love for her.

The pastor advised him to speak frankly with the young woman, and to tell her briefly of his past life. "She must sense that you love her and that something is holding you back," he said. "So you must clear the air. If you are going to spend your lives together, there must be no barriers between you." Still the young man hesitated.

At this point Barnhouse told him a story which is retold here in order to introduce the comment that was wrung from the young professor when he had finished. "Some time ago," he said, "I dealt with a man whose story was not much different from your own. He too had lived a life of sin and had been converted under conditions similar to those existing in a rescue mission. He had then married a fine Christian woman to whom he had briefly told his sordid story. He said that, after he had told his wife this, she kissed him and replied, 'John, I want you to understand something very plainly. I know my Bible well, and I know something of the workings of Satan. I know that you are a thoroughly converted man, John, but I also know that you have an old nature to which Satan will certainly appeal. He will do all that he can to put temptations in your way. The day may come—I pray that it never shall—when you shall succumb to temptation and fall into sin. Immediately the devil will tell you that you have ruined everything, that you might as well continue in sin, and that above all you should not tell me because it will hurt me. But, John, I want you to know that this is your home. This is where you belong. I want you to know that there is full pardon and forgiveness in advance for any evil that may come into your life.'"

As Dr. Barnhouse told this story the professor lowered his head into his hands. But when Barnhouse reached the end, the young man lifted his head and said reverently, "My God, if anything could ever keep a man straight, that would be it."[1]

This is the principle of 1 John 2:1, 2: forgiveness in advance for any sin that might come into our lives. This is God's promise, and it is given to us precisely that we might not sin. God is not shocked by human behavior, as we often are, for He sees it in advance, including the sins of Christians. Moreover, and in spite of this, He sent His Son to die for the sins of His people so that there might be full forgiveness. Such love is unmeasurable. Such grace is beyond human comprehension. But God tells us of that love and grace in order that we might be won by it and determine, God giving us strength, that we will not fail Him.

THE WORK OF CHRIST (vv. 1, 2)

Sometimes we do fail him, in spite of His assurance of pardon. What then? In that case, says John, we are to come to God to confess the sin and seek forgiveness, knowing that we are able to approach Him through the work of Christ as children approach a father. In this statement the reference to cleansing through the blood of Christ (1:7), the promise of forgiveness and cleansing for those who will confess their sins (1:9), and the call to holiness (2:1, 2) are tied together.

Jesus, our advocate

The work of Christ is the basis upon which the Christian may approach God for full forgiveness and cleansing. John uses three terms to describe it. The first is "advocate," or "one who speaks . . . in our defense." This is a legal term, in Greek as in English; but in the Greek language, unlike English, the word has a passive rather than an active sense. It means literally "one called alongside of" and describes anyone who is called upon to help another, particularly in a court of law. It is easy to see, then, how John can use the word of Jesus; for he simply means that Jesus is the One called in to help us before the judgment bar of God. As Barclay says, "We are not to think of him as having gone through his life upon the earth, and his death upon the

---

[1]The story is told by Donald Grey Barnhouse in *God's Methods for Holy Living* (Philadelphia: Eternity Book Service, 1951), pp. 72-74).

Cross, and then being finished with men." Rather, "He still bears his concern for men upon his heart."[2]

The word "advocate" does not occur outside the Johannine writings, but the ministry of Christ to which it refers occurs in many places. Jesus promised Peter that He would intercede for him that his faith might not fail in the aftermath of his denying his Lord (Luke 22:32). John 17 records a prayer to the same effect on behalf of all believers. Jesus declared that "whoever acknowledges me before men, the Son of Man will also acknowledge him before the angels of God" (Luke 12:8). Paul describes Jesus as the One "who was raised to life—is at the right hand of God and is also interceding for us" (Rom. 8:34).

There is one thing to be noted in John's use of "advocate," however. When the term is used in a legal sense today, we usually think of the work of a lawyer in presenting the full case of the defendant; that is, in defending the accused largely upon the merits of his case. In John the idea of merit on the part of the accused is entirely absent; rather the merit is on the part of the advocate. The former idea is illustrated by a use of the term in the early rabbinic tractate *Pirkē Aboth:* "He who does one precept [of the law] gains for himself one advocate, and he who commits one transgression gains for himself one accuser" (4:13). In the New Testament, it is entirely a question of God's grace.

Jesus, the righteous one

The second term used by John of Jesus is "righteous." Indeed, it is this word which is emphasized. In what sense is it used? It is possible that John is referring to that judicial righteousness which the Father has applied to believers on the basis of Christ's sacrifice of Himself for them, the meaning usually given to the term by Paul, as in Romans 10:4: "Christ is the end of the law so that there may be righteousness for everyone who believes." But this is unlikely for several reasons. First, it is awkward to understand the word in two senses in such a short space (in 1:9 of the Father and in 2:1 of the Son), which we must do if this interpretation is adopted. In the first case, the word refers to the justice of God's action in forgiving sin. Second, the idea of the sufficient grounds of our Lord's advocacy is adequately developed in the clause

---

[2]William Barclay, *The Letters of John and Jude* (Philadelphia: Westminster Press, 1958), p. 45.

which follows, which tells us that He is "the atoning sacrifice for our sins." So it is not needed here. Finally, the dominant idea in these verses is not justification on grounds of the righteousness of Christ. Rather, it is Christ's advocacy on the part of the believer who has sinned. For these reasons it, therefore, seems best to take the word as describing, not the legal righteousness which Christ has and is, which is offered to us in the gospel, but rather the righteousness of His character which governs the nature of His advocacy for us.

Not all advocates are like this, as any who have been to court know. Often they are unjust. Many times they serve their own interests rather than those of their client. Some use technicalities to escape the law's just censure. But Jesus does not work in this fashion. Rather, He is faithful to our cause and presents the case faithfully and with perfection.

Jesus, the atoning sacrifice

Finally, John calls Jesus "the atoning sacrifice for our sins", adding, "and not only for ours, but also for the sins of the whole world."

Instead of the word "propitiation," which occurs in the KJV, or "atoning sacrifice," which is used in the NIV, the RSV has "expiation," thereby following a rather modern trend in biblical scholarship. The word "propitiation" was used extensively in ancient pagan writings of the appeasement of an angry god by offerings. It had the sense of "placation" or "mollification." In these circles the idea of propitiation was very debased. But this is incompatible with the character of the Christian God, some scholars say. God is not an angry God, according to the Christian revelation. He is gracious and loving. Moreover, it is not God who is separated from us because of sin, but rather we who are separated from God. Or again, it is not He who is to be propitiated, but ourselves. According to such thinking, propitiation is therefore to be referred, not to what Jesus has done in reference to God, but rather to what has been done by God in Christ for our guilt. This has been "covered," "disinfected" (so Dodd), or "expiated" by His death; hence, the RSV translation and others. Those who adhere to such views note that, strictly speaking, the Bible never makes God the object of the propitiation.

But this is not the whole of the matter, as sympathetic as one may be with the concerns of such critics. In the first place, while it is true that we must not throw the Christian concept of God into the same barrel with the capricious and petulant character of the deities of the ancient world, at the same time neither do we want to forget His just wrath against sin, in accordance with which sin will be punished either in Christ or in the person of the sinner. Here the whole scope of the biblical revelation must be taken into account.

Second, although the word "propitiation" is used in biblical writings, it is nevertheless not used in precisely the same way it is used in pagan writings. In the pagan rituals the sacrifice was the means by which a man placated an offended deity. In Christianity it is never the man who takes the initiative or makes the sacrifice, but God Himself who out of His great love for the sinner provides the way by which His own wrath against sin may be placated. In 1 John 4:10, the only other passage in the New Testament which uses the exact form of the word found in 2:2, God's love is emphasized. This is the true explanation of why God is never the explicit object of the propitiation in the biblical writings. He is not the object because He is, even more importantly, the subject. In other words, God Himself placates His wrath against sin so that His love may go out to embrace and fully save the sinner.

It is in the Old Testament sacrificial system that the true idea of propitiation is most clearly observed, for if anything is conveyed through the system of sacrifices (in the biblical sense of sacrifice) it is that God has himself provided the way by which a sinful man or woman may approach Him. Sin means death. "The soul who sins is the one who will die" (Ezek. 18:4, 20). But the sacrifices teach that there is, nevertheless, a way of escape and of approaching God. Another may die in the sinner's place. This may seem astounding, even (as some have wrongly suggested) immoral; but it is what the system of sacrifices teaches. Consequently, the individual Israelite was instructed to bring an animal for sacrifice whenever he approached God; the family was to kill and consume an animal at the yearly observance of the Passover; the nation was to be thus represented by the high priest annually on the Day of Atonement when the blood of one offering was sprinkled upon the mercy seat of the ark of the covenant within the Holy of Holies in the Jewish temple. This latter ceremony may be what John is thinking of explicitly in this passage, for a cognate of "propitiation" is used of the very mercy seat upon which the blood of the sacrifice was sprinkled (*hilastērion,* Heb. 9:5). Besides, John referred to the shed blood of Christ just verses earlier (1:7).

Jesus is Himself the propitiation, then, and it is by virtue of His being this that He can be our advocate. "Our advocate does not plead our innocence; he acknowledges our guilt and presents his vicarious sacrifice as the ground of our acquittal," as Ross indicates.[3] Moreover, in this lies the Christian's confidence, for it is not on the grounds of our merit but solely on the basis of the finished work of Christ that we are bold to approach a righteous heavenly Father. Here Charles Wesley's "Arise, My Soul, Arise" is an excellent commentary.

> Arise, my soul, arise; shake off thy guilty fears;
> The bleeding Sacrifice in my behalf appears.
> Before the throne my Surety stands;
> My name is written on His hands.
>
> He ever lives above, for me to intercede;
> His all-redeeming love, His precious blood to plead;
> His blood atoned for all our race,
> And sprinkles now the throne of grace.
>
> Five bleeding wounds He bears, received on Calvary;
> They pour effectual prayers, they strongly plead for me.
> "Forgive him, O forgive," they cry,
> "Nor let the ransomed sinner die."
>
> The Father hears Him pray, his dear anointed One;
> He cannot turn away the presence of His Son:
> His Spirit answers to the blood,
> And tells me I am born of God.
>
> My God is reconciled, His pard'ning voice I hear;
> He owns me for His child, I can no longer fear:
> With confidence I now draw nigh,
> And "Father, Abba, Father!" cry.

The last phrase of verse 2 presents us with unusual problems, but it may be that the idea of the propitiatory sacrifice performed on the Day of Atonement, which underlies this passage,

---

[3]Ross, p. 150. The idea of propitiation is discussed at great length by Leon Morris in *The Apostolic Preaching of the Cross* (Grand Rapids: Eerdmans, 1956), pp. 125-185, and by Robert Law in *The Tests of Life* (Grand Rapids: Baker, 1968), pp. 156-183.

explains it. The phrase is "and not only for ours but also for the sins of the whole world." It is added to the description of Jesus as "the propitiation for our sins" to broaden it or somehow universalize it. This much is clear enough; but it is not clear in what sense this may be said to be true. Consequently, commentators have not found it easy to make plain either to themselves or others the precise nature of the universalism found here. They have in general developed one easy answer and one very common answer, but neither is satisfactory.

The easy answer is an affirmation of universalism in its full sense; that is, that Jesus actually died for the sins of every human being and that as a result each and every one is saved by Him. All will be in heaven. This is a popular interpretation for those who are disposed to universalism anyway on other grounds, but it is hardly supported by any biblical writer, including John. In fact, it is John who among all the New Testament writers most clearly distinguishes between Christ's own and the world (John 13:1; 17:9; 1 John 3:1, 10). Not all will be saved. So, whatever the phrase means, it clearly cannot be taken to imply a full-blown universalism.

The most common answer is that the death of Christ applies to the whole world potentially but that it becomes efficacious unto salvation only in the case of those who appropriate it through faith. Those who hold to this view most naturally view the text as an important refutation of the third distinctive tenet of Calvinism, commonly called "limited atonement," and they oppose it to the idea of election itself. This, however, is not entirely satisfactory. For if the atonement of Christ is to be taken as an atonement in potential only, then it is not actually an atonement. That is, it does not actually atone for any particular sin. Moreover, it is ineffective; for, unless one moves into the camp of the universalists, it does not actually save the world, since many who are in the world will perish.

What is the answer then? One answer is given by B. B. Warfield in an essay entitled "Jesus Christ the Propitiation for the World." According to Warfield, John is thinking of the salvation of the world in temporal terms rather than spatially. Thus, Jesus "came into the world because of love of the world, in order that he might save the world, and he actually saves the world"—but only eventually as the impact of the Christian message is increasingly proclaimed and believed on widely. "We are a 'little flock' now: tomorrow we shall be the world." At the end, though not at the beginning, Christ shall have a saved world to present to His Father.[4]

Warfield's answer could be the correct one, though there is reason to doubt whether the Bible teaches that the world as a whole will be saved (cf. 1 Tim. 4:1, 2; 2 Tim. 4:3, 4; 2 Peter 2:1-3; Jude 18). But a better answer may be possible. If John, as a Jew, is actually thinking of the propitiatory sacrifice as it was practiced in Israel, particularly on the Day of Atonement—and how could he not?—then it may well be of himself and other Jews as opposed to Gentiles that he uses the word "us" or "we" in this phrase. The contrast would therefore be, not between Christians and the as-yet-unsaved world, but between those Jews for whom Christ died and those Gentiles for whom Christ died, both of whom now make up or eventually will make up the church. This use of the first person plural pronoun is not impossible in that John has used it in several different senses already.

According to this view, what John wishes to say is that Jesus fulfilled the pattern set by the Old Testament sacrifices but that He did so in such a way that now Gentiles as well as Jews are saved.

This is a marvel and a cause for great praise, for, as Paul says as he concludes a similar series of observations at the end of the eleventh chapter of Romans, "God has bound all men over to disobedience so that he may have mercy on them all. Oh, the depth of the riches of the wisdom and knowledge of God! How unsearchable his judgments, and his paths beyond tracing out! 'Who has known the mind of the Lord? Or who has been his counselor?' 'Who has ever given to God that God should repay him?' For from him and through him and to him are all things. To him be the glory forever! Amen" (Rom. 11:32-36).

CONCLUSION

The conclusion of this train of thought is evident. If Jesus has done so much for us, and not only for us but also for men and

---

[4]Benjamin B. Warfield, *Selected Shorter Writings of Benjamin B. Warfield—I*, edited by John E. Meeter (Phillipsburg, N.J.: Presbyterian and Reformed Publishing Company, 1970), pp. 167-177. The article first appeared in *The Expositor*, XXI (1921), pp. 241-253.

women scattered throughout the whole world, and if this naturally leads us to praise Him, should it not also lead us to holiness? Should it not impel us to fulfill John's desire for his little children that they "not sin"? Of course it should, and as much today as ever. Indeed, we should say with Paul, "For Christ's love compels us, because we are convinced that one died for all, and therefore all died. And he died for all, that those who live should no longer live for themselves but for him who died for them and was raised again" (2 Cor. 5:14, 15).

1 John 2:3-6
Righteousness: The Moral Test

> We know that we have come to know him if we obey his
> commands. The man who says, "I know him," but does not
> do what he commands is a liar, and the truth is not in him.
> But if anyone obeys his word, God's love is truly made
> complete in him. This is how we know we are in him: Who-
> ever claims to live in him must walk as Jesus did.

Anyone who has worked with young Christians knows it often
happens that shortly after a person believes in Christ doubts set
in. The initial experience of the Christian is usually one of great
joy. He had been lost in the darkness of his own sin and ignorance; now he has come into the light. Formerly he had not
found God; now he has found him. But then, as time goes by, it
is also frequently the case that the new Christian begins to wonder if, in fact, anything has really changed. He thought that he
was a new creature in Christ; but, to speak frankly, he is really
much as he was. The same temptations are present; they may
even be worse. There are the same flaws of character. Even the
joy, which he once knew, seems to be evaporating. At such a
time the new Christian often asks how it is possible to be certain
that he is saved by God. He may ask, "How can I truly know that
I know God?"

To answer this question is one of the major purposes,
perhaps the major purpose, of 1 John. But it is only at this point,
rather than earlier, that the problem is dealt with directly. Until
now John has been stating largely the historical groundings of the

54

Christian faith and has been dealing with the reality of sin in Christians. Now, however, he begins to indicate in explicit language how a Christian may truly know that he is born again or, to use John's own language, how he may know that he knows God.

There are three answers or tests. These were highlighted years ago by Robert Law and have since been restated well by Stott.[1] First, there is the moral test, which is the test of righteousness. This is developed first in 2:3-6, the verses being studied in this present chapter, and is brought forward at several other points throughout the letter. The point here is that the one who knows God will increasingly lead a righteous life, for God is righteous. It does not mean that he will be sinless; John has already shown that anyone who claims this is lying. It simply means that he will be moving in a direction marked out by the righteousness of God. If he does not do this, if he is not increasingly dissatisfied with and distressed by sin, he is not God's child. The second test is social, the test of love. It is developed first in 2:7-11 and is also restated several times later in the letter. Finally, there is the doctrinal test, which is the test of truth. It is found in 2:18-27, among other places.

From what John has already said it is easy to understand the importance of this first test, for if a person claims to know God and yet does not live a righteous life, then he inevitably comes to justify the sinful things he does. In other words, he says that sin is not sin, or that God does not care about sin, or that what he does is not sin. So he becomes a hypocrite. John calls him a liar. His very presence begins to undermine true Christianity.

THE MORAL TEST (v. 3)

John introduces the first of the tests for Christian assurance in verse 3. But he does so, not by saying, "And by this we may know that we are born again" or "By this we may know that we are Christians," but rather by the idea of knowledge. He says, "We know that we have come to know him if we obey his commands." The reason is immediately apparent, for since the Gnostics made so much of the matter of knowledge, it is as if John is saying, "So you want to speak about knowledge; all right,

---

[1]Robert Law, *The Tests of Life* (Grand Rapids: Baker, 1968), pp. 208-278; Stott, *Epistles of John*, p. 53, and *passim*. See the discussion under "Introduction to 1 John," pp. 14-15.

then. What is it that characterizes the one who truly knows God?" The answer, as we have already seen and as he says here, is "righteousness."

This, of course, was not the idea of knowledge most characteristic of Greek thought. In the classical Greek period there was an almost unlimited confidence in human reason, somewhat similar to the confidence in reason which existed in Europe and England in the eighteenth century. The early Greeks believed that accurate knowledge of all things, including God, was attainable. That is, they believed that they could arrive at God by the mere process of reasoning. Plato in particular led the way in this. In his system of thought, knowledge became by definition a knowledge of the eternal and unalterable essence of things, not of changeable phenomena. That is, it was a knowledge of forms, ideas, or ideals; and religion, as Barclay notes, became "something not very unlike the higher mathematics."[2] With men of great intellect this attempt to know God was no doubt popular, but it could hardly be as equally popular or satisfying to ordinary people. Moreover, it had two flaws. First, it gave no adequate basis for ethics. A man could be a philosopher or "knowing one" and yet indulge in all the depravity which infested paganism. Second, an intellectual knowledge of God did not satisfy the whole man, for man is more than intellect. Man wants to relate to the infinite, not merely contemplate it. So while the god of Plato and others filled the mind, it did not warm the heart or stir the emotions, which man desires.

In the Hellenistic period, partly as the breakdown of the old Greek democracy and partly as the result of contact with the east under Alexander and his successors, an entirely new concept entered the Greek world. It was the idea that God could be known through emotional experience. If the mind did not satisfy, perhaps the senses would. So the mystery religions, with their promise of an emotional union with the god induced by lighting, music, incense, and liturgy, became popular. There was a twofold problem with this approach too, however. First, it did not last. It was transient. Second, it did not satisfy the mind. The worshiper had an experience; but what was the experience? He had a great weekend; but it did not mean much on Monday morning. In this period, then, the Greek had a choice between a cold rationalism

[2]Barclay, *Letters of John and Jude*, p. 49.

and a passing emotional experience, if he should want to know God.

In contrast to either of these two Greek ideas, John's understanding of the knowledge of God is essentially personal and practical. So it is satisfying. It is satisfying because it is knowledge, not of an idea or thing, but of a person, and because it issues in a profound change of conduct.

This is not unique with John, of course. Rather it is simply a reflection of the entire biblical system. For example, in Jeremiah the goal of religion is said to be the "knowledge of God," as the Greeks also claimed it was. But at the same time that this is said, the nature of that knowledge, which is entirely different from the Greek idea both in its nature and effects, is indicated. Thus, we find Jeremiah writing, "'Let not the wise man boast of his wisdom or the strong man boast of his strength or the rich man boast of his riches, but let him who boasts boast about this: that he understands and knows me, that I am the LORD, who exercises kindness, justice and righteousness on earth, for in these I delight,' declares the LORD" (Jer. 9:23, 24). Any Greek would agree with the first part of that sentence, the part that says that the knowledge of God is man's glory. But the second part, the part that speaks of God practicing kindness, justice, and righteousness, and delighting in those who emulate Him in these characteristics, would be foreign to the same Greek thinker.

In the same way, Jeremiah 31:34 speaks of the knowledge of God that God's people will possess in the latter days: "'No longer will a man teach his neighbor, or a man his brother, saying, "Know the LORD," because they will all know me, from the least of them to the greatest,' declares the LORD." But this verse is preceded by a statement of how this will become possible: "I will put my law in their minds and write it on their hearts. I will be their God, and they will be my people." Moreover, it is followed by the ethical statement, "I will forgive their wickedness and will remember their sins no more."

There is no knowledge of God without an accompanying righteousness, for God is righteous. This is John's point. It is the first test by which we may know that we know him. John is not insensitive to the concerns of his contemporaries. Did the Greeks want to come into touch with reality? So does John. Did the most sensitive people of his day want to know God? This is also John's aspiration. But the questions are: How do you know Him? And how do you know that you know Him? John's answer is that you know Him when you come into contact with a personality that changes your personality and specifically leads you to live a righteous life.

Why is the righteous life a proof that we know God? Because it is not natural to sinful man. Consequently, it is proof of a divine and supernatural working in our lives if we obey Him. Paul makes the same point when he follows his admonition to the Philippians to "work out" their salvation with the profound observation, "For it is God who works in you to will and to act according to his good purpose" (Phil. 2:13).

TWO TYPES OF MEN (vv. 4, 5)

At this point John introduces two types of men, as if to make the test concrete. On the one hand, there is the man who claims to know God but who does not keep His commandments. John calls him a liar. On the other hand, there is the man who obeys God out of a genuine love of Him. John does not even say that this man claims to know God; but he does know Him, as his conduct indicates.

Profession without obedience

John has harsh words for the person who claims to know God but who does not obey His commandments. He calls him a liar. That is, he is neither deceived by someone else nor confused by facts. Rather, he is openly professing something which he knows is not true and therefore should rightly be branded a deceiver. Moreover, says John, "the truth is not in him." This phrase may be no more than a restatement of the claim that the man professing to know God while actually disobeying His commandments is a liar, but it may also mean more than this. It may mean that the truth is not to be found in him in the sense that the one seeking truth should go, not to this man, but rather to another source. If this is the case, then the phrase obviously applies to the false teachers of John's day (whom true seekers after God should avoid) and to false teachers in our time also. It means that truth should be sought, not from the man who has intellectual qualifications alone, but rather from the man whose claim to know spiritual things is backed up by godlike conduct. Unless there is observable godliness, such a man's teachings about God should be distrusted.

Obedience flowing from love

The second type is the man who obeys God. He is not making great statements of how much he knows God, as the Gnostics did. At least John is not saying that he is making such statements. Nevertheless, he does know God.

Two points are made about this man. First, in this man, rather than the other, love for God is perfected. In Greek the phrase "love for God" contains a genitive ("love *of God*"), which may be taken in one of three ways. It may be a subjective genitive. If this is the case, God is subject, and the reference is to God's love for us. It may be an objective genitive. In this case, God is the object, and the reference is to our love for God. Finally, it can be a qualitative genitive, in which case the reference would be to divine love; that is, to love that is of the nature of God. The second meaning is best. The meaning is that if a man loves God, he will seek to please Him and keep His commandments.

Anything else is hypocrisy. A number of years ago when the so-called "new morality" was at the peak of its popularity, a number of theologians met to discuss it. Most were in favor. So the discussion centered on the value of being free of any rules and regulations. "But there must be some guidelines," someone said. This was discussed. At length it was decided that the only acceptable guideline was love. Anything that flowed from love was permissible. Anything was allowed so long as it did not hurt anyone. While the discussion was proceeding along these lines a Roman Catholic priest, who had been invited to the discussion and was in the room, became very quiet. At length it was noticeable. The others turned to him and asked what he thought. "Don't you agree that the only limiting factor in any ethical decision is love?" they asked him.

The priest replied, "If you love me, you will obey what I command" (John 14:15).

The second statement made about the man who obeys God is that he has confidence spiritually, for, says John, "This is how we know we are in him." It is uncertain whether the phrase "this is how" refers to what has gone before or to what follows. The

59

sentence contains no connecting particles, nor does the one following. So the passage itself is undetermining. Besides, to make the matter more confusing, John apparently uses the phrase "this is how" both ways. Most often it refers to what follows; but sometimes, as at 4:6, it clearly refers to the preceding. The KJV takes it in the latter sense, that is, as referring to the man who obeys God and who therefore has assurance that he is a Christian. Most modern versions view it as an introduction to the concluding verse of this section, finding support in the resulting parallelism between verses 3 and 4, on the one hand, and verses 5 and 6, on the other. Thus, the NIV translation reads, "This is how we know we are in him: Whoever claims to live in him must walk as Jesus did."

Despite the weight of opinion on the other side, I feel that in this instance the KJV is right, for verse 6 is not so much a restatement of the test by which we may know that we know Him as it is a conclusion or exhortation addressed to those who do. If this is so, then verse 6 is an independent wrap-up of the entire section, and the phrase "this is how we know we are in him" rightly belongs with the preceding as a second consequence in the life of the man who does obey God. The flow of thought is, therefore: 1) the man who obeys God can know: a) that his love for God is being perfected, and b) that he is "in" God. Therefore, 2) everyone who says that he abides in God ought to reassure his own heart and others by obeying Him.

CONCLUSION (v. 6)

This conclusion also comes to Christians living in our own time. Do we say we are Christians? Then, "Whoever claims to live in him must walk as Jesus did." The call is to emulate Jesus in our conduct. "Earlier," as Calvin said, "he had set the light of God before us as an example. Now he calls us also to Christ, to imitate him. Yet he does not simply exhort us to the imitation of Christ, but, from the union we have with him, proves we should be like him."[3]

To walk as Christ walked is to live, not by rules, but by an example. It is to follow Him, to be His disciple. Such a discipleship is personal, active, and costly. It is *personal* because it

---

[3]John Calvin, *The Gospel According to St. John 11-21 and The First Epistle of John* (Grand Rapids: Eerdmans, 1961), p. 247.

cannot be passed off to another. Indeed, we are to find ourselves with Christ, as Peter did following the Resurrection. Jesus asked Peter, "Do you love me?" When Peter replied "Yes," he was told, "Feed my sheep." This was repeated three times, and it began to irritate Peter. So to escape Christ's careful probing he turned to John, the beloved disciple, who was apparently standing some distance away and asked, "Lord, what about this man?" Jesus replied, "If it is my will that he remain until I come, what is that to you? Follow me!" In other words, there was no escaping the call to a personal discipleship for Peter.

To walk as Christ walked is also *active* because the Lord Himself is active. To be inactive is to be left behind.

Finally, it is *costly* as well, because the path that Jesus walked is the path to crucifixion. It leads to glory, but before that it leads to the cross. Such a path can be walked only by the one who has died to self and who has deliberately taken up the cross of Christ to follow Him.

Such a one, whether in John's day or our own, will always have confidence before God and will be sure that he knows Him. Here Dodd concludes most perceptively, "In this passage our author is not only rebutting dangerous tendencies in the Church of his time, but discussing a problem of perennial importance, that of the validity of religious experience. We may have the feeling of awareness of God, of union with him, but how shall we know that such experience corresponds to reality? It is clear that no amount of clearness or strength in the experience itself can guarantee its validity, any more than the extreme vividness of a dream leads us to suppose that it is anything but a dream. If, however, we accept the revelation of God in Christ, then we must believe that any experience of God which is valid has an ethical quality defined by what we know of Christ. It will carry with it a renewed fidelity to his teaching and example. The writer does not mean that only those who perfectly obey Christ and follow his example can be said to have experience of God. That would be to affirm the sinlessness of Christians in a sense which he has repudiated. But unless the experience includes a setting of the affections and will in the direction of the moral principles of the Gospel, it is no true experience of God, in any Christian sense."[4]

[4]C. H. Dodd, *The Johannine Epistles* (London: Hodder and Stoughton, 1946), p. 32.

There is more to be said, of course, as Dodd also indicates. In fact, more is to be said in the verses following, but thus far the test of one's experience holds. By the test of righteousness we may know that we know God and may assure our hearts before Him.

1 John 2:7-11
Love: The Social Test

> Dear friends, I am not writing you a new command but an old one, which you have had since the beginning. This old command is the message you have heard. Yet I am writing you a new command; its truth is seen in him and you, because the darkness is passing and the true light is already shining.
>
> Anyone who claims to be in the light but hates his brother is still in the darkness. Whoever loves his brother lives in the light, and there is nothing in him to make him stumble. But whoever hates his brother is in the darkness and walks around in the darkness; he does not know where he is going, because the darkness has blinded him.

In an appendix to his excellent book *The Church at the End of the 20th Century,* Francis Schaeffer speaks of love as "the mark of the Christian." His study is based upon John 13:34, 35, in which Christ is recorded as having imparted a new commandment to His disciples: "A new commandment I give you: Love one another. As I have loved you, so you must love one another. All men will know that you are my disciples if you love one another." Schaeffer's point is that "only with this mark may the world know that Christians are indeed Christians and that Jesus was sent by the Father."[1]

He is right. It may be added to this, however, that it is also

[1]F. A. Schaeffer, *The Church at the End of the 20th Century* (Chicago: Inter-Varsity Press, 1970), p. 153.

by love that *Christians* may know that they are Christians. That is, a Christian may know that he has been truly made alive by Christ when he finds himself beginning to love and actually loving those others for whom Christ died.

This is the theme of the next section of 1 John, for it is in these verses (2:7-11) that the aged apostle develops the second or social test for whether a person who considers himself to know God actually knows Him or does not. The first test is found in verses 3-6. It is the moral test, the test of righteousness. The third test is found in verses 18-27. It is the test of belief or sound doctrine. Here, however, the test is love. Does the one who professes to love God love others as well? If he does, he can be sure that he has been made alive by God. If he does not, John says, such a person has no more right to consider himself a child of God than does the one who says that he knows God but disregards His commandments.

The section is divided into two parts: first, the law of love and, second, the life of love. The second part contains three contrasting applications of the basic principle.

THE LAW OF LOVE (vv. 7, 8)

In the preceding verses John admonished believers to keep God's commandments. But this was a general statement. Now he brings forward one command specifically: the command to love. It is true that verses 7 and 8 do not contain the word "love" and that, in fact, it is only mentioned once in the entire section (in v. 10). But the commandment to love is what John obviously has in mind, as the reference to the "new commandment" of John 13 clearly indicates. The progression of thought is that if a person knows God, he will keep God's commandments, and that, if he keeps God's commandments, he will love others in accord with Christ's teaching.

Love as an old commandment

There is nothing fundamentally new in all this, however, for John reminds his readers that the command is that which they have had from the beginning. It is possible to take this last phrase in at least two ways. It may refer to the beginning of Christianity, as the same phrase seems to do in chapter 1. Or it may be taken as referring to the beginning of revealed religion, that is, to the commandment as it existed in the Old Testament era. It is probably best to take it in the latter sense, for it is easier to see an old-new contrast between the law of love as contained in the Old Testament and the law of love as restated by Jesus for Christians, than to imagine a contrast between what existed from the beginning of Christianity and what is nevertheless in some sense still new as John writes his letter.

The command to love is old in that it existed and was known before Christ's coming. In its simplest form it is found in Leviticus 19:18, which says, "Love your neighbor as yourself. I am the LORD." This is the verse to which Jesus referred when He was asked His opinion regarding the first and greatest commandment. He said that the greatest commandment was that recorded in Deuteronomy 6:5: "Love the LORD your God with all your heart and with all your soul and with all your strength." But the second, He said, was the one found in Leviticus 19:18.

Love as a new commandment

In what sense, then, is the command to love a new commandment? It is new in that it was raised to an entirely new emphasis and level by the teaching and example of Jesus. William Barclay suggests two ways in which this is true, to which we may also add a third.

First, in Jesus, love became new in "*the extent* to which it reached." In Christ's day love was not new, but at the same time there were few who would consider love to be an obligation beyond a fairly limited circle of close friends or, at the widest extent, one's nation. To the orthodox Jew the sinner was not to be loved. Rather, he was one whom God obviously wished to destroy. Nor were Gentiles to be loved. They were created by God for hell. By contrast Jesus extended His love to everyone. He became the "friend of sinners," a sympathetic listener and teacher of women (who were also despised), and eventually the One through whom salvation was extended even to the gentile world. His last words to His disciples were that they were to make disciples "of all nations" (Matt. 28:19) and that they were to be His witnesses "in Jerusalem, and in all Judea and Samaria, and to the ends of the earth" (Acts 1:8).

Second, in Jesus love became new in "*the lengths* to which it would go." Here one must look to the cross, for it is at the cross that the height and depth of God's love is seen, as it is not seen to the same degree anywhere else. To what length will the love of God go? To the length at which the very Son of God will take upon Himself a human form, die on a cross, and there bear the sin of a fallen race, so that in bearing the punishment for that sin He is actually alienated for a time from God the Father and thus cries out in deep agony, "My God, my God, why have you forsaken me?" (Mark 15:34). That is the extent to which the love of God goes. It is thus that love becomes an entirely new thing in Christ.

Third, in Jesus love is made new in "*the degree* to which it is realized." John indicates this by adding in verse 8, "its truth is seen in him and you, because the darkness is passing and the true light is already shining." In this verse "true" *(alēthes, alēthinos)* means "genuine," and the point is that the true or genuine love, like genuine righteousness, is now being seen not only in Jesus but in those who are made alive in Him as well. In this sense, what was not possible under the Old Testament dispensation is now possible; for the life of Jesus, which expresses itself in love, is in His people.

THE LIFE OF LOVE (vv. 9-11)

John has stated that the darkness is passing away and that the true light is shining; but, nevertheless, the darkness is not completely gone yet, nor is the light seen everywhere or in everyone. Therefore, he brings forward three examples of those to whom the test of love may be applied. There are two negative examples and one positive one.

Profession without love

The first example is of the person who "claims to be in the light but hates his brother." John says that he is "still in the darkness." The wording of this verse ("Anyone who claims") recalls the similar and somewhat parallel statements in chapter 1 ("If we claim," vv. 6, 8, 10), and its place in the argument corresponds directly with 2:4: "The man who says, 'I know him,' but does not do what he commands is a liar, and the truth is not in him." In this case, however, John does not say that the one professing to know God while actually hating his brother is a liar, though that is true also, but rather that he is in darkness and walks in darkness until now. In this verse the reference is obviously to John's Gnostic opponents, as is also the case in the other verses which begin "If we claim." The Gnostic claimed to be the enlightened one. But he is actually in darkness, says John, if he fails to love his brother.

Paul said the same thing in writing to the Corinthians about love: "If I have the gift of prophecy and can fathom all mysteries and all knowledge, and if I have a faith that can move mountains, but have not love, I am nothing" (1 Cor. 13:2). Plummer states, "The light in a man is darkness until it is warmed by love."[2]

Love arising out of light

The second example is the positive one. This is the person who shows that he abides in the light by loving his brother. John says that in this behavior "there is nothing to make him stumble."

The idea of stumbling may be applied in either of two ways. First, it may be applied to others in the sense that the one loving his brother not only walks in the light himself but also is free of having caused others to offend. This is the general meaning of the word in the rest of the New Testament. On the other hand, it can also apply to the individual himself in the sense that, if he loves, he walks in the light and therefore does not himself stumble. The context almost demands this second explanation, for the point of the verses is not what happens to others but rather the effect of love and hate on the individual himself. The negative equivalent of this statement occurs just one verse later. In these verses John introduces the important idea that "our love and hatred not only reveal whether we are already in the light or in the darkness, but actually contribute towards the light or the darkness in which we already are."[3] The one who walks in the light has more light day by day. The one who walks in darkness is increasingly darkened.

Hate leading to greater darkness

The last of John's examples is again negative and follows naturally upon what precedes it. He has spoken of the man who loves his brother and has shown the consequences of so walking. Now

---

[2]Plummer, *Epistles of S. John,* p. 95.

[3]Stott, *Epistles of John,* p. 94.

he returns to the case of the one who hates his brother and shows the consequences of that. There are three consequences. After these, John appends a final and summarizing explanation.

The first consequence is in the nature of an observation: the one who hates his brother is in darkness. This is the simplest expression of the test in its negative form. The second consequence is that he walks in darkness. This adds the idea of continuing action or a continuing sphere of activity. It is not just that the man who fails to love his brother is without knowledge of God; it is also that everything he does is in darkness and is characterized by darkness. He continues in it. Finally, John adds that although he continues in his darkened walk, he does so without any clear knowledge of a goal. He walks on, for the way of the ungodly is one of restless activity. But he "does not know where he is going" (cf. John 12:35).

There is only one explanation for this incredible state of affairs, a state where men walk in darkness even though the true light is shining and do not have a goal even though God's goal in Christ has been made clear. It is that men are blind and cannot see the light nor discern the goal. Clearly there is no hope for such except in God, who is able to give sight to the blind and direct the sinner's feet in the paths of righteousness.

CONCLUSION

This last verse introduces a term which may be applied to the life of love. It is the term "walk," which suggests practical steps. What is love after all? It is not just a certain benign feeling. It is not a smile. It is an attitude which determines what one does. Therefore, it is impossible to speak of love in the Christian sense without at least suggesting some of the actions which ought to flow from it, just as it is impossible to speak of the love of God without mentioning such things as the creation of man in His image, the giving of the Old Testament revelation, the coming of Christ, the cross, the outpouring of the Holy Spirit, and other realities.

What does love mean? What will happen if those who profess the life of Christ actually love one another? Francis Schaeffer, who was referred to at the beginning of this chapter, has several suggestions.

First, it will mean that when a Christian has failed to love his brother and has therefore acted wrongly toward him, he will go to him and say he is sorry. That sounds easy, but it is not, as anyone who has tried it knows. Nevertheless, this more than anything else expresses love and restores that oneness which Jesus said should flow from the fact that Christians do love one another and by which their profession is verified before the world.

Second, because the offense is often the other way, we are to show our love by forgiveness. This too is hard, particularly when the other person does not say, "I am sorry." Schaeffer writes, "We must all continually acknowledge that we do not practice the forgiving heart as we should. And yet the prayer is, 'Forgive us our debts, our trespasses, as we forgive our debtors.' We are to have a forgiving spirit even before the other person expresses regret for his wrong. The Lord's prayer does not suggest that when the other man is sorry, then we are to show a oneness by having a forgiving spirit. Rather, we are called upon to have a forgiving spirit without the other man having made the first step. We may still say that he is wrong, but in the midst of saying that he is wrong, we must be forgiving."[4]

John himself learned love at this point, for early in his life he was known as one of the "sons of thunder." He once wanted to call down fire from heaven upon those who rejected Jesus (Luke 9:54). But as he came to know more of that Spirit he was of, he came increasingly to call for love among the brethren.

Third, we must show love by practical demonstration, even when it is costly. Love cost the Samaritan in Christ's parable. It cost him time and money. Love cost the shepherd who endured hardship to hunt for his sheep. Love cost Mary of Bethany who, out of her love, broke the box of priceless ointment over the feet of Jesus. Love will be costly to all who practice it. But what is purchased thereby will be of great value, though intangible; for it will be proof of the presence of the life of God both to the individual Christian and to the watching world.

---

[4]Schaeffer, *The Church at End of 20th Century,* p. 145.

1 John 2:12-17
The Church and the World

I write to you, dear children, because your sins have been forgiven on account of his name.
I write to you, fathers, because you have known him who is from the beginning.
I write to you, young men, because you have overcome the evil one.
I write to you, dear children, because you have known the Father.
I write to you, fathers, because you have known him who is from the beginning.
I write to you, young men, because you are strong, and the word of God lives in you, and you have overcome the evil one.
Do not love the world or anything in the world. If anyone loves the world, the love of the Father is not in him. For everything in the world—the cravings of sinful man, the lust of his eyes and the boasting of what he has and does—comes not from the Father but from the world. The world and its desires pass away, but the man who does the will of God lives forever.

Most persons have had the experience of making a remark that was intended for one individual and of having an entirely different individual take it personally. It may even have been that the one who applied the remark to himself was the one who least needed it. Still he applied it to himself because he was sensitive and because he really wanted to learn from what was going on about him. An experience like this is so common that we can easily imagine that it was in John's mind as he began to write the next section of his letter. He had just said something intended for certain individuals, and he was afraid that the Christians, for whom he had not intended it, might take it wrongly.

John has been stating the tests by which the presence of the life of God within the individual may be discerned, and conversely he has spoken of those in whom it is not present. At times his words have been harsh. He has said that those who profess to know God but who fail to obey God's commandments are liars. He has added that those who say they love God but fail to love their brothers are in the dark, walk in the dark, and do not know where they are going. What would be the reaction of John's readers to these words? We can imagine some of them taking the words personally, as John undoubtedly imagined that some of them might do. They would admit that at times they did not obey God's commandments and did not love one another, and some would wonder if therefore they were truly born again. But this is not the way John wanted them to think. Indeed, he is writing his letter not to increase their doubt but to strengthen their assurance. As a result, at this point he interrupts his presentation of the tests to direct a personal word to his readers.

First, he assures them, in spite of what he has said, that he has no doubt of their having come to a knowledge of God. In fact, it is because they know God, rather than not knowing God, that he is writing to them. At the same time, however, he indicates the way in which his remarks are to be taken by Christians. The first of these points is established in verses 12-14. The second is made in verses 15-17.

Law says of these purposes, "The impulse to write thus does not spring from doubt of their Christian standing or of their progress in Christian experience, but that, on the contrary, it is his confidence in their Christian character and attainments that inspires him to write as he does. The motive of the address is, in the first place, apologetic and conciliatory—to obviate possible misunderstandings, or even possible offense." However, at the same time, "He secures a vantage ground from which to press the yet more stringent demands that are to follow."[1]

---

[1]Law, *Tests of Life*, p. 307.

71

1 John 2:12-17

JOHN'S READERS (vv. 12-14)

There are several problems connected with the interpretation of verses 12-14. But they must not be blown out of proportion, in that the message is fairly clear regardless of how one solves them.

The first problem involves those who are addressed in the passage. In these verses John makes six statements about his readers, arranged in two sets of three statements each. In each set the first remark is addressed to "dear children" (a different word is used in each case), the second to "fathers," the third to "young men." But how are these three categories of readers to be taken? Are these merely three different ways of looking at all Christians so that each remark applies to all believers? This is the view taken by Dodd and Barclay. Are there three separate categories so that some words are directed to those who are new Christians, others to those who are mature in the faith, and still others to those who are somewhere in between, the young men? This view is taken by Augustine and other early church fathers. It is also held by Henry, Stott, Bruce, and others. Or, finally, can it be that there are only two categories, that is, that John first addresses all his readers as "dear children" and then subdivides them into "fathers" and "young men"? This view, which is supported by John's use of the phrase "dear children" elsewhere, is held by Westcott, Law, Brooke, Ross, and other commentators.

Several facts support the twofold grouping of John's readers. The order (children, fathers, young men) is one of them. But in spite of this the distinct content of the remarks, at least in the judgment of the present writer, suggests three categories. The children are those who have recently come to the knowledge of God and of sins forgiven. The fathers have acquired the gift of spiritual wisdom, having lived longer in the faith and thus have come to know Him who is from the beginning in a deeper way. The young men are those who are bearing the brunt of the church's spiritual warfare. We must apply John's words to Christians in each of these three categories.[2] Nevertheless, as we

[2]Calvin wisely notes the difficulty most people have in doing this. "Indeed, such is our malignity that few think that what is directed at all belongs to themselves. The old for the most part steal away as if they had exceeded the age of learning. Children refuse to hear, as if they were not yet old enough. Middle-

adopt this grouping we must remember that in a quite different and secondary sense each Christian life also has analogies with youth, young manhood, and age so that what is said may also be applied to most Christians generally.

The second problem cannot be explained so easily, but is probably even less significant. In these verses John changes the tense of the verb "I write." In the first three instances he uses the present form ("I am writing"); in the second three instances he uses the past or aorist form ("I have written"). It has been suggested that John is here referring to an earlier letter or that he was interrupted at this point and then picked up in the past tense to speak of what he had written, but these ideas are only conjecture. More likely John is simply thinking of the words he is writing when he uses the present tense and of what he has already written when he uses the aorist. It is also possible that the second section merely employs the epistulary aorist, which has the same effective meaning as the present tense, for stylistic purposes.

Dear children

John's first remarks are addressed to "dear children." Whether we take this as referring only to those who are young in the faith or to all believers the meaning is the same, for all who have believed in Christ have known this experience. John says that it is twofold; they have had their sins forgiven for Christ's sake, and they know the Father. These almost without exception are the first conscious experiences of the new Christian, for, having believed on Jesus as the Son of God and Savior, the newborn child of God knows that his sins are now forgiven through the work of Jesus on the cross and in the same moment comes to know God, whom before he did not know and even feared. He now calls God "Father" (cf. Rom. 8:15, 16).

The testimony of Charles H. Spurgeon to the nature of his conversion is a good illustration of this point. He had been converted suddenly at a fairly early age after several years of conviction of sin. In these years he had known great misery but, having

aged men do not attend, because they are occupied with other cares. Therefore, lest any should exempt themselves, he accommodates the Gospel to the use of individuals. And he mentions three ages, the most common division of human life" (p. 251). It is, however, better to take the terms as referring to stages of spiritual maturity rather than of physical development, as Calvin does.

come to Christ, he found all things changed. "When my eyes first looked to Christ, he was a very real Christ to me; and when my burden of sin rolled from off my back, it was a real pardon and a real release from sin to me; and when that day I said for the first time, 'Jesus Christ is mine,' it was a real possession of Christ to me. When I went up to the sanctuary in that early dawn of youthful piety, every song was really a psalm, and when there was a prayer, oh, how I followed every word! It was prayer indeed! And so was it, too, in silent quietude, when I drew near to God, it was no mockery, no routine, no matter of mere duty; it was a real talking with my Father who is in Heaven."[3]

In these references John writes to the newborn in Christ to assure them that he is writing, not because they are not saved (which some of his remarks might lead them to question), but because they are and because he wants them to progress in their Christianity. The book should have the same value today.

Fathers

John's two statements to the spiritually mature of his congregations, the fathers, are identical; what is more, they are also quite similar to the second of his statements to children. There is one difference, however, and in this difference lies the distinct nature of John's reference. John said to the children that he has written to them because they have "known the Father." Now he says to the fathers that he is writing to them because they have "known him who is from the beginning." Obviously the new element is the reference to time ("from the beginning"), and this suggests the idea of God's unchanging faithfulness together with the spiritual trust and wisdom which such knowledge brings. It is the fathers who, as the result of a lifetime of spiritual experience, have known the eternal One and have come fully to trust Him. John writes to these because, having known God in this way, they will be able to rejoice in the truths that the aged apostle enunciates and support him in what he says.

Brooke, Burdick and some others believe that the phrase "him who is from the beginning" must refer to Christ, in that the opening verses speak of Christ in similar language. But it is not certain that the words "that which was from the beginning" refer

---

[3]Spurgeon, *Autobiography,* p. 99.

74

to Christ even there.[4] Besides, the context suggests that the reference is to God the Father, since the Father is referred to explicitly in verse 13. There is not, of course, any essential difference between the two interpretations.

Young men

John's lengthiest comments are reserved for the young men, and it is easy to see why this is so. These are the ones most energetically engaged in the business of Christian living and who are expected to be the church's first line of defense in case of attack. Indeed, in view of the threat which occasioned the letter, one can say that the young men are to be the major opponents of the then incipient Gnosticism.

The author says three things of these men. First, he says they are strong. This is the natural virtue of young manhood, but we might have expected John to encourage them to be strong rather than simply stating that they are. This is not John's approach, however. Rather, he wishes to assure them of that which they have already attained and of the fact that under God they are able to meet Satan's attacks. It is interesting to note at this point that the verbs in these six statements ("are" and "lives" excepted) are in the perfect tense, indicating a continuing result of past action. In other words, as Stott notes, "John is laying emphasis on the assured standing into which every Christian has come, whatever his stage of spiritual development."[5]

Second, John explains why the young men are strong. It is not that they are strong in themselves, for he is speaking spiritually now and not physically, and no one is spiritually strong by himself. It is rather that God has Himself made them strong through His Word which is abiding in them. These men have understood the gospel. They have assimilated its demands, including obedience to God and the need to love the brethren, and they are using their knowledge. It is possible that John is thinking of Psalm 119:9 as he writes: "How can a young man keep his way pure? By living according to your word." He may also be thinking of that future day of full victory and of those victors of whom he writes in Revelation 12:11, "They overcame him by the blood of the Lamb and by the word of their testimony." Clearly

---

[4]See pages 24-25.
[5]Stott, *Epistles of John*, p. 98.

these victors have taken "the sword of the Spirit, which is the word of God" (Eph. 6:17).

Third, John tells of the results that come from the fact that the young men have been strong; namely, they "have overcome the evil one." This is his point of emphasis, for the words are repeated twice, in each case in the last and emphatic position. Victory! This is what is called for. Consequently, believers must learn that the forgiveness of sins and the knowledge of God which they have enjoyed from the initial moments of their conversion are not the sum total of Christianity. Rather they must seek to grow strong so that they may take their proper and needed place in the Christian warfare.

An Appeal to John's Readers (vv. 15-17)

The first part of John's long parenthesis, verses 12-17, was written to reassure his readers, for John did not want them to think that he was questioning their salvation. Rather, he has written to them because their sins have been forgiven and because they do know the Father. If they miss this truth, they have misunderstood him. On the other hand, John does not want them to think that what he has written regarding the tests of life has no relevance for Christians, for this would be a misunderstanding too. Thus, he now goes on to show how what he has said should be applied to their lives. They are not to doubt their salvation, but rather, being assured of it, are to press on in those areas which give evidence of their transformation and which indeed bring the greatest measure of personal blessing. What is the Christian to do? Quite simply, he is to refuse to love the world and its values and instead love God and the will of God. In stating this John also gives two reasons why this is the only sane course for any Christian.

Love not the world

John's appeal to his readers is stated negatively, but the positive side must be understood also. Christians must not love the world. At the same time it must also be said that they are to love God and do His will. Indeed, it is only as the love of God fills them and the will of God motivates them that the world can be conquered, just as in the preceding verse it is only as the Word of God abides in them that Satan can be overcome.

With the exception of one passing reference in 2:2, this is the first time in the letter that John has used the word "world" *(kos-*

76

mos). But now it occurs six times in just these three verses, and it will occur many more times later on. On the whole, it is one of the most important terms in the Johannine vocabulary. What is the "world"? The answer to that question is a complex one, for the word itself has a wide range of meaning. At times, though this is a very minor usage, John seems to mean little more than the "universe," as in John 1:10. This, of course, is the basic meaning of the Greek word. In the early history of the Greek language *kosmos* meant "an ornament" (this meaning is preserved in English in the word "cosmetic"), then later the "universe" or "world globe," as the ornament of God. In this early period *kosmos* could also mean "that which is well constructed," "well ordered," or "beautiful."

In time the application of the word to the world led also to a further development by which it came to denote "the world of men." This use is also present in John, occurring at times without apparent moral overtones. It is said of the world in this sense that God loved it and gave His only begotten Son for it (John 3:16), that it is the object of His saving purposes (John 3:17), that Jesus gave Himself as a propitiation for it (1 John 2:2), and that Christ is its Savior (John 4:42; 1 John 4:14). It must be understood of this use of the word that it refers to the human race collectively and not necessarily to each individual, otherwise the verses in question would imply a universal salvation of all men which is, however, repudiated elsewhere.

The third major use of the word is one which involves the ethical dimension; and it is not only the most common, it is also the most significant usage in John's writings. The idea here is of the world of men in rebellion against God and therefore characterized by all that is in opposition to God. This is what we might call "the world system." It involves the world's values, pleasures, pastimes, and aspirations. John says of this world that the world lies in the grip of the evil one (1 John 5:19), that it rejected Jesus when He came (John 1:10), that it does not know Him (1 John 3:1), and consequently that it does not know and therefore also hates His followers (John 15:18-21; 17:14). It is in this sense that John speaks of the world in the passage before us.

If the first sense of the word is used, Christians are to receive and be thankful for the world, for it is God's gift. Jesus Himself was appreciative of the world in this sense. If the second sense is used, Christians are to love the world and seek to evangelize it, for God also loves the world. In the third sense, the sense we have here, Christians are to reject the world and conduct their lives according to an entirely different set of values.

When John says that Christians are not to "love the world or anything in the world," he is not thinking then so much of materialism ("things") as he is of the attitudes that lie behind materialism. For he knows, as we should all know, that a person without worldly goods can be just as materialistic as a person who has many of them; and, conversely, a rich person can be quite free from this and any other form of worldliness. John is actually thinking of selfish ambition, pride, the love of success or flattery, and other such characteristics. Law recognizes this in his excellent rephrasing of the apostle's appeal. He writes, "Do not court the intimacy and the favour of the unchristian world around you; do not take its customs for your laws, nor adopt its ideals, nor covet its prizes, nor seek fellowship with its life."[6] The NEB says, "Do not set your hearts on the godless world or anything in it."

Two reasons

John does not say this merely to have Christians be different, however. He has perfectly good reasons for saying what he does. The first reason why Christians are not to love the world or the things that are in the world is that love for the world and love for the Father are incompatible. God is set over against the world's sin and values. Consequently, it is impossible to both love and serve God and at the same time love that which He hates and which opposes Him. Does the believer love God? Then he must serve Him. As Jesus said, "No one can serve two masters. Either he will hate the one and love the other, or he will be devoted to the one and despise the other. You cannot serve both God and Money" (Matt. 6:24).

The truth of this statement becomes even more evident when the nature of the world system is analyzed, as John now proceeds to do in three succinct and memorable phrases: "the cravings of sinful man, the lust of his eyes and the boasting of what he has and does."

It may be, as John uses the phrase, that "the cravings of sinful man" refers to those sinful desires which arise out of man's

---

[6]Law, *Tests of Life*, p. 148.

fleshly or carnal nature. We can think here of the grosser sins. But in John's writings, as throughout Scripture, "sinful man" or "flesh" usually has a broader connotation by which is meant the whole of man's nature as it is apart from God's grace in Christ Jesus. Therefore it is more likely that "flesh" is to be understood broadly in this context. In this case the phrase would refer simply to all godless desires. As Barclay notes, "It is to live a life which is dominated by the senses. It is to be gluttonous in food; effeminate in luxury; slavish in pleasure; lustful and lax in morals; selfish in the use of possessions; regardless of all the spiritual values; extravagant in the gratification of worldly, earthly and material desires. The flesh's desire is forgetful of, blind to, or regardless of the commandments of God."[7] Clearly, we do not need to think of this as concerning particularly gross sins alone, though they are part of it. Rather, we may include all activity which is oblivious to God and insensitive to the needs of other people.

The second phrase refers naturally to covetousness. But again, this must be understood in a broader sense than a desire merely to possess things. The "lust of his eyes" certainly refers to the desire to "keep up with the Joneses" in regard to the appearance of the home, the second car, the vacation cottage, and other material considerations. But it also refers to the desire to keep up with the Joneses in terms of the husband's status at work, the wife's position in the Women's Association, the social acceptability of the children, and all other such nonmaterial but nevertheless worldly values. These are the things that the Christian is not to love. In other words, he is to be content to be overlooked for the promotion, do without the external symbols of success, be thought unsophisticated or unglamorous if such actually contributes to the glory of God and the living out of the will of God for the individual Christian.

Finally, worldliness is here characterized as "the boasting of what he has and does." The unique quality of this phrase lies not so much in keeping up with the Joneses as exceeding them. This characteristic, while the hardest of the three to define, is probably also the most subtle, for it is easy to see how quickly a perfectly laudable ambition may slide over into pride that glories not so much in doing well as in being better than one's fellows. An example is that of the student who tries desperately to be the best

[7]Barclay, *Letters of John and Jude*, p. 68.

in his class. This can be done in a proper way. If he has been given the talent by God and applies the talent in order that God might be honored by his achievement or better served by it, his ambition is good. On the other hand, if he finds himself thinking that he is rather superior and therefore entitled to an extra measure of deference or respect, then his ambition is at base satanic, for it arises from him who is the prince of this world and of this world's godless system. The same kind of satanic ambition can affect men in business, wives in the home, or ministers in the pulpit. Indeed, Paul even warned us that some of Satan's tools would wear doctoral robes and teach theology (2 Cor. 11:14, 15).

These, then, are the ideals which are accepted and even prized in the world but which are antithetical to Christianity. To love God is to move away from such values. To love the world is to increasingly drift from love for God and thereby also lose love for others.

The second reason why the Christian is not to love the world is the one which closes the passage. It is that all that is in the world is transitory and therefore headed for destruction. The world is passing away, John states. So are its values and those who are characterized by its values. How foolish, then, to pin one's hopes on the world system, however attractive it may appear or however rewarding.[8]

But does nothing at all abide? Yes, says John. The one who does God's will abides forever. The object of his love, even the Father, abides forever. His love itself, having its source in God, abides forever. His works, being an aspect of the work of God, abide forever, for He is the possessor of eternal life and heir to all God's riches in Christ Jesus. The conclusion is that Christians should therefore love God and serve Him fervently.

CONCLUSION

Do we love and serve God fervently? Then we must turn from all that would keep us from such love and service. When Jesus called men to be His disciples, He challenged them with the

---

[8]Westcott has a long and valuable note on "The Two Empires: the Church and the World," in which he demonstrates their fundamental antipathy to one another and contrasts the decline of the Roman Empire, as one expression of the world's kingdom, with the victorious progress of Christianity (pp. 249-282).

words "Follow me." This meant that they had to leave their nets or money tables or whatever else had been occupying their attention and time up to that moment. Similarly, when we are called to embrace the truth of the gospel, we must reject error. When we are called to righteousness, we must turn from unrighteousness. When we are called to love God, we must turn from all lesser loves and loyalties. To fail to do this does not mean that we thereby lose our relationship to God, but it does mean that we are unfaithful to Him and disgrace our calling. It is like a marriage. Adultery does not change the legal status of the marriage, but it destroys the fellowship and is dishonorable. As Christians we are married to Christ. Therefore, we must not dishonor that relationship by adultery, or even by flirting with the world.

1 John 2:18-27
Truth: The Doctrinal Test

Dear children, this is the last hour; and as you have heard
that the antichrist is coming, even now many antichrists have
come. This is how we know it is the last hour. They went out
from us, but they did not really belong to us. For if they had
belonged to us, they would have remained with us; but their
going showed that none of them belonged to us.

But you have an anointing from the Holy One, and all
of you know the truth. I do not write to you because you do
not know the truth, but because you do know it and because
no lie comes from the truth. Who is the liar? It is the man
who denies that Jesus is the Christ. Such a man is the
antichrist—he denies the Father and the Son. No one who
denies the Son has the Father; whoever acknowledges the
Son has the Father also.

See that what you have heard from the beginning remains in you. If it does, you also will remain in the Son and
in the Father. And this is what he promised us—even eternal
life.

I am writing these things to you about those who are
trying to lead you astray. As for you, the anointing you received from him remains in you, and you do not need anyone to teach you. But as his anointing teaches you about all
things and as that anointing is real, not counterfeit—just as it
has taught you, remain in him.

It is a characteristic of our time, often pointed out by contemporary Christian apologists, that men and women no longer strictly
believe in truth. To be sure, they do use the term in a certain

colloquial sense, referring to that which is the opposite of false; nevertheless, most twentieth-century men do not mean that when a thing is said to be true it is therefore true absolutely and forever. They usually mean that it is true for some people, though perhaps not for others, or that it is true now, but not necessarily also for tomorrow or the day after. The consequences of this are a great deal of uncertainty and a noticeable sense of lostness in the universe of ideas and objects by modern men.

To men and women conditioned by this twentieth-century mind it is somewhat of a surprise to find that Christianity, particularly in its New Testament expression, moves within an entirely different set of presuppositions. But surprise or not, it is clear that when the Bible speaks of truth it means truth absolutely; that is, truth which is binding upon everyone and which is true both now and forever. It is in this sense that God is "true," that Christ is "the truth," and that the Bible is said to contain "true" propositions. Moreover, according to the Bible, such truth can be known now. It can be known by believing it. That is, it can be known by taking God at His word, as that word is recorded in the Bible, and by acting upon it. In 1 John the aged author of that book even says that knowing the truth is one evidence of the new life of God within the Christian.

At this point the reader of the letter will recall that one of John's purposes in writing it, perhaps even the major purpose, is to help Christians become sure of their salvation. To do this he is offering three tests by which the presence of new life within the Christian may be recognized. The first two have already been given. They are the test of righteousness and the test of love. Now, after a brief parenthesis to reassure and encourage his readers, John brings forward his third and final test, which is the test of truth. How may those who consider themselves Christians be sure they really are Christians? In these verses John answers that they may reassure themselves on the basis of their attitude toward the truth of God as revealed in Jesus. They can be certain of their salvation if they believe that Jesus is God incarnate and if they continue in that conviction.

In this section John follows a threefold outline. First, he develops a contrast between the antichrists of his day and God's true children, a contrast which is at the same time a contrast between falsehood and error (vv. 18-21). Second, he defines the heresy of the antichrists, which is the chief heresy of all (vv. 22, 23). Third, he encourages those who are Christians to make use of their two most valuable defenses against heresy, namely, the truth of the gospel and the Holy Spirit (vv. 24-27).

ANTICHRISTS AND GOD'S CHILDREN (vv. 18-21)

It is a logical step from verse 17, in which John has mentioned the world which is passing away, to "the last hour" with which this section commences. But John's thought is not primarily upon the last hour. He is thinking mainly of the false teachers, the Gnostics, who had left the churches to whom he is writing in order to found their own church. He calls them "antichrists" and contrasts them with God's true children.

The antichrists

The word "antichrist" occurs in the Bible only in the letters of John and that only five times in four verses (1 John 2:18, 22; 4:3; 2 John 7); but though the word is infrequent the idea of antichrist is frequent and is an important one. It is part of a widespread belief in John's day that at the end of history there was to be a final struggle between the forces of good, focused in God, and the forces of evil, focused in a being of superior intelligence and cunning. John's manner of referring to antichrist indicates that his readers were already familiar with these concepts.[1]

In the Bible the idea of antichrist is first seen in Daniel. In Daniel 7, for example, there is a vision of four great beasts, in the context of which antichrist is described as "a little horn" who destroys three other horns. In the language of these visions, a horn is an earthly king or world ruler. So the vision means that this last evil figure will be a king who is able to overcome three other kings. When the vision goes on to say that this horn possesses "a mouth that spoke boastfully" (v. 8), it means that he will have great oratorical ability. The activity of this figure in profaning the temple, an act partially fulfilled by Antiochus Epiphanes in 168 B.C., is described in Daniel 11:31 and 12:11.

If Daniel alone were consulted, one might think that An-

---

[1]There is an excellent discussion of the development of the antichrist concept in Brooke ("Additional Note," pp. 69-79). He discusses it in relation to both extrabiblical and biblical texts.

tiochus Epiphanes had fulfilled the prophecies regarding antichrist completely. But this is not the case in that the Book of Revelation both amplifies upon Daniel's prophecy and looks for a further fulfillment. Thus, in Revelation 13 Daniel's vision of the beasts and horns reappears; only here the beasts are fused into one, thereby suggesting that antichrist will combine the strengths of each of three former world kingdoms in his own.

Similarly, in Mark 13:22, 23 Jesus also prophesied concerning a future fulfillment: "False Christs and false prophets will appear and perform signs and miracles to deceive the elect—if that were possible. So be on your guard; I have told you everything ahead of time."

In 2 Thessalonians 2:3, 4 the concept occurs again. Here the apostle Paul writes of antichrist as "the man of lawlessness," who, we are told, "opposes and exalts himself over everything that is called God or is worshiped, and even sets himself up in God's temple, proclaiming himself to be God" (v. 4). These references are all related to each other, as a careful reading of the passages in question shows. Moreover, they seem to picture antichrist filling a religious function as well as a political role.

The names given to this terrifying figure in these prophecies point to his totally evil nature and demonic goals—a horn, a beast (even *the* beast), the man of lawlessness or perdition, and antichrist—but we need not think, just because these names are used, that antichrist must therefore be repulsive. Here the meaning of the word "antichrist" is important. It is formed of two words: "Christ" and the prefix "anti," which can mean either "the opposite of" or "instead of." Those who have taken the former meaning tend to view antichrist as the total counterpart to Jesus and have therefore sometimes identified him with the worst tyrants of history. Some support for this is found in the fact that if John had not meant "the opposite of," if he had meant rather "a substitute Christ," he could have used the word "pseudochrist" as he does "pseudoprophet" in 4:1. On the other hand, the word "antichrist" may have been a fixed term, rather like a popular name, with the consequence that John was really not at liberty to alter it. Besides, in the context of the chapter it is surely significant that the antichrists are identified, not as those who are outside the church, but as those who at least for a time were within it. In other words, they are not the outright pagan opponents of Christianity but rather those who were attempting to destroy the faith from within by pretending to be Christians.

When John writes that "many antichrists have come" he is not saying, then, that the final singular figure of antichrist is in the world, though, of course, that could have been a possibility. Rather, he is saying that the spirit that will characterize the final antichrist is already working in those who have recently left his readers' congregations. The future antichrist will be a substitute for Christ, as much like Jesus as it is possible for a tool of Satan to be. Similarly, these Gnostic teachers appear to be angels of light but are actually satanic in both their works and outlook.

Being faced with a major defection in their ranks, the Christians of Asia Minor might be tempted to be discouraged, but now John adds that the defection has a good purpose. These "went out" from us, he says, in order that it might show "that none of them belonged to us." In other words, the defection has the effect of purifying the church and revealing both truth and error in true colors.

It is interesting to note, as Stott does, that 1 John 2:19 has an incidental but very important bearing upon two great Christian doctrines: the perseverance of the saints and the nature of the visible church. The bearing of the verse upon the first doctrine is seen in the statement that if the false teachers were really members of the body of Christ, they would have continued with other members of the body of Christ. This implies that perseverance is the ultimate test of genuine participation in the life of Christ. Those who are saved will persevere. On the other hand, the doctrine is not given in order to lull anyone into a false sense of security before God. As Bruce writes, "When Paul, not without reason, says to the Corinthian church, 'Do you not realize that Jesus Christ is in you?—unless indeed you fail to meet the test!' (2 Cor. 13:5), he implies that all those in whom the risen Christ is present by his Spirit will indeed meet the test, while those who fail to meet the test, who show themselves 'reprobate' (*adokimoi*), prove by that fact that the root of the matter was never in them, whatever appearance of genuineness they may once have presented."[2]

The second doctrine upon which the verse throws light is that of the church, for it gives warrant for a distinction between

[2]Bruce, *Epistles of John,* p. 69.

the visible and the invisible church. It must be granted that Christians should pray that the church be as pure as it is possible for the church on earth to be, and work toward that goal. But when this is said, it must at the same time also be acknowledged that the church on earth will always contain tares as well as wheat and that Christians must exercise the utmost care in how they deal with them. The great temptation, particularly for those who are most serious about the church and its doctrine, is to root up the tares. But those who incline to this must remember that in Christ's parable (Matt. 13:24-30) it was precisely this course that was forbidden to the householder's servants. They said, "'Do you want us to go and pull them up [that is, the tares]?' 'No,' he answered, 'because while you are pulling the weeds, you may root up the wheat with them.'" The time for separation was to be at the time of the final harvest when the wheat should be gathered into barns and the tares burned.

The implication of Christ's parable and John's statement is that some Christians are so much like non-Christians and some non-Christians so much like Christians that it is impossible to tell the difference between them in this life. Moreover, in Christ's judgment the protection and nurture of all his followers within the church, regardless of their outward appearance or degree of sanctification, are of such value that he would rather tolerate an impure church than forfeit them. The followers of the Lord should therefore do likewise, though, of course, they will be greatly relieved when some who are not genuine believers reveal this fact by their departure from the church. We must bear in mind that John is not talking about a mere exchange of one denomination for another—the one who does that is not by that act revealed to be an unbeliever—but rather of a departure which is at the same time a rejection of the fundamental truths of Christianity.

God's children

Over against the antichrists who have left the church John sets God's true children. These are distinguished by two essential characteristics: first, they have been anointed by the Holy One and, second, they all know the truth centered in Jesus Christ.

The contrast that John makes is far sharper in the Greek language than in any English version, for the effect of his wording is to say that the Christians to whom he is writing are true "Christs" as opposed to the "false Christs" who have left their number. The word "Christ" or "Messiah" means "anointed one." Similarly, the word that lies behind the word "anointing" in the phrase "you have an anointing from the Holy One" is *chrisma,* which is related to the word "Christ." So to say that the believers have all received an anointing (literally, "You have an anointing") is in some sense equivalent to saying that they are now Christs in this world. This may be applied personally by all believers, for all who have truly been anointed by God are as Christ and must act as Christ in their own situation. Jesus said, "As the Father has sent me, I am sending you" (John 20:21). John later writes, "In this world we are like him" 1 John 4:17).

John also says that those who are truly God's children "know," by which, as the next verses show, he means that they know the truth concerning Jesus Christ with all its consequences. The KJV gives an unfortunate translation at this point, being based, as it is, upon what is probably a faulty Greek text. The KJV translators read the Greek word *panta,* which means "all things," and therefore derived the translation "and ye know all things." Actually, the word should probably be *pantes,* meaning "you all," and the translation should therefore be as the RSV, NEB, NIV, and other more modern versions have it, namely, "you all know." The point is not that Christians know everything. They certainly do not. But rather that all who are Christians at least know the full, absolute, and reliable truth concerning Jesus. Whatever their other doubts may be, they at least have no doubt at the point of Christ's person. Once again we should notice that John's purpose in writing is not to impart fresh truth but rather to bring his readers to the point of using more effectively that which they already know.

THE CHIEF HERESY (vv. 22, 23)

The mention of lies versus truth in verse 21 leads John naturally to an analysis of the Gnostics' errors. It is not their errors in general that he seizes upon but rather the fundamental error which is their denial that Jesus is the Christ. Indeed, as he states it, this is not only the Gnostics' error but also the most fundamental error that can be made by anyone. Therefore, it also has the most serious consequences. In writing about this denial of Jesus as the Christ John calls it *the* lie, and the one who embraces it *the* liar. The KJV weakens this greatly by its mistaken translation, "Who is a liar but he that denieth that Jesus is the Christ?"

To gain the full force of John's statement one must recognize that the confession "Jesus is the Christ" does not mean merely that Jesus is the Messiah of the Old Testament expectation. This is involved, of course, but much more is involved. For if this were all the statement means, it is hard to see how the Gnostics could be opposed to it. Here the context throws light on the statement, for in the same verse and in the next verse John goes on to speak of Jesus as the Son, that is, as the Son of God, and of knowing the Son in the Father and the Father in the Son. In other words, it becomes clear from the context that John is thinking of a confession of Christ's full divinity. It is the belief that God became incarnate in Jesus as the Christ. This, incidentally, also makes sense of the historical situation in respect to the Gnostics, for the one thing that is most certainly known about them, particularly the form of Gnosticism popularized by Cerinthus in Asia Minor, is that they believed that the divine Christ, conceived as an emanation from the highest and superior God, came upon the man Jesus at the time of His baptism and left Him before His crucifixion.

This type of Gnosticism is not so foreign to some forms of modern biblical criticism, for it is reflected in the kind of scholarship that would drive a wedge between what is called "the historical Jesus" and the "Christ of faith."

Another form of this basic confession is also possible. That is, it may be extended to include all that the Father has said about Jesus in the Bible. Here Calvin is quite incisive. He writes, "I readily agree with the ancients, who thought that Cerinthus and Carpocrates are here referred to. But the denial of Christ extends much further; for it is not enough to confess in one word that Jesus is the Christ, but he must be acknowledged to be such as the Father offers him to us in the Gospel. The two I mentioned gave the title of Christ to the Son of God, but imagined he was a mere man. Others followed, like Arius, who adorned him with the name of God but despoiled him of his eternal divinity. Marcion dreamed that he was a mere phantom. Sabellius imagined that he differed in nothing from the Father. All these denied the Son

89

of God, for none of them really acknowledged the whole Christ, but adulterated the truth about him so far as they were able and made for themselves an idol instead of Christ." Calvin then adds, "We now see that Christ is denied whenever the things that belong to him are taken from him. And as Christ is the end of the Law and the Gospel and has within himself all the treasures of wisdom and understanding, so also is he the mark at which all heretics aim and direct their arrows. Therefore, the apostle has good reason to make those who fight against Christ the leading liars, since the full truth is exhibited to us in him."[3] According to Calvin, to confess that Jesus is the Christ is to confess the Christ of the Scriptures. To deny that Christ, by whatever means, is the heresy.

Moreover, it is a heresy with terrible consequences, as one might expect. First, says John, to deny the Son is to deny the Father. No doubt, the false teachers would have pretended to be worshiping the same God as the Christians. "We only differ from you in your views about Jesus," they might have said. But John says that this is impossible and quite obviously so, for if Jesus is God, then to deny Jesus as God is to deny God. Moreover, it is also to forfeit the presence of God in one's life or, as we could also say, to have no part of Him or He of us. John uses the phrase "has the Father." In biblical language this is the equivalent of saying that the one who will not confess Jesus as the Christ remains unregenerate and therefore under God's just condemnation. On the other hand, the one who finds Christ finds the Father also and both possesses and is possessed by Him.

DEFENSE AGAINST HERESY (vv. 24-27)

Twice in this section John has identified the denial of Jesus by the false teachers as the work of antichrist, that is, as the work of a terrifying demonic influence upon the congregations to whom he is writing. But if that is so, then the Christians might well ask, But what can we do against it? How can we guard ourselves against this adversary? John's answer is that Christians are to make use of the two main weapons of defense that have been given to them.

---

[3]Calvin, *John 11-21*, pp. 259, 260.

The Word of God

The first of the Christians' weapons is the word which they had heard from the beginning. Clearly, this refers to the gospel or basic apostolic teaching which they had heard at the beginning and which they had believed. In its fullest sense, however, it refers to the entire teaching of the Word of God. They are to let this Word abide in them and therefore guide and form them. By contrast, they are not to neglect it or minimize it while running off in a search for some new thing. For their part, Christians are to do as Paul advised Timothy: "But as for you, continue in what you have learned and have become convinced of, because you know those from whom you learned it, and how from infancy you have known the holy Scriptures, which are able to make you wise for salvation through faith in Christ Jesus. All Scripture is God-breathed and is useful for teaching, rebuking, correcting and training in righteousness, so that the man of God may be thoroughly equipped for every good work" (2 Tim. 3:14-17).

The Holy Spirit

By itself the apostolic teaching is not enough to keep Christians in the truth, however important and indispensable it may be, for the Gnostics had also heard the truth and yet had departed from it. The other element, which John's readers have and the false teachers do not have, is the Holy Spirit who indeed teaches the Christian by making the Word come alive for him. John refers to the Holy Spirit by the phrases "the anointing" and "his anointing" (cf. v. 20). In these verses John touches upon one aspect of that which became known at the time of the Reformation as the priesthood of all believers or, from the other side, the perspicuity of the Word. It is the truth that the believer in Christ is not dependent upon a higher order of churchman, whether priest or Gnostic, to interpret the Word of God for him. Rather, through the indwelling Spirit he has the means of understanding the Word for himself and of using what he finds there to combat heresy.

When John says that the Christians of his day "do not need anyone to teach" them, the statement must be understood in its context. It does not mean, for instance, that there is no value at all in teaching or that there is no such thing as a teaching ministry in the church. In fact, as Bruce observes, "What is John himself doing in this letter if he is not 'teaching' his readers?"[4] It only means that any valid and therefore useful teaching of the Lord's people must be done by those who are themselves among the Lord's people and that, if Christians are confronted by the false teaching of unbelievers, they have within themselves the means of exploring the Scriptures and thus dividing truth from error. In knowing the truth they can remain firm.

CONCLUSION

The obvious conclusion of this section is for those who are not yet Christians. These must know that they will find a solid basis for the living of their lives only in the truth concerning Jesus. But there are lessons for Christians too.

First, Christians must learn that questions concerning truth matter. Unfortunately there is a tendency in some Christian circles to minimize thought and to substitute for it either ethical demands, sometimes conceived quite legalistically, or subjective experiences, such as so-called "second blessings" or "tongues" or the mere obligation to "love." Not all of these substitute items are bad, of course. In fact, the tests of life, which John is giving, include the test of obedience and the test of love. But in addition to these there is also the very important test of truth; and it is so important that John can even declare that those who do not hold to the truth concerning Jesus are of antichrist. Truth, as it is contained in the Scriptures and as it is revealed in Jesus Christ, is an objective standard. It provides a basis for making judgments, and it reveals error. Consequently, Christians should be concerned with truth, should seek to understand it with increasing fullness, and should proclaim it to the world.

Second, there is the matter of Christian responsibility where truth is concerned. It is true that believers have an "anointing" and have no need that anyone should "teach" them. But this may not be construed as an excuse for failing to remain in the truth by conscious effort and determination. Here the key term is "abide" or "remain" (*mēno* in Greek), which occurs five times in the last verses of this section and with which the passage closes. True, the Word abides in all Christians, but for this reason they are to allow it to abide in them increasingly. The Holy Spirit also abides in them, but they are also to abide in Him or Christ.

---

[4]Bruce, *Epistles of John,* p. 76.

Third, there are the means by which every Christian should achieve victory over error in life: the Word of God and the indwelling of the Holy Spirit. Both are necessary. Without the Spirit, knowledge of the Word becomes but a bitter orthodoxy. Without the Word, the experience of the Spirit can lead to the most unjustified and damaging of excesses. The only safeguard against either and therefore the only sure defense against heresy is to have abiding within us both the Word from which we learn and the Holy Spirit who teaches it to us.

1 John 2:28-3:3
God's Children

And now, dear children, continue in him, so that when he appears we may be confident and unashamed before him at his coming.

If you know that he is righteous, you know that everyone who does what is right has been born of him.

How great is the love the Father has lavished on us, that we should be called children of God! And that is what we are! The reason the world does not know us is that it did not know him. Dear friends, now we are children of God, and what we will be has not yet been made known. But we know that when he appears, we shall be like him, for we shall see him as he is. Everyone who has this hope in him purifies himself, just as he is pure.

A generation ago it was popular to speak of the message of the Bible as being summarized under the two phrases "the fatherhood of God" and "the brotherhood of man." The phrases expressed the thought that all men are equally children of God and therefore brothers within one divine family. All that was needed, so the thinking went, was for men and women to realize this and live accordingly. In reacting to such views it must be acknowledged that there are such concepts as the fatherhood of God and the brotherhood of man in the Bible. But the point must be added in order to be accurate that neither of these apply to all men. Brotherhood is a concept reserved for Christians only; these have become brothers and sisters to one another, but not to everyone, though they do have a responsibility to all men. Similarly, the fatherhood of God applies only to those who have been reborn into God's spiritual family through faith in Jesus Christ.

These points have been evident in John's letter in several earlier sections, especially in John's use of the words "Father" and "children." But now he seems to make the contrast especially sharp as, in these verses, he directs a challenge to those who are indeed God's special children and breaks out into near rhapsody at the thought of what God is doing and will yet do for them.

These verses are somewhat difficult to fit into a neat outline of the letter. Some commentators regard them as the opening words of an entirely new section of the epistle. Others split them, as did those who established the chapter division. Dodd begins a new section with verse 29. Brooke calls verses 28 and 29 "transition" verses. Obviously, there is truth in each of these views and there will be little difference in interpretation regardless of how one regards them. To the present writer, however, it seems best to treat this entire section somewhat as a parenthesis, a parenthesis which is at the same time a summary of the first presentation of the tests and an introduction to the second. The tie with the preceding is seen in the carrying over of the word "continue," in order to give it even more emphasis, and in the introductory phrase *kai nun,* which is generally used to introduce a deduction based on conditions which have just been stated. The phrase "and now" might be better translated by "since this is so" or "this being the case." The link to what follows is in the word "righteousness," which dominates these verses and chapter 3 as far as verse 10.

RIGHTEOUSNESS AND THE LORD'S RETURN (vv. 28, 29)

John has already spoken of righteousness and the need to be obedient to Christ earlier in chapter 2 and of the need to abide in Him just one verse before this. Although he repeats the ideas here, he nevertheless does so in a new context which is that of Christ's return. John's point is that those who are Christ's ought to abide in Him and live righteous lives in order that they might have confidence and not be put to shame at Jesus' return.

The reference to the personal return of the Lord Jesus Christ to earth is unmistakable. So it is a puzzle how some commentators can regard the second coming of Jesus as a rather primitive apocalyptic idea which was present in the early days of the Christian proclamation but which was soon dropped by more thoughtful writers such as the apostle John. It has often been observed that the most explicitly prophetic passages of the synoptic Gospels, particularly the Olivet discourse of Matthew 24, 25, Mark 13, and Luke 21, are dropped by John, being replaced rather with the farewell discourses in which teaching about the coming of the Holy Spirit is prominent. This is supposed to suggest that John viewed the return of Jesus as being fulfilled rather in the coming of the Spirit and in the present enjoyment of eternal life. But this theory is not substantiated even by John's handling of the gospel material. And this text alone refutes it.

Actually, the doctrine of Christ's return is prominent throughout the whole of the New Testament. It has been observed by some that in the New Testament one verse in twenty-five deals with the Lord's return. It is mentioned 318 times in the 260 chapters of the New Testament. It is mentioned in every one of the New Testament books, with the exception of Galatians, which deals with a particular doctrinal problem, and the very short books such as 2 and 3 John and Philemon.

Mark's Gospel, which is probably the earliest of the Gospels, contains three distinct references plus other indirect ones. For instance, in chapter 8, after Peter has given his great confession of faith, there is the reply by Jesus in which He foretells His death and resurrection, calls His followers to faithful discipleship, and concludes, "If anyone is ashamed of me and my words in this adulterous and sinful generation, the Son of Man will be ashamed of him when he comes in his Father's glory with the holy angels" (v. 38). Similarly, in chapter 13 He says, "At that time men will see the Son of Man coming in clouds with great power and glory" (v. 26). He adds, "No one knows about that day or hour, not even the angels in heaven, nor the Son, but only the Father. Be on guard! Be alert! You do not know when that time will come" (vv. 32, 33). In chapter 14 he tells those who at His trial asked Him if He was the Christ, "I am. And you will see the Son of Man sitting at the right hand of the Mighty One and coming on the clouds of heaven" (v. 62).

Matthew and Luke repeat much of this material from Mark, sometimes with variations. But John, as the other Gospel writer, adds material uniquely his own. For instance, in the fourteenth chapter he quotes Jesus as saying, "Do not let your hearts be troubled. Trust in God; trust also in me. In my Father's house are many rooms; if it were not so, I would have told you. I am going there to prepare a place for you. And if I go and prepare a place for you, I will come back and take you to be with me that you also may be where I am" (vv. 1-3). Again, at the end of the book, when Peter asks Jesus about the destiny of the unnamed disciple, saying, "Lord, what about him?" Jesus answers, "If I want him to remain alive until I return, what is that to you? You must follow me!" (John 21:22). Clearly these verses and those that follow assume the Second Coming.

Paul's letters are full of this same teaching. He wrote of our being caught up in the clouds "to meet the Lord in the air" (1 Thess. 4:17). He reminded the Philippians that "our citizenship is in heaven. And we eagerly await a Savior from there, the Lord Jesus Christ" (Phil. 3:20). Peter called the return of Jesus Christ "a living hope" (1 Peter 1:3). Paul called it "the blessed hope" (Titus 2:13). In Revelation the apostle John declares, "Look, he is coming with the clouds, and every eye will see him" (Rev. 1:7). He ends with the words, "He who testifies to these things says, 'Yes, I am coming soon.' Amen. Come, Lord Jesus" (Rev. 22:20).

All these texts testify to the prominence of the doctrine of the Lord's return throughout the New Testament. But the unique aspect of the reference before us is that John refers to it here, not as a mere point of doctrine considered in itself, but rather as an incentive for living a righteous life. Righteousness, like purity of doctrine, is to come only by abiding in Christ. But we are encouraged to do that by knowledge of the fact that one day we will have to give an account before Him.

This, then, is a very practical doctrine. Sometimes believers have treated the doctrine of the return of Christ as if it were an escape valve from having to face the harsh realities of life. These say, "No matter that ungodliness is everywhere apparent, no matter that men and women are suffering from persecution and hunger, no matter that the church is unfaithful to God's written revelation of His will and ways; soon Jesus will return, and nothing else will matter." Some unfortunately have even rejoiced when conditions in the world have gotten worse; for, they say, "It is a sign of a not-too-distant Second Coming." But this is wrong,

97

and John at least will not stand for it. What happens when a Christian actually understands that Jesus is returning and that he must give an account before Him? The answer is that he "purifies himself," even as Christ is pure (1 John 3:3). Moreover, it is the one who understands these things that is most often down in the heart and heartbreak of the city, working to bring the liberating power of the gospel to broken men and women, and in the far reaches of the world in order to tell those who have not heard the gospel about the world's Savior.

In the last words of chapter 2, John says that it is by doing righteousness that the one who is really born of God demonstrates that he is born of Him. The idea here is of inherited family traits. God is righteous.[1] Consequently, everyone who is born of God must show traits of that righteousness.

THE LOVE OF THE FATHER (vv. 1-3)

Thoughts of the return of Jesus apparently led John to reflect on the certainty of the final outcome of the Christian's salvation and of the love of God which lies behind it. Moreover, as this is so meaningful and so wonderful, John immediately bursts into praise to God for the greatness of His love in thus making us His children. Here the phrase "how great" (literally, "behold, of what country") implies great astonishment, as if the love of God is so unparalleled in human experience that John cannot even tell from what country it comes. It is beyond explanation. On the other hand, it is not an impractical thing, for the love of God determines both what we are now and what we shall be.

What we are

First of all, the love of God determines what we are now; and what we are now is God's children. It is not just that we receive the designation "children of God," though that is also true. John does not want his phrase to be understood as implying that limitation. We actually *are* children of God by the new birth. This was God's intention for us as His people from the beginning, as we shall see. Yet from the perspective of human life following the

---

[1]The "he" of this verse must refer to the Father, in line with such texts as Psalm 11:7 and the phrase "born of him," which always refers to the Father rather than to Christ. Cf. Stott, *Epistles of John*, p. 117.

fall it is so inconceivable that it can only bring forth wonder and praise in the one who has been born again.

It is no accident that the Bible often uses the image of birth in speaking of how God has called men and women into His spiritual family. God has given human birth as an illustration of what the new birth means. In human birth there is first a conception in which the seed of the father unites with the egg of the mother to begin a new life. There is a period of gestation in which that which was begun in such a quiet and small way begins to grow and take form. At last there is the actual birth. In the birth the first cries of the child are heard, and those who stand by rejoice in a new human being. In the same way, men and women become God's children when God the Father of His own will takes the seed of His Word and plants it within the heart, causing it to unite with the ovum of saving faith, which together begin to grow. At this stage of God's work those without cannot tell whether spiritual life is present or not. But in time the life within grows and the actual birth takes place. As those standing by hear the public confession of Christ by the newborn they know of the new life and rejoice in it with the Father (cf. 1 Peter 1:23; James 1:18).

It is in line with this conception of salvation that John writes in the prologue to the Gospel, in words that bear a similarity to this section of the Epistle, "Yet to all who received him, to those who believed in his name, he gave the right to become children of God—children born not of natural descent, nor of human decision or a husband's will, but born of God" (John 1:12, 13).

What we shall be

God did not bring children into spiritual life to thereafter abandon them and let them go to hell. He brought them into life in order to make them completely like Jesus and take them with Him into heaven. Therefore, John cannot stop his rhapsody with the mere thought of what we are but rather goes on to reflect on what we shall be when Christ shall appear and we shall be made like Him.

What we shall be is not completely known to John, a fact which throws light on how 1 John 2:27 should be taken. But enough is known to cause wonder. "What we will be has not yet been made known," John says, "But we know that when he appears, we shall be like him, for we shall see him as he is" (3:2).

Here there is an important sequence. First, Jesus Christ shall appear. This is the Christian's earnest expectation. Second, we shall see Him. It will not be a mere spiritual, still less an impersonal return. Rather, "This same Jesus, who has been taken from you into heaven, will come back in the same way you have seen him go into heaven" (Acts 1:11). Third, we shall be made like Him. In this latter expression John seems almost to suggest that there is something in the mere sight of the glorified Christ that will purge His followers of sin and conform them at last to His own perfect image.

That day will see the perfection of God's eternal purpose concerning His chosen ones. Here Bruce writes brilliantly, "These first two verses of 1 John 3 celebrate the accomplishment of God's eternal purpose concerning man. This purpose finds expression in Genesis 1:26, where God, about to bring into being the crown of creation, says: 'Let us make man in our image, after our likeness.' In other words, he declares his intention of bringing into existence beings like himself, as like himself as it is possible for creatures to be like their Creator. In words which echo the language of Genesis 1, the status and function of man in the purpose of God are celebrated in Psalm 8:5ff.: 'thou hast made him little less than God, and dost crown him with glory and honor. Thou hast given him dominion over the works of thy hands; thou hast put all things under his feet.' But Genesis 3 tells how man, not content with the true likeness to God which was his by creation, grasped at the counterfeit likeness held out as the tempter's bait: 'you will be like God, knowing good and evil.' In consequence, things most *unlike* God manifested themselves in human life: hatred, darkness and death in place of love, light and life. The image of God in man was sadly defaced. Yet God's purpose was not frustrated; instead, the fall itself, with its entail of sin and death, was overruled by God and compelled to become an instrument in the furtherance of his purpose.

"In the fulness of time the image of God, undefaced by disobedience to his will, reappeared on earth in the person of his Son. In Jesus the love, light and life of God were manifested in opposition to hatred, darkness and death. With his crucifixion it seemed that hatred, darkness and death had won the day, and that God's purpose, which had survived the fall, was now effectively thwarted. But instead, the cross of Jesus proved to be

God's chosen instrument for the fulfillment of his purpose. . . . This purpose is stated by Paul in terms which go back far beyond the act of creation in Genesis 1: 'those whom he foreknew he also predestined to be conformed to the image of his Son, in order that he might be the first-born among many brethren' (Rom. 8:29). The children of God, who enter his family through faith in his Son, display their Father's likeness, because of their conformity to him who is the perfect image of the invisible God''[2]

Now, as God's children, we are made like Christ progressively. In that day we shall be fully like Him, for we shall see Him no longer dimly but "face to face" (1 Cor. 13:12).

CONCLUSION

After such rapturous thoughts the Christian is in danger of floating away on a cloud of mysticism, but John does not allow this. Nor does Scripture allow it anywhere. "Is this your hope?" John seems to ask. "Then show it," he concludes. For "everyone who has this hope in him purifies himself, just as he is pure" (v. 3).

This is what Dodd calls the "all-important corollary of the Christian hope."[3] It is simply that if we are to be like Christ hereafter, then we must act like Christ now, imitating Him now, particularly in the area of our personal morality. Moreover, it is not even a mystical and somehow glorified Christ that we are to imitate, for John admits that he does not yet know what we shall be, having not yet seen Christ face to face in His glory. The Christ we are to imitate is the Christ of history. It is the Christ of the opening pages of the Epistle, the Christ who was seen and heard and touched and indeed proclaimed from the beginning as the heart of the apostolic gospel. That is the Christ who is coming back and to whom we must answer for how we have lived and how we have employed the talents that He has entrusted to us.

---

[2]Bruce, *Epistles of John,* pp. 85, 86.
[3]Dodd, *Johannine Epistles,* p. 71.

1 John 3:4-10
The First Contrast:
Righteousness and Sin

Everyone who sins breaks the law; in fact, sin is lawlessness. But you know that he appeared so that he might take away our sins. And in him is no sin. No one who lives in him keeps on sinning. No one who continues to sin has either seen him or known him.

Dear children, do not let anyone lead you astray. He who does what is right is righteous, just as he is righteous. He who does what is sinful is of the devil, because the devil has been sinning from the beginning. The reason the Son of God appeared was to destroy the devil's work. No one who is born of God will continue to sin, because God's seed remains in him; he cannot go on sinning, because he has been born of God. This is how we know who the children of God are and who the children of the devil are: Anyone who does not do what is right is not a child of God; neither is anyone who does not love his brother.

In conversations with those who are not yet Christians, Christians are often puzzled by the fact that the other person sometimes professes to believe all that the Christian believes yet also believes things that seem, at least to the Christian, to be incompatible with Christianity. For example, the Christian believes that Jesus is the unique Son of God. The one who is not yet a Christian says that he believes this too but adds that he also believes that all men are sons of God, like Jesus. Or again, the Christian affirms that men and women are lost apart from Christ and are saved only through faith in His atoning death for them.

The First Contrast: Righteousness and Sin

The non-Christian agrees but adds that he also thinks that men and women have to earn their salvation. This problem is common because it is based upon a widely held but erroneous view of truth. In this view many incompatible things are possible, for truth is relative. In the biblical view, by contrast, truth is absolute; therefore, to be meaningful any truth must be accompanied by corresponding denials. To return to the examples just given, if Jesus is God's unique Son, then other persons are not, at least not in the same sense. Or again, if salvation is by grace through faith, then other methods of salvation are excluded.

If truth does not have this character, then anything means everything and all is meaningless. If truth does have this character, then it is possible to separate truth from error and live accordingly.

To separate truth from error is one of the goals of the author of 1 John, as we have seen. Consequently, it is frequently the case that the letter's affirmations and teachings are accompanied by strong repudiations and denials. An excellent example is found in the first chapter, where, after having stated that God is light, John immediately adds, "in him there is no darkness at all" (v. 5). He goes on to say that those who know God must walk in the light as He is light. But John first denies: 1) that a person can know God and still walk in darkness, 2) that sin in a particular individual can be eradicated, and 3) that it is possible for a person never to have sinned. This procedure is now followed in the next major division of the letter.

After his opening remarks, which conclude in his call to holiness to all God's people, John introduced a series of three tests by which the child of God can know that he truly is a child of God. These are righteousness, love, and truth, and what John has had to say about them is clear. It would seem that John himself was not satisfied, however. Consequently, in the next major section of the letter he introduces these three themes again, but this time with contrasts, obviously to sharpen his meaning and to set himself apart from those who would agree with his statements but at the same time affirm their opposites. In these verses we have three contrasts: first, the contrast between righteousness and sin (3:4-10); second, the contrast between love and hate (3:11-18); third, the contrast between truth and error (4:1-6). The last two of these are separated by a parenthesis dealing with the subject of doubt (3:19-24), just as in the initial presentation of the tests, love and truth were separated by a parenthesis dealing with the church and worldliness.

The first of these contrasts may be subdivided as containing statements about sin and its origins, the work of Christ, sin and the Christian life, and an appeal for clear thinking and for righteousness.

SIN AND ITS ORIGINS (vv. 4, 8a)

John has a habit of presenting his themes in parallel passages with slight variations, and such is the case here as he contrasts sin with righteousness. Verses 4-7 deal with the nature of sin, the work of Jesus Christ in opposition to sin, the incompatibility of continuing in sin while living the Christian life, and the practical conclusion that the one who does right is righteous. But this, with slight variations, is also the outline of verses 8-10, which deal (more specifically) with the origin of sin, the work of Jesus Christ in defeating the devil, the fact that the true child of God cannot continue in sin, and the conclusion that the children of God are known by righteousness just as the children of the devil are known by sin. To get the full thrust of his teaching it is therefore wise to consider the two sections together under a combination of these four headings.

In verse 4 the author defines sin as lawlessness and says that everyone who commits sin is guilty of it. This is not the most comprehensive definition of sin that might be given, but neither is it "somewhat superficial," as Dodd indicates. By lawlessness John naturally recalls thoughts of God's Old Testament law by which sin is revealed in its full sinfulness. As the Westminster Shorter Catechism states, "Sin is any want of conformity unto, or transgression of, the law of God." So the law shows how far short men fall from God's standards. On the other hand, what John says is actually more complete and therefore also more profound than this, for he does not say that sin is merely the breaking of a divinely revealed law. Rather, he indicates that sin is the spirit of lawlessness itself, which lies behind the rebellion.

At this point John's understanding is clearly one with that of the apostle Paul, who writes in Romans that "before the law was given, sin was in the world" (Rom. 5:13). The proof, as Paul indicates, is that death is sin's consequence and that men and women died before the law was given.

This definition of sin means that sin is simply the desire to have my own way. It is this which causes me to transgress the law of God when the law is given. This desire expresses itself in the stubbornness of even the smallest child or the rebellion of a young person in his teens. It is the disposition that causes some to break the speed limit when driving, cheat on income tax, use an employer's time for personal affairs, attempt to get ahead at the expense of others, and so on. It is what Isaiah described when he declared, "We all, like sheep, have gone astray, each of us has turned to his own way; and the LORD has laid on him the iniquity of us all" (Isa. 53:6). This is what characterizes every man or woman apart from the transformations produced by God's grace. When a Sunday school teacher once asked a little boy to define sin, he answered, "I think it is anything you like to do." He was not far wrong. At least he was right in the sense that in our natural state we all want to do that which, in part if not completely, is opposed to the holy will of God.

When we begin to speak of sin in the areas of a person's personal desires, however, the immediate impulse is to begin to defend those desires, pointing out that they do not necessarily hurt anyone and that much that we desire is good and not wrong. But that is just what we must not do, for if we do, we are actually minimizing sin and placing ourselves wrongly within the camp of those who, as we think, do not need a Savior. Moreover, John will not allow this chain of reasoning, for in his second discussion of sin, in verse 8, he shows that all sin is of the devil, however mild or seemingly harmless, and he shows the fundamental connection between the devil and the one sinning. Sin may be mild in any particular case. But it is in the devil's way and leads to more transgressions. On the other hand, righteousness is God's way, and it alone reveals the godlike character of the one practicing it.

As we read this section we detect what must be a further reference to the tendency of the Gnostic teachers to underestimate sin or excuse it. Perhaps the Gnostics excused sin as being essentially negative in nature; that is, as being connected with what is finite. Again, they may have related it only to their bodies and not to their minds, which they may well have said were above any dispositions to sin. But John will not have this. Sin is not merely negative. It is willful rebellion. Moreover, it involves the mind as that in which rebellion originates. It is only when we see this that we begin to abhor sin and turn from it to seek a Savior.

THE WORK OF CHRIST (vv. 5, 8b)

John reminds his readers that it is the characteristic of the devil to sin. Now he also reminds them that it is a characteristic of Christ to take away sin. He states this in two forms, corresponding to the parallel structure of these verses. First, Jesus appeared to take away the sins of His people; second, Jesus appeared to destroy the works of the devil.

But how can He do this? Obviously, He did it by dying in place of the sinner, becoming a propitiation for his sin, as John said earlier. In the earlier reference, 1 John 2:2, John had the breadth of Christ's sacrifice uppermost in his mind, stressing that Jesus died for the gentile world as well as for Jews.[1] Here he seems to be thinking specifically, for the Greek reads literally "the sins"; that is, the individual sins of the particular people for which He died. "The taking away of the sins can be accomplished only by one who is himself sinless," as Bruce notes.[2] Hence, the reminder: "in him is no sin" (v. 5). It is not by works that a man is saved, still less by any minimizing of sin or by wishful thinking. A person is saved by faith in Jesus Christ. And this is made possible by the fact that He who was sinless and who therefore did not need to die for His own sin, took our sin upon Himself and died for it, the just for the unjust, so that the God of the universe, who must do right, saw sin punished and therefore opened the gates of heaven for those who believe on Jesus.

In itself this act does not destroy the works of the devil, which are many. But it is the first step. Indeed, it is as Christians come to Christ and are united to Him by faith that they receive the power to turn from sin and the devil's works and thus begin to live a holy life before God. The devil's works are not yet totally destroyed. But Christ's appearance was the first step in their

---

[1]On the surface the words seem to imply an even greater breadth than this; that is, Jesus died not only for those who should believe on Him but for all men. However, see the discussion of this verse on pages 48-52.

[2]Bruce, *Epistles of John,* p. 89.

complete destruction. Now the Christian can live in that knowledge and can escape from sin's tyranny.

SIN AND THE CHRISTIAN LIFE (vv. 6, 9)

If the coming of Christ the first time was to put away sin and destroy the works of the devil, it follows that the one who is united to Christ by faith must not sin but rather must live a holy life. If he does not, he is obviously working against Christ. John writes, "No one who lives in him keeps on sinning. No one who continues to sin has either seen him or known him. . . . No one who is born of God will continue to sin, because God's seed remains in him; he cannot go on sinning, because he has been born of God."

Can a Christian sin?

The point that John makes is inescapable, for it is made strongly: Sin has no place in the Christian life. However, the fact that he makes it strongly produces a problem. John says that the one who abides in Christ does not sin. But is that really true? Can we say that? Or again, since John has already written, "If we claim we have not sinned, we make him out to be a liar and his word has no place in our lives" (1:10), can we even believe that John is consistent? Ought we not rather simply to discount his words on sin entirely? The difficulty in dealing with these and similar questions has produced a wide variety of interpretations of these verses by commentators.[3]

1. The first interpretation goes back to the days of the early church and is reflected by some Reformation theologians. It restricts the "sin" in this passage to particularly heinous sins—murder and the like. In Catholic theology the distinction is expressed as that between mortal and venial sins. It is enough to answer in reply to this interpretation that, in addition to the fact that John is obviously not making any such distinctions in the passage, Christians do on occasion commit heinous sins. Besides, in the Bible's evaluation sins such as murder are not necessarily more evil than sins of the spirit such as pride, of which all are guilty.

2. A second view is that what is sin in an unbeliever is not so

---

[3]The various interpretations are summarized rather fully by Stott, *Epistles of John,* pp. 130-136, and by Law, *Tests of Life,* pp. 223-230. The following summary is based on Stott's analysis.

regarded by God in the life of a believer. But this is simply not true. Sin is sin, wherever it is found. Moreover, it is probably the development of this precise double standard by the Gnostics that John is opposing.

3. Some have distinguished between the old nature and the new nature in a believer, arguing that the new nature cannot sin because it is from God. This is true in a sense and may even be supported by statements such as "Flesh gives birth to flesh, but the Spirit gives birth to spirit" (John 3:6), drawn from the Gospel. But it is dangerous, for it can easily suggest that the individual is not responsible for the sins of the old nature or that he need not fight against them. One might argue that Paul makes such a distinction in Romans 7. But whether it is actually this distinction or not, it is surely a sufficient answer to note that John at least is not making any such distinction here. Indeed, he is calling for the individual Christian to turn from sin to righteousness; he is not calling upon the Christian to allow one nature rather than the other to dominate him.

4. A more recent and quite widespread interpretation of these verses is that John is here speaking of an ideal. But if this is so, the question must then be asked, "Did he expect Christians to attain the ideal in this life?" If he did, we have not escaped the problem; we have only changed its contours. On the other hand, if he did not, then his entire moral test becomes meaningless.

5. There is a qualified form of the idea of an ideal characteristic of the holiness movement. It is the view that John is indeed stating an ideal but that it is an attainable ideal to the extent that the Christian truly "lives" in Christ (v. 6). Here Stott's reply is incisive. He notes that, while this is a possible interpretation of verse 6 (in which the Christian clearly has an obligation to abide in Christ), nevertheless it is obviously inadequate as an interpretation of verse 9 (in which all Christians, rather than just some, are included). The only way around this latter difficulty is to suggest that one can be born of God and be sinless, then, as a result of sin, cease to be born; in other words, to be born and unborn repeatedly. But this is contrary to John's teaching and runs against his entire emphasis upon the Christian's need to be sure of his salvation. The Christian could hardly be sure of his salvation if each sin he committed alienated him from God's family.

6. The sixth view is that the sin which the Christian cannot do is willful or deliberate sin. But this is only a variation of the first interpretation and is disproved by the acknowledged conduct of all too many Christians. We do sin willfully and deliberately. Consequently, we should not be under any illusions regarding our need to confess our sin and seek cleansing.

7. The last and only adequate interpretation of these verses is that the sin which a Christian cannot commit is lasting or habitual. Here the interpreter is assisted by the tenses of the Greek verbs, all of which are present tense. If John had used an aorist tense as he does, for instance, in 2:1, he would have been referring to a specific sin committed at some particular point. This Christians do, as the earlier reference tells us. The cure for it is confession before Jesus Christ, our great High Priest and advocate. In this passage, however, John uses the present tense three times to indicate, not a particular sin once committed, but rather a continuance in sin over an indefinite period. Each phrase indicates this. In verse 6 he says that "No one who lives in him keeps on sinning," that is, "continues in sin indefinitely." In verse 9 he says that "No one who is born of God will continue to sin." In English this distinction seems somewhat superficial and even unjustified, but it is not so in the Greek language, in which John wrote. In Greek John is simply saying that although a Christian may sin, and in fact often does sin, it is nevertheless impossible for him to go on persisting in sin indefinitely. Were this not so, righteousness could not be considered a true test of whether or not one is truly a child of God.

God's seed

The reason John gives for why a Christian cannot continue to persist in sin is that "God's seed remains in him." This can be taken in a variety of ways, but it should probably be taken as a reference to the very nature of God abiding in the Christian, as some modern versions do.

On the one hand, since the antecedents of the pronouns are not specified, the phrase could mean that God's people [God's spiritual progeny] abide in God. But this, while true, is not quite the point John wishes to make here. This would be a point in favor of the doctrine of the eternal security of the believer, but John is arguing rather that those who belong to God show that they belong to God in that they do not continue in sin. A second possibility is that the phrase "God's seed" refers to the Word of God, which abides, at least in part, within every believer. This is an attractive view, particularly since the idea of the indwelling Word or seed occurs elsewhere. An example is 1 Peter 1:23, "You have been born again, not of perishable seed, but of imperishable, through the living and enduring word of God." But there is nothing in John's writings to make us think that he either used this image or thought in this way. Failing these explanations, it is best to think only of the nature of God within the believer, a nature which because it is opposed to sin will not let the believer rest in sin but rather constantly exposes sin and prods him toward holiness.

Herein lies the explanation of John's initial test and the reason behind it. If a person has truly been born of God, then something radical has happened to him. He has received a new nature and is therefore and for that very reason launched on a new course. The course is a course in holiness. Therefore, if he does not go on in holiness, this indicates that he has never in plain fact been born again. On the other hand, if he does go on, he can be encouraged by this fact and take confidence. It is this test more than any other that presumably enabled the apostle John to dismiss the Gnostic teachers as unbelievers.

AN APPEAL FOR RIGHTEOUSNESS (vv. 7, 10)

John's final statements, both for verses 4-7 and for verses 8-10, are in the nature of an appeal for sound thinking. They provide a conclusion. "Dear children, do not let anyone lead you astray. He who does what is right is righteous, just as he is righteous. . . . This is how we know who the children of God are and who the children of the devil are: Anyone who does not do what is right is not a child of God; neither is anyone who does not love his brother."

The Gnostics with their keen minds and sophistry were capable, not only of making their own sinful conduct seem right, but also of confusing the Christians in regard to who was and who was not God's child. But John does not want anyone to be confused. Therefore he draws the issue in as black and white tones as possible. To begin with, he indicates that in spiritual terms there are only two groups of people, those who are God's children and those who are not, and he indicates by his language that it is only by a new birth that one enters the former of the two groups. The issue is therefore not one of knowledge, as the Gnostics affirmed. Nor is it one of progression along a certain religious scale. One does not grow into Christianity. From the divine side, one enters into Christianity only by being born of God. On the human side, one enters it through believing on Jesus Christ as Savior and Lord. Nothing must cloud these facts. Indeed, they must be stated in the sharpest of terms.

But there is also a second issue that John wants his readers to see sharply. It is that there must be evidence for whether or not a person belongs to God's family. It is not a matter of mere profession, for many will say that they are Christians though they are not.

Here is a word particularly suited to our own day. Today as the result of the widespread impact of Christianity upon western life and culture many claim to be Christians who are not and who therefore obviously do not have the evidences of the new birth in their lives. They think they are Christians. But this is largely a negative conviction. It is because they are not Moslems or Jews or atheists, not because there has been a genuine work of God in their lives with its inevitable consequences. To all such John sounds a somber warning. "Anyone who does not do what is right is not a child of God." He is of the devil! Let no man deceive you! It is a warning for all who have not been born again to turn from all forms of sin and seek the Savior.

111

1 John 3:11-18
The Second Contrast: Love and Hate

This is the message you heard from the beginning: We should love one another. Do not be like Cain, who belonged to the evil one and murdered his brother. And why did he murder him? Because his own actions were evil and his brother's were righteous. Do not be surprised, my brothers, if the world hates you. We know that we have passed from death to life, because we love our brothers. Anyone who does not love remains in death. Anyone who hates his brother is a murderer, and you know that no murderer has eternal life in him.

This is how we know what love is: Jesus Christ laid down his life for us. And we ought to lay down our lives for our brothers. If anyone has material possessions and sees his brother in need but has no pity on him, how can the love of God be in him? Dear children, let us not love with words or tongue but with actions and in truth.

At no point is the contrast between one of John's tests and its opposite more important for contemporary men and women than the contrast between love and hate. This is so simply because the meaning of love has become so debased in modern culture that practically anyone will claim to have love, according to his own definition. A popular song says, "Everybody loves somebody sometime." If this is correct and if the meaning given to love in this song is John's meaning, then everyone can claim to have met John's test and be a Christian.

This is not the kind of love about which John is speaking, of course. Consequently, it is of great importance to follow his reasoning in this section of the letter as he contrasts love with hate and works out the origins, nature, and practical consequences of both. On the one hand, hate originates with the devil and indicates the existence of a bond with him. It expresses itself in jealousy and ends in murder. On the other hand, love originates in God and indicates the existence of a bond with God. It expresses itself in self-sacrifice and in many practical demonstrations of concern for those in need. These two points of emphasis—the origin and nature of hate and the origin and nature of love—form the two main sections of the passage.

In presenting his analysis John is conscious of the fact that he is presenting nothing new. Indeed, he is glad of that, for the commandment itself is "the message you heard from the beginning." It is interesting in this connection to note that nearly everything he says is stated elsewhere in Scripture, so that John may be said almost to be quoting it. The commandment to love is, of course, Christ's command to his disciples, recorded in John 13:34. The story of Cain comes from Genesis 4 and is a totally accurate analysis of that story. John's statement that Cain "belonged to the evil one" reflects Jesus' words regarding those who were trying to murder Him: "You belong to your father, the devil, and you want to carry out your father's desire. He was a murderer from the beginning" (John 8:44). Verse 13 echoes John 15:18,19: "If the world hates you, keep in mind that it hated me first. If you belonged to the world, it would love you as its own. As it is, you do not belong to the world, but I have chosen you out of the world. That is why the world hates you." There are also a number of lesser references (cf. John 3:7; 5:28, 38). The phrase "to lay down one's life" is frequent in and unique to the Johannine writings (cf. John 10:11, 15, 17, 18; 13:37, 38; 15:13).

THE EXAMPLE OF CAIN (vv. 12, 13).

Love between Christian brothers suggests hatred between brothers as its contrast. So John turns to the example of Cain and Abel. Cain is the only proper name (except for the names of Christ or God) occurring in this letter and the only explicit Old Testament reference in the three epistles. Cain was a murderer, by which he showed his spiritual lineage. He was of the evil one, John says. And why did he murder his brother? Was it because his brother was a great sinner and deserved to be slain? On the contrary, it was because his brother was righteous and his own deeds were evil. In other words, the ultimate act of murder grew out of a basic heart attitude, an attitude of hate and jealousy.

Here John is in perfect accord with the Lord's teaching regarding murder, as found in the Sermon on the Mount. Jesus said, "You have heard that it was said to the people long ago, 'Do not murder, and anyone who murders will be subject to judgment.' But I tell you that anyone who is angry with his brother will be subject to judgment. Again, anyone who says to his brother, 'Raca,' is answerable to the Sanhedrin. But anyone who says, 'You fool!' will be in danger of the fire of hell" (Matt. 5:21, 22). In Christ's day the rulers of Israel had taken the sixth commandment of the Decalogue, which said "You shall not kill (murder)," and had combined it with a verse in Numbers that demanded death for anyone who unlawfully took another person's life (Num. 35:30). The implication was that the sixth commandment referred to nothing more or less than this ultimate and external act. "But is this what murder is?" asked Jesus. Is it nothing more or less than this ultimate act? Is there no guilt connected to the man who would like to kill his brother but is afraid to do it or is too weak to carry it out? "No," said Jesus. True murder is that which is conceived in the heart. For from within, out of the heart of man, come "evil thoughts, sexual immorality, theft, murder, adultery, greed, malice, deceit, lewdness, envy, slander, arrogance, and folly. All these evils come from inside and make a man 'unclean'" (Mark 7:21-23). Consequently, a person is guilty before God for heart attitudes as much as for the outward, visible actions that flow from his sin. By God's definition hatred is as much murder as the unlawful taking of another's life.

John has taken Cain as his great example of hatred because Cain's murder of Abel is a perfect contrast to Christ's giving of Himself for His brethren, which is to come next. But we must not miss the fact that the nature of Cain is seen in many examples of jealousy and hatred even though actual murder does not always flow from it.

This truth is now unfolded in verse 13, for John moves easily from the actions and attitudes of Cain toward Abel to the attitude of the world toward Christians. "Do not be surprised, my brothers, if the world hates you." Cain is the prototype of this world; the devil is the prince of this world, as he was the spiritual father of Cain. It is therefore only to be expected that the spiritual progeny of Cain will continue to hate and persecute the spiritual progeny of Abel. As Matthew Henry notes, "The great serpent himself reigns as the God of this world. Wonder not then that the serpentine world hates and hisses at you who belong to that seed of the woman that is to bruise the serpent's head."[1]

CHRISTIAN LOVE (vv. 14-18)

Just as the presence of jealousy and hatred in a life indicates that the person involved is of the world and not of the family of God, so also do love and self-sacrifice indicate that such a one has now passed out of the world and into God's family. John turns now to an analysis of Christian love, elaborating his statements over against the background of the world's hatred and murderous designs. In this section he restates and elaborates upon the social test itself, digs deeper into love's essential nature, and finally suggests two ways in which the Christian may show love practically.

The social test

Once again John brings forward the social test, but this time he does so in the context of a black and white contrast with the world's hatred. In the Greek text the opening pronoun is in a prominent position and is therefore emphasized. It has the effect of saying, "Whatever may be the attitudes and actions of the world, we who are Christians are different; we love one another. This is evidence of the fact that we are God's children."

In John's statement of these ideas in verses 14 and 15 some important truths are passed over quickly. It is profitable to reflect on them. First, when John says that the one who does not love "remains in death" he indicates that men and women are spiritually dead in trespasses and sins to start with and not that they die later through sinning. In other words, this is an indirect expression of the doctrine of original sin which is so unpopular with

---

[1]Matthew Henry, *Matthew Henry's Commentary on the Whole Bible* (Old Tappan: Revell, n.d.), p. 1077.

some churchmen. Men do not begin neutral, as we might say, and then either choose or reject God. They start as sinners and express their sin in everything they think and do.

Second, there is a passing reference to the supernatural nature of the new birth. When John says Christians are those who "have passed from death to life," he is indicating that becoming a Christian involves something much like a resurrection. No one grows into Christianity, in other words. Christianity is a divine creation or recreation, by which God of His own free will plants spiritual life within a person who otherwise is dead spiritually.

Third, the impartation of the divine life is of necessity accompanied by the characteristics of the One who gave it, above all by love, so that the one who does not love cannot be assured that he is of God's family (whatever his beliefs or upbringing) and so the one who does love can know that he is of the brethren.

John's reference to "brothers" involves a special emphasis. We might have expected him to use the term "beloved," as he did in the corresponding section earlier (2:7). But he says "brothers" instead, which suggests the idea of families. On the one hand, there is the world's family with Satan as its father. On the other hand, there is the family of Christians with God as its father. The hatred of the world is seen not merely in the hatred itself but in the fact that it principally hates Christians. For in hating them it hates Christ ("Why do you persecute me?" Acts 9:4). Similarly, the love of Christians is seen not merely in a general love for all mankind, though they have that also, but rather in a particular love for the brethren.

If Christians really do love one another, then they will not spend so much time criticizing one another, as is often the case. They will not abandon the assembling of themselves together while substituting some kind of private religion. They will not neglect one another's needs. Instead, they will find themselves uniting together in a spiritual fellowship in which the Lord is worshiped and they themselves are mutually encouraged in the Christian life.

The example of Christ

As John has been writing of Christian "love" he has been using the greatest of all Greek words for love, *agapē*. This now brings him inevitably to that supreme example of *agapē* love, the sacrifice of Jesus Christ as He gave Himself for our salvation. The love about which John is speaking cannot be analyzed apart from this event. Indeed, it cannot be known apart from it, for it is at the cross and only at the cross that this greatest of all loves is fully demonstrated.[2]

It is interesting to notice in this connection that there is hardly a verse in the New Testament that speaks of God's love that does not also speak (or the context does not also speak) of the cross. For instance, there is John 3:16: "For God so loved the world that he gave his one and only Son, that whoever believes in him shall not perish but have eternal life." Galatians 2:20: "I have been crucified with Christ and I no longer live, but Christ lives in me. The life I live in the body, I live by faith in the Son of God, who loved me and gave himself for me." Romans 5:8: "But God demonstrates his own love for us in this: While we were still sinners, Christ died for us." First John 4:10: "This is love: not that we loved God, but that he loved us and sent his Son as an atoning sacrifice for our sins." In each of these verses the cross of Christ is made the measure of God's love as well as the primary means by which we become aware of it.

What is it that gives the love of God as seen at the cross its special character? Primarily it is the element of self-sacrifice on behalf of those who are totally undeserving and even undesirious of the sacrifice.

Here the continuing contrast between Cain the murderer and Christ the Savior is seen in its sharpest focus. Life is the most precious possession anyone has. Cain showed his hate by killing

---

[2]There are four major words for "love" in the Greek language, as C. S. Lewis (*The Four Loves,* Harcourt, Brace & World, 1960) and others have pointed out. The first is *eros*. It refers to sexual love and has given us our English words "erotic" and "erogenous." The Bible is aware of this kind of love, of course; but by the time of the writing of the New Testament this love had become so debased in pagan practice that the word was apparently excluded from use in the Bible as something contaminated. The second word is *storgē*. It refers to family love. It is not included in the New Testament either, although it could be. The third word is *philia*, which is preserved in our English words "philanthropy," "philharmonic," "Philadelphia," and others. It denotes strong, brotherly affection. It might be described as the highest love of which man, unaided by God, is capable. The fourth word, *agapē*, is love which loves without variableness. It loves even when the object of that love is unlovely or hateful. It loves even when the loved one turns away. Westcott has an extended note on "St. John's Conception of Love" (pp. 130-134).

117

righteous Abel. Jesus revealed His love by sacrificing His own life for those foul creatures of sin He chose to make His brethren.

Love for others

But what does this supreme example of self-sacrifice have to do with Christians? It has everything to do with them, for John does not hesitate to point out that it is precisely in this self-sacrifice of himself that Christ is to be their example. Did He give of Himself? Then "we ought to lay down our lives for our brothers."

It is not often the case, at least today, that a Christian literally has opportunity to die in place of a Christian brother or sister. So John (who knew this even for his own more perilous times) will move on to more common matters in the next verse. Nevertheless, we should not pass over the idea of self-sacrifice too quickly. True, we do not often have opportunities literally to die for others. But we do have opportunities to "die to self" or, as we might also say, "sacrifice our own interests" constantly.

This is true of all forms of Christian work, involving both time and money. To make the gospel of Christ known worldwide involves sacrifice on behalf of God's people. They must live less lavishly than they otherwise might in order that money might be available to send Christian workers to tell others about Christ. They must be willing to sacrifice their sons and daughters to go if God should so lead them. They must go themselves if God directs it.

Another area in which self-sacrifice must be practiced is in the Christian home, particularly in love between a husband and wife. Today's culture glorifies self-satisfaction. It teaches that if one is not personally and fully gratified in marriage, one has a right to break it off, whatever the cost to the other spouse or to the children. But this is not God's teaching. God teaches that we must die to self in order that the other person might be fulfilled, for it is only as that happens that we will find the fullness of God's blessing and personal satisfaction.

The title of Walter Trobisch's little book, *I Loved a Girl,* is an illustration of this point. The book is a collection of letters between a young African boy and Trobisch, his pastor, after the boy had made love to a girl and had written to his pastor about it. One of the pastor's letters says this, "One phrase in your letter struck me especially. You wrote, 'I loved a girl.' No, my friend.

118

You did not love that girl; you went to bed with her—these are two completely different things. You had a sexual episode, but what love is, you did not experience. It's true you can say to a girl, 'I love you,' but what you really mean is something like this: 'I want something. Not you, but something from you. I don't have time to wait. I want it immediately.' . . . This is the opposite of love, for love wants to give. Love seeks to make the other one happy, and not himself.

"Let me try to tell you what it really should mean if a fellow says to a girl, 'I love you.' It means: 'You, you, you. You alone. You shall reign in my heart. You are the one whom I have longed for; without you I am incomplete. I will give everything for you and I will give up everything for you, myself as well as all that I possess. I will live for you alone, and I will work for you alone. And I will wait for you. . . . I will never force you, not even by words. I want to guard you, protect you and keep you from all evil. I want to share with you all my thoughts, my heart and my body—all that I possess. I want to listen to what you have to say. There is nothing I want to undertake without your blessing. I want to remain always at your side."[3] This is the standard of love that blesses homes and makes them stable. But it is only learned, as Trobisch later notes, from God as He is revealed in Jesus Christ.

A third area in which self-sacrifice should be practiced is in professional Christian relations. Terrible battles again and again divide the churches. These are usually portrayed as doctrinal battles, as they sometimes are. But more often they are simply personality struggles fueled by jealousy. Choir members can be jealous of one another and hate one another even when they are singing in praise of God. Ministers can be jealous of other ministers, so much so that they rejoice in the others' failures. Those in one denomination can have the same jealous hatred for those in another and can seek to undermine their ministry. These things ought not to be.

It is important, then, that we do not too quickly pass over the matter of the Christian's obligation to emulate Jesus' giving of himself. But neither do we want to linger there forever, for it is also true that the Christian is called to show love in less exacting

---

[3]Walter Trobisch, *I Loved a Girl* (New York: Harper and Row, 1965), pp. 3, 4.

ways. Suppose that one believer sees another believer in need, says John. And suppose that the first believer has the means to supply what the other is lacking. Well, then, he must supply it. For "If anyone has material possessions and sees his brother in need but has no pity on him, how can the love of God be in him?" (v. 17). Here is practical Christianity. A person may claim to be filled with God's love and to be so motivated that he would gladly give his life for others. But this can be no more than sentimentality. What John wants to know is how we treat our individual brother (singular, not plural) and how we meet his particular, very tangible need.

His final words are a true conclusion. "Dear children, let us not love with words or tongue but with actions and in truth" (v. 18). It is not by words alone that love is shown. It is not by words alone that those who are without Christ are won to Him, important as words are. It is by deeds, for these back up the words and give them content.

1 John 3:19-24
How to Deal With Doubt

This then is how we know that we belong to the truth, and how we set our hearts at rest in his presence whenever our hearts condemn us. For God is greater than our hearts, and he knows everything.

Dear friends, if our hearts do not condemn us, we have confidence before God and receive from him anything we ask, because we obey his commands and do what pleases him. And this is his command: to believe in the name of his Son, Jesus Christ, and to love one another as he commanded us. Those who obey his commands live in him, and he in them. And this is how we know that he lives in us: We know it by the Spirit he gave us.

At first glance it is somewhat surprising to find that John interrupts his second presentation of the tests—righteousness, love, and truth—to deal with doubt, at least so late in the letter. But when we reflect on John's pastoral concern for his readers and on the nature of normal Christian experience, it is not really so puzzling. To be sure, John has developed his argument concerning the basis for Christian assurance in a masterly way. But as a pastor he knows that in spite of all he has said there will still be some who feel condemned in their own eyes and who are therefore depressed by this and lack assurance. This self-condemnation can be due to a number of factors. It can be a matter of disposition; some people are just more introspective and melancholy than others. It may be a question of health; how a person feels inevitably affects how he thinks. It may be due to

121

specific sin. It may be due to circumstances. But whatever the cause, the problem is a real one and is quite widespread. How is a believer to deal with such doubt? How can he overcome depression? John apparently recognized this problem as a real one in his time and therefore wisely interrupts his argument at this point to deal with it.

How does a Christian deal with doubt? Although there are many causes for it, there is only one answer. It is: by knowledge. The Christian must simply take himself in hand and confront himself with what he knows to be true concerning God and God's work in his life. In other words, faith (which is the opposite of doubt), being based on knowledge, must be fed by it. This is the point that John develops at the close of this third chapter.

He does it in a broad way, however, as the outline indicates. First, he deals with the "condemning heart," John's own term for describing the problem. In these verses he offers two ways by which we may "set our hearts at rest in his presence." Second, he deals with the results that flow from having thus dealt with our heart: confidence of access to God and confidence that our prayers will be answered. Finally, he deals for the first time in the letter with the witness of the Holy Spirit, treating it, however, not as some additional source of confirmation but rather as expressing itself in the three tests already elaborated.

This parenthesis in his argument (3:19-24) corresponds to a parenthesis on the church and the world (2:12-17), occurring at a similar point in his first elaboration of the tests in chapter 2.

THE CONDEMNING HEART (vv. 19, 20)

The meaning of verses 19 and 20 is clear enough in a general way, but the grammar of the verses is difficult. As a result there have been many slightly differing interpretations. The causes of the difficulty are two. First, the Greek verb *peithein*, which occurs in the phrase "and set our hearts at rest in his presence," has more than one meaning. The most common meaning is "to convince" or "to persuade," in which case the verb is usually followed by a phrase containing the truth of which one is to be persuaded. In this case, there is indeed such a phrase. In fact, there are two of them: "whenever our hearts condemn us" and "for God is greater than our hearts." But neither of these gives a satisfactory sense of the passage. If they are the truth of which we are to be persuaded, the passage must mean that our love of the brethren (v. 18) convinces us of the greatness of God, which is just not true. "The consciousness of a sincere love of the brethren does not furnish the basis of the conviction of the sovereign greatness of God."[1] In responding to this some have suggested that the content phrase must be supplied. That is, we are to insert something like "that we are of the truth" or "that we are of God." But the objection here is that it is surely odd to have to supply mentally the very phrase which the verb leads one to expect to be expressed clearly.

The other meaning of *peithein* is "to reassure" or "to assure." This meaning is rare. It occurs elsewhere in the New Testament only in Matthew 28:14—"If this report gets to the governor, we will *satisfy* him and keep you out of trouble." But in spite of its infrequency, this is probably the meaning to be adopted (so RSV, NASB, and others). In this case the two main clauses following the verb need not be interpreted as supplying the content of that of which we are to be persuaded, and may give other meanings.

What the phrases do mean is, however, connected with the other major grammatical difficulty. In each case the phrase is introduced by the apparent conjunction *hoti*. This may mean "because." In fact, in the second instance it obviously means "because," for that phrase—"God is greater than our hearts, and he knows everything"—gives us a truth by which we may reassure our consciences. In the first instance, however, the meaning "because" is clumsy and disrupts the passage as a whole. The solution, in this case, seems to be to take *hoti* as the relative pronoun *ho* plus *ti*, which words together with the following *ean* form an idiomatic expression meaning "in matters where" or "whenever." This solution is adopted by most of the modern commentators and by many contemporary translations, including the NIV.

If these solutions to the grammatical difficulties of the passage are followed, the sense is as the NIV presents it. In this case, two references are made by which the doubting Christian may reassure or pacify his heart. The first looks back to what has just been said concerning love as it expresses itself in deeds. The sec-

---

[1] Westcott, *Epistles of John*, p. 117.

123

ond looks forward to God's verdict of acquittal, a verdict to be trusted regardless of one's own doubts or misgiving.

Love in action

It is not usual in John's writing for the phrase "this then" to refer to what has come before. Usually it refers to what follows. Still the reference to what has already been said is possible; and, what is more, it is demanded by the context here.[2] It is important to note, however, that in referring back to the test of love John is not referring to love merely in some generally emotional or subjective sense. For this would be little help to the doubting Christian. Indeed, it may be precisely this that he is doubting. He may be asking, "But do I really love the brethren? Do I love enough?" He may even be remembering acts that did not express love and for which his heart condemns him. No, John is not referring to love in a general sense but rather to love in the precise and visible sense about which he has just been speaking. He has spoken of the essence of love as self-sacrifice. He has spoken of the need to meet specific needs of specific Christians. He concluded, "Dear children, let us not love with word or tongue but with actions and in truth." Now he says, "Remember that, when you doubt. Do not look at your failures. Christians have many of them. Look rather at those specific acts of love which the Holy Spirit of God within you has led you to perform. Let these be evidence, and cease doubting."

Here an active taking hold of oneself and reminding oneself of objective personal acts flowing from the divine nature is striking, for John is not saying that we are to indulge our feelings of doubt or encourage introspection. We are not even to pray about the matter; for, as he is about to show, confidence of being able to pray and of being heard in prayer comes after we have assured our hearts before him. We are not even to "let go and let God," as some say. We are to seize our minds, and by the grace of God turn ourselves around. The first way we are to do that is by focusing on specific past acts of the divine love.

God's verdict

There is a second truth which we may also use to reassure our

---

[2]Another obvious case is at 4:6, where "this is how" must refer to verse 5. Verse 7 begins an entirely new section.

hearts. The first by its very nature was related to ourselves specifically; it had to do with God's specific work in our own individual life. The second is more general in that it refers in equal measure to all who are God's children. It is simply that whatever our hearts may say, God knows us better than even we ourselves do and, nevertheless, has acquitted us. Therefore, we should reassure ourselves by His judgment, which alone is trustworthy, and refuse to trust our own.

It is necessary to note that a weighty tradition of interpretation going back to some of the Greek fathers and echoed by the Reformers takes the judgment of God, not as being more merciful than that of our hearts, but as being more rigorous. That is, the verse is to be taken as a warning against presumption rather than as a cause for reassurance. Calvin expresses this view by saying, "From the contrary he proves that those who have not the testimony of a good conscience bear the name and appearance of Christians in vain. For if anyone is conscious of guilt and is condemned by the feeling of his own mind, far less can he escape God's judgment. Therefore it follows that faith is overturned by the disquiet of an evil conscience."[3] This, of course is perfectly true in one sense. Indeed, John gives warnings against presumption elsewhere. The difficulty is that it does not seem to be John's intention in the passage to awaken a sense of sin which might lead some almost to self-despair. It is to reassure his readers. For this reason, then, we must take the verse as presenting an additional truth by which the questioning heart may be comforted; namely, that God who knows all has nevertheless acquitted us before the bar of His justice on the basis of the sacrifice of Christ. Our confidence is to be found, therefore, not in our experience, but in His acts and word.

Paul's expressions of confidence in Romans 8 are a perfect commentary on John's arguments. 'What, then, shall we say in response to this? If God is for us, who can be against us? He who did not spare his own Son, but gave him up for us all—how will he not also, along with him, graciously give us all things? Who will bring any charge against those whom God has chosen? It is God who justifies. Who is he that condemns? Christ Jesus, who died—more than that, who was raised to life—is at the right hand of God and is also interceding for us" (Rom. 8:31-34).

---

[3]Calvin, *John 11-21*, p. 278.

CONFIDENCE BEFORE GOD (vv. 21-23)

It would be possible for someone who does not have much understanding in spiritual matters to argue that all that has been said about doubt and the condemning heart is of little importance. "For what does it matter if some doubt in spiritual matters?" he might argue. "Let them doubt. It will not hurt them, and it might even make them more humble or easier to live with." This would be false reasoning, however, as John now shows. For whether one has confidence before God or lacks confidence before God necessarily affects one's relationship to Him. Indeed, the one who stands condemned by his heart can have no confidence to stand before God at all, and he can have no confidence that his prayers will be either heard or answered. John treats the whole matter from the positive perspective, however, showing what blessings the Christian can expect if his heart does not condemn him.

Access to God

The first advantage of an uncondemning heart is what John calls "confidence before God." But this must be understood, not in the sense of confidence of things in general, but in the sense of confidence of one's standing before God and therefore of access to Him. The Greek phrase literally says, "confidence toward God," meaning that confidence by which we turn trustingly toward Him. It is one fruit of justification in the Christian life (Rom. 5:2).

This is the second time in the letter that the word "confidence" *(parrēsia)* has been used, and it will occur twice more. In the first instance and in the third it refers to confidence before God in the day of His judgment: "And now, dear children, continue in him, so that when he appears we may be confident and unashamed before him at his coming" (2:28), and "Love is made complete among us so that we will have confidence on the day of judgment" (4:17). In this instance and in the last (5:14) it refers to confidence in prayer. It is, as Westcott says, "the boldness with which the son appears before the Father, and not that with which the accused appears before the Judge."[4] Dodd calls attention to the fact that in ancient times the word rendered "confidence"

---

[4]Westcott, *Epistles of John,* p. 118.

stood for the most valued right of a citizen in a free state to speak his mind. He adds that "although the meaning of the word became wider and more vague in course of time, yet there always hangs about it this special association with the thought of freedom of speech, unhampered by fear or shame."[5]

Prayers answered

It is not only confidence in being able to approach God freely and speak our mind that should delight us, however. This would be wonderful enough even if this were all, but it is not. There is more. Not only does the one whose heart does not condemn him have confidence in being able to approach God, but he also has confidence that his prayers will be answered: "And [we] receive from him anything we ask, because we obey his commands and do what pleases him."

This, of course, is a most remarkable statement, for it is a claim that prayer will be answered, not just for some Christians in some instances, but in every instance for any Christian who will meet certain conditions. The conditions are: 1) that we obey His commandments, and 2) that we do what pleases Him.

It is possible that these two conditions are identical. Certainly they are related, for obeying the commandments of God is doing what is pleasing to Him. Still there is probably a difference. To "obey his commandments" is to adhere to an external standard. That is, it involves certain objective statements. John is going to refer to two of them in a summary way in the next verse. To "do what pleases him" may go beyond this in indicating a desire to serve and please God even in those areas where no specific commandment applies. In this case, it would be the attitude of a child seeking to please his father in little thoughtful ways, as well as by doing all that the father has specifically commanded. It is when these two elements are present, obeying His commandments and seeking to please Him, that the Christians can pray with total confidence.

John is not inventing any special doctrine at this point. Rather he is only taking at face value what he had learned from Jesus. Jesus had said, "I tell you the truth, my Father will give you whatever you ask in my name. Until now you have not asked for anything in my name. Ask and you will receive, and

---

[5]Dodd, *Johannine Epistles*, p. 93.

your joy will be complete" (John 16:23, 24). In these verses the phrases "keep his commandments," "do what pleases him" and "ask . . . in my name" point to an attitude in which the will of the one praying is subjected to the will of the Father.

But what are the commandments that one is to fulfill if he is to enjoy the privilege of having all his prayers answered? At this point John must have thought of the rabbis with their many points and refinements of points of law and he must have turned from this approach to the simpler and yet much more rigorous approach outlined from the beginning by Jesus. There is really only one commandment, John answers in verse 23; he uses the singular of the word. It has two prongs: faith in Christ and love for one another. Here "his command" means, "the Father's commandment," which Jesus reiterated. Jesus said, "The work of God is this; to believe in the one he has sent" (John 6:29); He called love for God and man the first and second most important summations of the law (Mark 12:28-31). John's reference to faith involves the full expression "to believe in the name of his Son, Jesus Christ," which means that we are to commit ourselves fully to the Jesus of history who is the very Son of God.

There is a difference in tense between the two words "believe" and "love," though both are related. "Believe" is an aorist and therefore refers to an act completed in the past. "Love" is in the present tense; so it involves a continuing attitude. In linking the words in this precise way, John comes remarkably close to Paul's classic definition of true religion, "For in Christ Jesus neither circumcision nor uncircumcision has any value. The only thing that counts is faith expressing itself through love" (Gal. 5:6).

THE WITNESS OF THE HOLY SPIRIT (v. 24)

In the last verse of chapter 3, John introduces two new ideas into the letter, neither of which has even been suggested up to this time. He mentions the idea of a mutual abiding, of Christ in the Christian and of the Christian in Christ; and he mentions the Holy Spirit, through whom the abiding is effected. Because of the development to come in chapter 5, the idea of the witness of the Holy Spirit is the more important of the two new concepts.

In mentioning the Holy Spirit we might think that John is

here introducing a new and subjective criterion by which the Christian may assure his heart before God, much as Paul seems to do in Romans 8:15, 16. But this is not the case, for it is not as a subjective witness that the Spirit is mentioned. Here Stott concludes wisely, "The Spirit whose presence is the test of Christ's abiding in us, manifests himself objectively in our life and conduct. It is he who inspires us to confess Jesus as the Christ come in the flesh, as John immediately proceeds to show (iv. 1ff.; cf. ii. 20, 27). It is also he who empowers us to live righteously and to love the brethren (cf. iv. 13; Gal. v. 16, 22). So if we would assure our hearts when they accuse and condemn us, we must look for evidence of the Spirit's working, and particularly whether he is enabling us to believe in Christ, to obey God's commandments and to love the brethren; for the condition of abiding is this comprehensive obedience (24a), and the evidence of abiding is the gift of the Spirit (24b)."[6]

This, of course, returns us to the starting point of this chapter; for it reminds us that the cure of doubt is not to be found in some subjective experience, but rather in knowledge. It is to be found in knowledge of the workings of God in our lives and of His verdict of acquittal of sinners through the work of Christ.

---

[6]Stott, *Epistles of John*, p. 151.

1 John 4:1-6
The Third Contrast: Truth and Error

Dear friends, do not believe every spirit, but test the spirits to see whether they are from God, because many false prophets have gone out into the world. This is how you can recognize the Spirit of God: Every spirit that acknowledges that Jesus Christ has come in the flesh is from God, but every spirit that does not acknowledge Jesus is not from God. This is the spirit of the antichrist, which you have heard is coming and even now is already in the world.

You, dear children, are from God and have overcome them, because the one who is in you is greater than the one who is in the world. They are from the world and therefore speak from the viewpoint of the world, and the world listens to them. We are from God, and whoever knows God listens to us; but whoever is not from God does not listen to us. This is how we recognize the Spirit of truth and the spirit of falsehood.

One Sunday evening after I had preached to the congregation of Tenth Presbyterian Church in Philadelphia on the need to test Christian teaching by the Scriptures, a young man came up to me with a very interesting story. Two summers before he had been active in a summer music camp sponsored by one of America's large universities. As a Christian he had longed for some effective Christian witness to the music students. So he was glad when, through the help of other Christian students and with the permission of the university officials, he was enabled to begin a Bible study group and a Sunday worship service. In his judgment these were quite effective. At any rate, quite a few of the students became Christians.

The following summer the work was begun anew and with high expectations, for the students had learned that the new conductor of the student orchestra was also a professing Christian. The young man who was telling me the story indicated that he had invited the conductor to the Bible study and the services and had asked him to take part. Unfortunately, the conductor did more than take part. He took over! Then he turned the meetings into an expression of a rather extreme form of Christian worship in which many so-called "charismatic gifts" were evident. The effect, far from being good, was divisive. The fellowship of the Christians was destroyed. Many open doors were closed. Eventually, because of the excesses, university officials banned all Christian meetings from the summer campus. The conductor felt that he had been persecuted; and when the young man protested that he had carried on a Christian work for the whole preceding summer without any harassment, he was told that this was because he had not been sufficiently bold or spiritual in his testimony. The young man wanted to know what I thought. It seemed to him that the work had been ruined unnecessarily. But was he right? Perhaps he really was not spiritual enough? If he was sufficiently filled with the Holy Spirit, would he not have found himself more in sympathy with the orchestra conductor?

I gave the young man some guidelines, much along the lines of the various tests of life that we have been studying from 1 John. But I tell the story, not for the sake of my response, but to make the point that the problem we are about to consider from John's time was not unique to his time. It is found in our own age also.

We do not know precisely what was happening to the churches to which John was writing. We know that at the least there was a schism in which those who professed to have a greater knowledge in spiritual matters withdrew from the original Christian assembly. But did they go out professing to have received a higher or purer revelation of the truth than had the others? We do not know. But if they left, it is not hard to imagine that they would have pretended to be more in tune with the leadings of the Holy Spirit or more obedient to Him. In addition to this, it may also have been the case that what they said and did

131

(and perhaps also what others said and did) was accompanied by various supernatural phenomena such as speaking in tongues or the performing of miracles. At least we know that such phenomena took place in other churches and by other individuals. What were the Christians to do in such circumstances? Did supernatural phenomena automatically authenticate the ones performing them? Some must have thought so, for when John begins the fourth chapter of his letter by saying, "Dear friends, do not believe every spirit, but test the spirits to see whether they are from God," he implies indirectly that some were at least tending to accept whatever teaching claimed to be given under such supposed inspiration.

In these verses John deals with this problem and, therefore, also with our own. His reply has three parts. First, there is the command to test those who claim to be inspired. Second, there is a standard to be used in testing them. Third, there is an application of these ideas to the problem of distinguishing between true and merely professing Christians. In this last section John deals once more with the radical distinction between the church and the world and shows the relation of each to the apostolic doctrine.

The contrasts in this section are therefore between the Holy Spirit and false spirits, belief and unbelief, and in a summary way (v. 6) between the truth and error.

TRUE AND FALSE PROPHETS (v. 1)

John begins with the statement that there are false prophets as well as true prophets and with a command for Christians to distinguish between them. At the same time he indicates what is the important point in so distinguishing. It is not whether supernatural phenomena are present, for the devil can also appear to do miracles. It is a question of the source of the prophet's inspiration. Is it of God? In that case, the prophet is a true prophet. If it is not of God, then he is not to be believed or followed, however great his wisdom or however striking his activity.

When John says that many false prophets are gone out into the world he is not necessarily thinking of his day alone. Indeed he would know that there have always been false prophets and that God's people have always had the task of distinguishing between those who are of God and those who speak either of themselves or by the power of the devil. The Old Testament contains a magnificent example in the case of Micaiah and the prophets of King Ahab, recorded in 1 Kings 22. King Ahab of Israel had been trying to persuade King Jehoshaphat of Judah to join him in battle against Syria in order to annex a piece of real estate known as Ramoth Gilead, but Jehoshaphat was skeptical. He wanted to ask whether the venture was blessed by the Lord by inquiring of a prophet. When he expressed this desire Ahab responded by calling together 400 of the court prophets, who then testified to a man: "Go, for the LORD will give it into the king's hand" (v. 6).

At this point Ahab was pleased; but Jehoshaphat was dissatisfied, for he sensed that these men were merely paid mouthpieces kept by Ahab for propaganda purposes. Jehoshaphat asked, "Is there not a prophet of the LORD here whom we can inquire of?" (v. 7). Ahab admitted that there was a man named Micaiah, but he said that he hated him because he never prophesied anything good about Ahab. Ahab did not want to hear Micaiah. Nevertheless, at Jehoshaphat's insistence this unpopular prophet was called. At first the prophet ridiculed the kings, saying word for word exactly what the false prophets had prophesied. But everyone understood what he was doing, and Ahab finally called, "How many times must I make you swear to tell me nothing but the truth in the name of the LORD?" (v. 16).

At this point Micaiah replied as God had instructed him: "I saw all Israel scattered on the hills like sheep without a shepherd, and the LORD said, "These people have no master. Let each one go home in peace'" (v. 17). This was clearly a prophecy of the death of Ahab, and it was obviously unpopular. Micaiah was imprisoned. But as he was being taken to prison he called out, "If you ever return safely, the LORD has not spoken through me" (v. 28). Moreover, he challenged all the people to take note of his prophecy.

Here is precisely the problem with which John was dealing in his churches. It is the question of who is right. And there is one test—a most important test—by which true and false prophets may be distinguished: fulfillment. Whose prophecies come true? Will Ahab be killed or will he not? Will Israel be scattered or will she return victorious? In this case Micaiah was vindicated. This is the test that Jeremiah gives: "But the prophet who prophesies peace will be recognized as one truly sent by the LORD only if his prediction comes true" (Jer. 28:9). Or, to present it from the negative side, it is also the test given to the people in Deuteronomy: "If what a prophet proclaims in the name of the LORD does not take place or come true, that is a message the LORD has not spoken. That prophet has spoken presumptuously. Do not be afraid of him" (Deut. 18:22).

But suppose that the prophecy of a false prophet does just happen to come true. It is conceivable. Or suppose that the prophecy is of such a general nature or involves such didactic material that it is just not capable of being tested in this way. What then? In that case, says Deuteronomy, the prophet is to be tested by whether or not he leads the people to serve false gods. "If a prophet, or one who foretells by dreams, appears among you and announces to you a miraculous sign or wonder, and if the sign or wonder of which he has spoken takes place, and he says, 'Let us follow other gods' (gods you have not known) 'and let us worship them,' you must not listen to the words of that prophet or dreamer. The LORD your God is testing you to find out whether you love him with all your heart and with all your soul" (Deut. 13:1-3).

THE TEST OF THE TRUE PROPHET (vv. 2, 3)

John has already indicated that behind every prophet stands a spirit, either the Spirit of God or the demonic spirit of antichrist (v. 3). He has spoken of the need to test the spirits by their origin. But how are they to be tested? How can a normal Christian know whether the spirit is of God or of antichrist? Here John applies precisely the test given in Deuteronomy 13, though in terms appropriate to the situation occasioned by the Gnostic challenge. "What do they say about Christ?" is John's question. Do they acknowledge that Jesus is the Christ come in the flesh or do they deny this? If they deny Christ, they are not of God no matter how marvelous their activity.

John's test has both a positive and negative expression, as is also the case with the similar test held forth by Paul in 1 Corinthians: "Therefore I tell you that no one who is speaking by the Spirit of God says, 'Jesus be cursed,' and no one can say, 'Jesus is Lord,' except by the Holy Spirit" (1 Cor. 12:3).

There are three possible ways in which the confession of

verse 2 may be taken, as Brooke indicates.[1] 1) "Jesus Christ" may be the object, and the phrase "has come in the flesh" may be the predicate. In this interpretation the confession would be to the effect that "Jesus Christ is come in the flesh"; that is, that He was a real man. This statement would be directed against some form of Docetism, the view that Christ was a spirit who only seemed to be a true man. 2) "Jesus" may be the subject, and the rest of the phrase may be the predicate. This would give the meaning, "By this you know the Spirit of God: every spirit which confesses that Jesus is Christ come in the flesh is of God." It would involve the identity of the historical Jesus as the incarnate Messiah. 3) The entire phrase may be taken as one connected and comprehensive accusative, the view favored by Brooke himself. This would be the simple confession of "Jesus Christ incarnate."

Brooke feels that the third interpretation is "the simplest construction" and should be preferred unless it is "too awkward." But there are two reasons why the second interpretation is better than this. First, the single subject "Jesus" accords with the same single subject in the negative statement in verse 3. It also accords well with a similar confession of Jesus as the Christ in John 9:22. Second, the confession of Jesus as Christ come in the flesh most clearly refutes what is known of the Gnostics' views. They wished to deny that the historical Jesus was the incarnate Christ, probably suggesting instead that the divine Christ merely descended upon the historical Jesus at His baptism and left Him before the Crucifixion. John, by contrast, regards the denial of Jesus as the incarnate Christ as the chief of all errors and seeks to combat it.

Here Dodd makes an excellent observation, contrasting this passage with the test of a true prophet in Deuteronomy 13. "The fundamental doctrine of Judaism is monotheism; no utterance, however inspired, which contradicts the principle of monotheism can be accepted as true prophecy. The fundamental doctrine of Christianity is the Incarnation; no utterance, however inspired, which denies the reality of the Incarnation, can be accepted by Christians as true prophecy."[2] In Christianity the incarnate Christ is central. Consequently, believers may tolerate no system which

---

[1]Brooke, *Critical Commentary*, pp. 108, 109.
[2]Dodd, *Johannine Epistles*, pp. 102, 103.

denies either His eternal godhead or historical humanity. As Bruce says, "No matter how charming, how plausible, how eloquent the prophets in question may be, the test of their witness to Christ and His truth is the test by which they must be judged."[3]

THE CHURCH AND THE WORLD (vv. 4-6)

At this point the contemporary reader may well feel that the discussion has become somewhat theoretical and even unreal. We are not often confronted today by those who claim to be prophets, he might argue. Our difficulty is rather of knowing on the purely human level whether or not a teacher speaks truly. Can we test those who speak on this level? Can truth be distinguished from error here? The objection is valid, of course, and the questions are good ones. Consequently, we are not surprised to find John turning to deal with the matter on this level in the remaining verses.

The outline to these verses is to be found in the emphasized pronouns which begin verses 4, 5, and 6. With the exception of verse 4 this is preserved even in most of the English versions.

Verse 4 begins with "you." It is a reference to those who are of God, that is, to Christians. John says two things of these persons. First, he says that they have overcome the false teachers. He is not referring to a physical contest by these words, nor even to a struggle in the area of morality. It is rather an intellectual battle in which the Christians have been victorious. The false teachers had been seeking to deceive these believers, but they had not succeeded. Merely by testing them and refusing to be taken in by their lies, the Christians have conquered. Second, John indicates why the Christians have been victorious. It is not that they were stronger in themselves, for they probably were not. The Gnostics were the ones who were the intellectual giants. Rather it was that God was in the Christians and that He who was in the Christians is stronger than he who is in the world. This last phrase recalls the statement of Elisha to his young servant when the latter was terrified at the armies of Syria who had surrounded them: "Don't be afraid," the prophet answered. "Those who are with us are more than those who are with them" (2 Kings 6:16).

---

[3]Bruce, *Epistles of John,* p. 105.

In this case the reference was to the angels of the Lord who had surrounded Elisha.

Verse 5 begins with "they." This refers to the false teachers who, John says, are of the world because what they say is of the world. It is the world's philosophy even though it may be dressed in Christian language and be presented by those who claim to be Christian teachers.

The last verse, verse 6, begins with "we." This "we" is not the same as the "you" who "are from God" in verse 4. In verse 4 the "you" is all Christians. In this verse "we" must refer, not to all Christians, but to the apostles, as the direct counterpart to the false teachers of verse 4. In other words, this "we" is the same as the "we" that begins the letter, which verses insist most strongly upon the apostolic teaching and testimony. What does this mean? It simply means that those who are of God and those who are of the world may be distinguished by their response or lack of response to the apostolic teaching. "Whoever knows God listens to us; but whoever is not from God does not listen to us. This is how we recognize the Spirit of truth and the spirit of falsehood." If this were a mere individual talking, the claim would be presumptuous. But it is not. This is one of the apostles citing the collective testimony of all the apostles and making that testimony the measure of truth and sound doctrine.

The tragedy of our time is that we do not have enough men and women to proclaim and defend that doctrine. So the truth is not clearly defined, and the way is not clearly illuminated. The doctrine of the apostles, the only true doctrine of the church, illuminates it; and the incarnation of God's Christ defines and gives a focal point to that doctrine. It is for us to determine whether or not we believe that doctrine and, if we do, to respond to it. There are not three ways, according to the apostle. There are not four, or five, or more. There are only two ways: the way of truth and the way of error, the way of Christ and the way of antichrist. We are called to serve Christ, and those who are truly of God will do so.

1 John 4:7-21
An Exhortation to Love One Another

Dear friends, let us love one another, for love comes from God. Everyone who loves has been born of God and knows God. Whoever does not love does not know God, because God is love. This is how God showed his love among us: He sent his one and only Son into the world that we might live through him. This is love: not that we loved God, but that he loved us and sent his Son as an atoning sacrifice for our sins. Dear friends, since God so loved us, we also ought to love one another. No one has ever seen God; but if we love each other, God lives in us and his love is made complete in us.

We know that we live in him and he in us, because he has given us of his Spirit. And we have seen and testify that the Father has sent his Son to be the Savior of the world. If anyone acknowledges that Jesus is the Son of God, God lives in him and he in God. And so we know and rely on the love God has for us.

God is love. Whoever lives in love lives in God, and God in him. Love is made complete among us so that we will have confidence on the day of judgment, because in this world we are like him. There is no fear in love. But perfect love drives out fear, because fear has to do with punishment. The man who fears is not made perfect in love.

We love because he first loved us. If anyone says, "I love God," yet hates his brother, he is a liar. For anyone who does not love his brother, whom he has seen, cannot love God, whom he has not seen. And he has given us this command: Whoever loves God must also love his brother.

To this point much of John's letter has been given over to developing the three tests by which a person who has become a child of God may know that he truly is a child of God. They are: the moral test, which is righteousness; the social test, which is love; and the doctrinal test, which is the test of truth or of belief in the Lord Jesus Christ as God incarnate. The tests have been developed one by one, but it has been obvious even as John talks about them that they belong together and that each is important.

But which is most important? In one sense this obviously is an illegitimate question, for any approach to the tests is illegitimate if it allows us to minimize one of them. For example, if we say doctrine is most important, we thereby imply that we do not need to live a righteous life or love one another, and we are clearly on the wrong track. Or again, if we say love is so important that we do not need either obedience or doctrine, that too is wrong and dangerous. On the other hand, there are senses in which a question about the most important test is valid. We can ask it in terms of our need, for instance: Which do we most lack? Or we can ask it in terms of John's interests: Upon which does John lay most emphasis as he writes this letter? Interestingly enough, the answer to both these forms of the question is love, for we need to love, and it is upon love that John himself seems to lay the greatest emphasis.

This does not mean that John neglects doctrine. The apostle who composed the fourth Gospel in order that those who read it might "believe that Jesus is the Christ, the Son of God" is not going to minimize the truths concerning Jesus Christ, nor any other doctrines. Nor does it mean that he neglects the need to live a righteous life. John has already said that the person who claims to know God and who does not live a righteous life is a liar. However, it does mean that John saw a lack in this area and therefore also saw that the need to show love demanded great emphasis. We remember that John was writing to those who had resisted the Gnostic errors and excesses. They had not abandoned the truth, nor had they fallen into loose living. But did they love? Did they really love one another?

In seeing why John presses the point as he does, particularly in this section of the letter, we also see why the point must be pressed today precisely among the most orthodox and moral sectors of the Christian church. For we recognize that it is possible

139

for a group of Christians to be very orthodox in theology and moral in outward behavior and yet have very little love for one another.

Nowhere does John stress the need to love more than in these verses from the fourth chapter. It is not the first time that he has considered the test of love, of course. The test occurs first in 2:7-11, in which it is related to the "true light." The test occurs a second time in 3:11-18, in which it is related to "eternal life." Each of these has been important, but in a sense both have been a preparation for this third development of the test, in which it is related, neither to light nor life, but to the very nature of God, which is love. This statement (that "God is love," 4:8, 16) is probably the high-water mark of the Epistle, and these verses are its "sublimest height."[1]

The verses fall into three easily discernable sections: first, the exhortation to love one another, repeated three times (vv. 7-12); second, the connection between love and sound doctrine (vv. 13-16); third, the perfection of love seen in confidence before God in the day of judgment and in love for the brethren (vv. 17-21). The last two sections are a further elaboration of a statement John makes in closing the first section.

LET US LOVE (vv. 7-11)

John begins with a passionate exhortation to his readers to "love one another," a phrase which is repeated three times, in verses 7, 11, and 12. This is his great concern, and the reasons for that concern are given in connection with this threefold repetition. The first reason is that love is of God's own nature; therefore, Christians are to "love one another." The second reason concerns God's gift in Christ; therefore, Christians are to "love one another." The third reason concerns God's present activity in and through His people; for this reason, too, Christians are to "love one another." Up to this point love has been seen mostly as a duty binding upon believers. Now it is seen for what it most truly is, a driving disposition arising out of the divine nature which by God's grace is now also within the Christian.

The first reason: God's nature

The first reason why Christians must love other Christians is that

---

[1]Law, *Tests of Life*, p. 246.

the very nature of God is love and that this demands it. John states this in two forms, saying that "love comes from God" and that "God is love." The first of these indicates that God is the source of all love. If this is so, then the one who loves must love with that love which comes from God and, therefore, he must be born of him. If he does not love, he does not know God. The second form of John's statement is that "God *is* love." This is more profound than the former, for it regards love not merely as a gift or attribute of God but in the deepest sense as God's own nature. It is to be taken alongside those two other unequivocal statements of John which tell us that "God is spirit" (John 4:24) and that "God is light" (1 John 1:5).

John links love to the nature of God in a very subtle way in these verses, and this should not be missed. It is seen in the fact that each of these statements regarding love and our need to love is linked to one of the persons of the Trinity, so that the entire Trinity is involved. In verses 7 and 8 the reference is to God the Father; it is this that we have just been considering. In verses 9-11 the reference is primarily to God the Son. God loved us so much that He died for us, and therefore we should love one another. Finally, in verse 12, in the phrase "God lives in us," the reference is to God the Holy Spirit; and again the conclusion is the same: love one another. In other words, God the Father is love, God the Son is love, God the Spirit is love. Therefore, if we know the God who is Father, Son, and Holy Spirit, we will love. It is difficult to see how the matter could be made simpler than this or more pressing upon the conscience of the Christian.

The second reason: God's gift

The fact that the Trinity is involved in these statements leads naturally to the second of John's reasons why Christians must love other Christians. The second reason is God's gift of Jesus Christ His Son for our salvation. The parallel between this and the first of John's reasons is striking. If we know God the Father, we will love. If we know the Son, we will love. Or again, if we know God's nature, we will love. If we know God's gift, we will love. In these verses John reminds us that spiritually we were dead men and women before God the Father sent Jesus to die for us. But when Christ died for us and when by the work of the Holy Spirit we were made alive spiritually, we were able to be-

141

lieve on Christ and recognize the love of God in Christ which stood behind His sacrifice. Consequently, having thus come to know love and take the measure of love, we are to love. "Dear friends, since God so loved us, we also ought to love one another."

There are three aspects to the love of God in the gift of Christ that give us this measure. First, there is the fact that God gave *His Son* (v. 9). That is, God gave the best there was to give. Nothing could be greater than this. Nothing that can possibly be imagined can exceed this gift, for this is that "indescribable gift" for which Paul can only give thanks as he writes to the Corinthians (2 Cor. 9:15).

The second factor that enables us to measure the great love of God in Christ is that God gave His Son *to die* (v. 10). If God had merely sent Jesus to teach us about Himself, that would have been wonderful enough. It would have been far more than we deserved. If God had sent Jesus simply to be our example, that would have been good too and would have had some value— though, of course, no one would ever have lived up to that example. These things would have been good. But the wonderful thing is that God did not stop with these but rather sent His Son, not merely to teach or to be our example, but to die the death of a felon, that He might save us from sin. This is the fact that overwhelms the biblical writers and emerges almost without fail whenever they speak in depth of the love of God. "What, then, shall we say in response to this? If God is for us, who can be against us? He who did not spare his own Son, but gave him up for us all—how will he not also, along with him, graciously give us all things? . . . For I am convinced that neither death nor life, neither angels nor demons, neither the present nor the future, nor any powers, neither height nor depth, nor anything else in all creation, will be able to separate us from the love of God that is in Christ Jesus our Lord" (Rom. 8:31, 32, 38, 39).

The final factor is that God gave His Son to die *for sinners*. As John says, "This is love: not that we loved God, but that he loved us and sent his Son as an *atoning sacrifice for our sins*" (v. 10). Who are those for whom Christ died? Not lovely people by God's reckoning, but sinners, those who had rebelled against God and hated Him. Indeed, they were those who would crucify His Son out of hatred for Him. And such are we all. Consequently, the measure of God's love is seen in the fact that He gave His Son to die for such as ourselves.

The term of endearment ("dear friends") with which John begins this last verse takes us back to the identical term with which he began this section: "Dear friends" (v. 7). It is as if, in exhorting his readers to love one another, John indicates that the exhortation is no less necessary for himself and that he must love and indeed does love them.

The third reason: God's present activity

The third reason why Christians are to love one another is seen in what Stott calls "God's present and continuous activity of love."[2] It is not just that love is to be seen as that which constitutes God's eternal nature or even that which is revealed definitively in past history at the cross of Christ. It is also that which is continuously present as God continues to work in and through His people. It is this about which John speaks in verse 12, saying, "No one has ever seen God; but if we love each other, God lives in us and his love is made complete in us."

That no man has ever seen God is evident. The Old Testament theophanies, including the apparently contradictory statement in Exodus 24:10, did not involve the full revelation of God as He is in Himself but only a suggestion of what He is in forms that a human being could understand. But how, then, is a person to know Him? The reply of this verse is almost breathtaking, for it is John's clear statement that although God cannot be seen in Himself, He can be seen in those in whom He abides and in whom His love is perfected. How are men and women who do not yet know God to know Him? he seems to ask. The answer is: When we who do know him love one another. Bruce writes well on this point saying, "The love of God displayed in his people is the strongest apologetic that God has in the world. When his love is planted in their hearts, and he himself thus dwells within them, his love is 'perfected' in the complementary response which it finds in them, towards him and towards their fellows. It is in this way that they are not only holy and merciful as he is holy and merciful, but, as enjoined by their Lord in the Matthaean version of the Sermon on the Mount, 'perfect' as their 'heavenly Father is

---

[2]Stott, *Epistles of John*, p. 163.

perfect' (Matt. 5:48), and all through that perfection of love poured out for them in the sacrifice of the cross."[3]

These are the three reasons why Christians are to love one another: first, because God is love and we are of God; second, because God loved us in Christ and so revealed His love to us; and third, because God is at work in us by His Spirit to bring that love to completion.

LOVE AND SOUND DOCTRINE (vv. 13-16)

In the last verse of the preceding section John has concluded that if we love one another, two things may be said to follow: first, that God abides in us, and second, that God's love is perfected in us. These two conclusions give the outline for the next two sections of this chapter. In the first section (vv. 13-16) God's indwelling of the Christian is discussed in greater detail; in the second (vv. 17-21) the perfection of love is analyzed. That the indwelling of the Christian by God is the theme of the first section is evident from the threefold repetition of the idea: once in verse 13 ("we live in him and he in us"), once in verse 15 ("God lives in him and he in God"), and once in verse 16 ("whoever lives in love lives in God, and God in him").

It is not easy to give a simple outline to this section of the chapter, however, as it was, for instance, for verses 7-12 on the basis of the threefold repetition of the phrase "love one another." Still, the major ideas are obvious. First, we know that we dwell in God and God in us because of the Spirit, whom He has given to us (v. 13). Then, second, we know that He has given us the Spirit because we have come to believe in Christ and love the brethren (vv. 14-16).

The gift of God's Spirit

John's first point is that believers know that they dwell in God and God in them because of the Holy Spirit whom God has given to them. By this John emphasizes that God is always first in spiritual things and that apart from His gracious activity by the Holy Spirit to open blind eyes to perceive the truth and move rebellious wills to turn from sin to the Savior, no one would believe in Christ or love the brethren. In the next few verses John is going to talk of belief in Christ and love of the brethren, but we must not think, as some commentators have, that these are con-

[3]Bruce, *Epistles of John,* p. 109.

ditions by which we are enabled to dwell in God or remain in Him. To believe in Christ and to love the brethren are not conditions by which we may dwell in God but rather are evidences of the fact that God has already taken possession of our lives to make this possible.

The Holy Spirit's gifts

This leads directly to John's next point, for, having said that it is always God who is first in spiritual things, the question with which He next wants to deal is this: Is God thus at work spiritually in me? In answer to this question he, therefore, now argues that if God is at work, the evidences for it will be seen in a combination of love and sound doctrine. In other words, we may know that we have the Spirit because we have come to confess Christ and dwell in love.

The confession of Christ is mentioned first because it is at the point of confession that the Christian life may properly be said to begin.[4] "And we have seen and testify that the Father has sent his Son to be the Savior of the world. If anyone acknowledges that Jesus is the Son of God, God lives in him and he in God" (vv. 14, 15). Once again, as in numerous spots throughout the letter, John phrases his confession of Christ in words which would be especially challenging to those faced with the Gnostic heresies. He emphasizes that God the Father sent the eternal Son to be the Savior and that the historical Jesus is that eternal Son.

This should not obscure the fact that there are additional theological riches in the verses, however. For one thing, there is the doctrine of a lost world which needs a Savior. This "world," as was pointed out in the earlier discussion of 2:15-17, means the world of men as it is in rebellion against God. A second doctrine is the full deity of Jesus Christ. A third is the focal point of His mission, which was to be the "Savior of the world." It was for this that God "sent" Him, says John. A fourth is the matter of God's own motivation in the work of salvation, which is "the love God has for us" (v. 16).

---

[4]Both the verb "have seen" (perfect) and "testify" (aorist subjunctive) point to a single original perception of who Christ is and what He has done and confession of Him as such. This original perception and confession are then followed by continuing efforts to "testify" (present) to these truths for others' benefit.

The second evidence of the Spirit's activity is love for God and one another, for John concludes by saying, "God is love. Whoever lives in love lives in God, and God in him." In other words, the love to which Christians were exhorted in verses 7-12 is now said not only to be a most solemn duty but also to be a striking evidence of the Spirit's activity.

Here certainly, in a combination of the ideas of the internal work of the Holy Spirit, belief in Christ as the Son of God and Savior, and the supreme point of Christian ethics which is a two-pronged love both for God and man, is a high point of the Epistle. John is dealing with the subject of assurance (as he has been throughout) and has expressed it under several aspects. There is a subjective side, but it is without those unreliable, so-called spiritual experiences on which so many depend: tongues, miracles, feelings, and so forth. There is also an objective side, but this is not without those tender expressions of love which temper mere orthodoxy and validate it. Dodd writes of these verses: "This closely knit statement therefore places the reality of the Christian experience of God beyond question, guarding against the dangers of subjectivism on the one hand, and of mere traditionalism on the other; placing equal and co-ordinate stress on love to God, which is the heart of religion, and love to man, which is the foundation of morality, without allowing religion to sink to the level of mere moralism, or morality to be dissolved in mysticism. The passage is the high-water mark of the thought of the epistle."[5]

LOVE'S PERFECTION (vv. 17-21)

In verses 13-16 John has developed the first of two ideas introduced for the first time in verse 12, the indwelling of the Christian by God. Now he returns to the second of those two ideas, the perfection of love, and explains what he means practically. Earlier, when he had said, "If we love each other, God lives in us and his love is made complete in us," the reader might well have been left with the question of how such a thing could be possible. God's attributes are perfection; He is perfection. Consequently, we might wonder how God's love could be perfected in us, or anywhere else for that matter. Now John explains his meaning, showing that his emphasis was not so much upon that love that

[5]Dodd, *Johannine Epistles,* p. 118.

God has in Himself (which obviously is already perfect) but rather upon our love both for God and one another. This has its source in God and is brought to completion by Him. "Made complete" here does not mean totally without flaw in a moral or any other sense. It means "whole" or "mature," and it refers to that state of mind and activity in which the Christian is to find himself when the love of God within him, expressing itself in the believer's own love, has accomplished that which God fully intends it to accomplish.

No doubt there are many aspects of love's perfection, but from this greater number John singles out two. First, there is confidence in view of God's coming judgment (vv. 17, 18). Second, there is love of the brethren (vv. 19-21).

Confidence

This is the third time in the letter that the word "confidence" (parrēsia) occurs, and it will occur once more. In two of the four instances it refers to confidence before God in reference to prayer (3:21; 5:14). In the other two instances, one of which is this text, it refers to confidence before God in view of Christ's return and the execution of His righteous judgment against sin (2:28; 4:17).

The idea of God's judgment is an unpopular one today, but it is not necessarily less popular than it was in John's time. The problem is simply that men and women do not like the idea of having to account to God for their actions. So they tend to discount the idea, hoping that the day of judgment might just go away. But judgment is the only logical idea of the three ideas usually associated with the end times. In most systems of theology the end events focus around three things: the return of Christ, the Resurrection, and the judgment. But neither the return of Christ nor the Resurrection are logical. Jesus came once and was rejected. He was crucified. If He never came back, this would be logical; and no one, least of all ourselves, could blame Him. Yet against logic He is returning. The resurrection is not logical either, for even the Bible declares of our bodies, "Dust you are and to dust you will return" (Gen. 3:19). Logically no one could expect more. But judgment? That is the most logical event the future holds for any man or woman.

Moreover, the day of judgment is as fixed in God's eternal timetable as any other day in world history. This is the significance of the word "day." Technically speaking, the day of judgment is not necessarily a twenty-four-hour period. At all events, it certainly includes a series of judgments upon the earth (Rev. 6-16), the beast and the false prophet (Rev. 19:20), the gentile nations (Joel 3:14; Matt. 25:31-46), Israel (Ezek. 20:33-44), and all individuals at the judgment of the great white throne (Rev. 20:11-15). The reason it is called a "day" is that it is fixed in God's timetable and will surely come.[6]

In view of this logical and unalterable day in which the thoughts and deeds of men and women are to be judged, an individual might well fear. But John says that in the case of Christians perfect love casts out terror. This does not mean that love for God is the ground of our acceptance before Him. The only possible ground is the death of Christ for us and faith in Him. It means rather that by love for God any unreasonable fears are quieted and we come to rest in the fact that the One who was for us in Christ will allow nothing to destroy the eternal relationship which the death of Christ established (Rom. 8:31-39).

It is possible to be a Christian and still be filled with fear in view of God's judgment. Some branches of the Christian church even encourage such fear on the part of their adherents. But the fear is unnecessary, and mature love defeats it. Bengel, in one of his excellent Latin expressions, gives the proper course of progress in the Christian life: "neither love nor fear, fear without love, both fear and love, love without fear." The sinner must begin by fearing the God against whom he has sinned; but, having believed in Christ who has atoned for sin, he may put away fear and grow in confidence before Him.

Love of the brethren

The second area in which love finds perfection is in reference to our love for the brethren; for it is there, according to John, that real love is to be seen and measured.

---

[6]There is a similar situation in John's references to the "hour" of Jesus Christ (John 2:4; 7:30; 8:20; 12:23, 27; 13:1; 16:32; 17:1). It is clear from these passages that the "hour" involves more than a sixty-minute period. At the very least it involves the three days beginning with the Crucifixion and concluding with the Resurrection; and it may involve the forty days following the Resurrection, inasmuch as the exaltation of Christ, which is involved in the "hour," would seem to include the Ascension. It is called Christ's "hour," then, not because of its length but because the events which it includes were fixed in God's timetable.

An Exhortation to Love One Another

John begins this section by a broad statement: "We love because he first loved us." But lest a person apply this to a love for God exclusive of a love for human beings, John immediately goes on to show that anyone who is attempting to separate the two is a liar, for love cannot be so differentiated. John's reasoning at this point is interesting. He argues that it is easier to love men than God; therefore, if there is no love for men, love for God is absent also, regardless of what the person professing to love God may say verbally. How many Christians really believe that it is easier to love men than God? Possibly it is a very small number, for our natural inclination is to think that it is easier to love God simply because He is worthy of our love and that it is difficult to love men because they are not lovable or lovely. Yet this passage says exactly the opposite, implying, no doubt, that unless we are really loving our Christian brothers and sisters on the horizontal level we are deluding ourselves in regard to what we consider to be our love for God on the vertical. Unless we can love men and women we cannot love God. Unless we actually do love them, we do not love the One who created them and in whose image they were and are created.

We can put this in other terms. Earlier in this book we considered the difference between *philia*-love and *agapē*-love. *philia*-love is strong brotherly affection. It might be described as the highest love of which man in himself is capable. *Agapē*-love is divine love. It might be described as the love of which only God and those who are indwelt by God are capable. These verses are the equivalent of saying that a person cannot practice *agapē*-love unless he can first practice *philia*-love. Without the love of men the love of God is impossible.

It is possible, moreover, that another conclusion may be drawn from this text. It is the conclusion that it is in learning to love men that we learn to love God. On the one hand, there are undoubtedly those who loudly profess to love God but who do not love their Christian brothers and sisters. John rightly calls such liars. But on the other hand, it is also possible that there are many who recognize that they do not really love God (at least not as much as they would like to) and who wonder how they might learn to love Him better. "I cannot see Him," they might argue. "At times he seems so far away and so unreal. How can I learn to love Him? How can I make progress in this that I know to be my privilege and Christian duty?" On the basis of these verses we are justified in arguing that John might well reply to such that a Christian learns to love God by loving those he can actually see. This does not replace the revelation of God's love at the cross of Jesus Christ, of course. It is there that we learn what love is. Nevertheless, it does supplement it practically, for it is by practicing a real and self-sacrificing love for one another that we learn to love the One who sacrificed Himself for us.

CONCLUSION

At the beginning of this chapter the question was asked, "Which is the most important of John's three tests: righteousness, love, or truth?" We answered that love was the most important, but at this point we have several additional insights for knowing why.

The first reason is obviously that we need love most, particularly in the so-called evangelical churches. These have sound doctrine, at least to a point. There is a measure of righteousness. But often, sadly, there is very little love. Without it, however, there is no true demonstration of the life of Christ within or true worship of the Father. The second reason is that Jesus Himself made love the first and second of the commandments. The first commandment is love for God (Deut. 6:4). The second is love for one another (Lev. 19:18). The two properly belong together. As Jesus said, "All the Law and the Prophets hang on these two commandments" (Matt. 22:40). The third reason is that it was the realization of this double love in us for both God and man that was the object of Christ's coming. This is what John seems to speak about in the opening verses of the letter when he says, "We proclaim to you what we have seen and heard, so that you also may have fellowship with us. And our fellowship is with the Father and with his Son, Jesus Christ" (1:3). That is, the coming of Christ is proclaimed so that those who hear of His incarnation and death might believe in Him and thereby learn to love both God and one another.

The devil is the one who disrupts. The Lord Jesus Christ is the One who draws together. Moreover, in the drawing together into fellowship, love is the key factor. Little surprise then that we have this commandment from Him: "Whoever loves God must also love his brother."

1 John 5:1-5
The Three Tests Combined

Everyone who believes that Jesus is the Christ is born of God, and everyone who loves the father loves his child as well. This is how we know that we love the children of God: by loving God and carrying out his commands. This is love for God: to obey his commands. And his commands are not burdensome, for everyone born of God has overcome the world. This is the victory that has overcome the world, even our faith. Who is it that overcomes the world? Only he who believes that Jesus is the Son of God.

At the end of the preceding chapter John spoke sharply about the need to love, saying, "If anyone says, 'I love God,' yet hates his brother, he is a liar. For anyone who does not love his brother, whom he has seen, cannot love God, whom he has not seen." But it is entirely possible that a person might try to escape this demand by asking; Who is my brother? Just whom precisely am I to love?

The full answer to this question, as Jesus showed in His story of the good Samaritan, is everyone. Each man is made in God's image and is to be the proper subject of our solicitations and love. But there is a closer and even more demanding sense in which the Christian's brother or sister is any other Christian, and it is this rather than the broader dimension that concerns John here. True, Christians often fail to love those who are in the world and so fail to win them to Christ. But it is also scandalously true that Christians often fail to love Christians. They believe in brotherhood, no doubt. But they restrict it to their own particular company of believers. Sometimes this is a social division, as when Christians associate with and love only those in the upper-middle class or, by contrast, only those within a lower level of society. At other times the division is by denomination, so that if they are Baptists, their brothers and sisters are Baptists; if they are Presbyterians, their brothers and sisters are Presbyterians; if they are Independents, their brothers and sisters are all Independents. At still other times, Christians will hold closely to those only within some rigid theological persuasion. Is this right? Can Christian brotherhood and the love that goes with it be so restricted? John gives the answer to these questions in the opening verses of chapter 5, when he says clearly, "Everyone who believes that Jesus is the Christ is born of God, and everyone who loves the father loves his child as well." In other words, membership in the family of God is not limited by anything other than confession of Jesus as the Christ. Consequently, the love of Christians for their brothers and sisters should extend to all who thereby give evidence of being God's true children.

It is not only a love-unity between all who are truly born of God that John has in mind in these verses, however. It is also a unity among the tests that he has been developing throughout the greater portion of this letter. Beginning in chapter 2 and continuing through chapter 4, John has discussed each of the three tests twice. He has discussed the moral test, which is righteousness, in 2:3-6 and 3:4-10. He has discussed the social test, which is love, in 2:7-11 and 3:11-18. Finally, in 2:18-27 and 4:1-6, he has discussed the doctrinal test, which is described either as truth or as belief in Jesus as the Christ. We must not think that these may be considered independently of one another, however, just as we are not to think of them without their opposites. Consequently, in this section of the letter, even as he continues his thoughts about love, John combines the three tests—righteousness, love, and truth—indicating as he does so that ultimately it is impossible to have any one without the others. In this combination and in these verses John summarizes the tests and thereby concludes this, the major portion of his letter.

The link that holds the tests together seems to be the new birth, which is mentioned in verses 1 and 4. This deserves mention by itself. The second element in the verses is the tests themselves, which may be considered in their mutual relationships.

The Three Tests Combined

CHILDREN OF GOD (v. 1).

The idea of spiritual birth or being "born of God" ties these verses together, for the concept occurs in verses 1 and 4, and it is from this that the realities involved in the three tests are developed. In John's understanding, the potential child of God is first made alive by God as a result of which he comes to believe on Christ, pursue righteousness, and love the brethren.

Which comes first, faith or life? The question is often asked in discussions of the differences between Calvinistic and Arminian theology, for it expresses the question of whether men choose God by deciding to believe on Christ or whether God first chooses men by making them alive in Christ, as a result of which they believe. John's first verse answers this question in reference to the new birth. In none of the English versions is the full sense of the verse adequately communicated, for the differences in tense are not as striking in English as in Greek. In the Greek text the word "believe" is present tense, indicating a present, continuing activity. The word "born" (in the phrase "born of God," also translated "is a child of God," RSV) is in the perfect tense. The perfect tense indicates a past event with continuing consequences. In other words, as Stott writes, "Our present, continuing activity of believing is the result, and therefore the evidence, of our past experience of new birth by which we became and remain God's children."[1] We believe and, in fact, do everything else of a spiritual nature precisely because we have first been made alive. If this were not the order, then the tests of life would have no value as indicators that an individual is truly God's child.

The image of conception and birth is a wonderful picture of what is involved in God's activity in bringing forth life in those who thereby become His children. This was suggested briefly in the discussion of 1 John 2:28–3:3.

First, it is a reminder of the fact that the initiative in begetting spiritual children is God's. James indicates this in writing "He chose to give us birth [literally, 'engendered us'] through the word of truth, that we might be a kind of firstfruits of all he created" (James 1:18). In other words, it is the Father's choice to beget a child, spiritually as well as on the human level. John says the same thing when he writes in the prologue to the Gospel,

---

[1]Stott, *Epistles of John*, p. 172.

"Yet to all who received him, to those who believed in his name, he gave the right to become children of God—children born not of natural descent, nor of human decision or a husband's will, but born of God" (John 1:12, 13). Second, the means of the new birth is suggested; for, as James says, this is by the word of truth, meaning the words of Scripture or of the gospel. In Peter this function of the Word is even compared explicitly to that of the male life germ or semen, which permeates the ovum of saving faith within the heart as the result of which a spiritual conception takes place and birth follows. Peter writes, "You have been born again, not of perishable seed, but of imperishable, through the living and enduring word of God" (1 Peter 1:23).

The Three Tests (vv. 2-4)

When a birth takes place the individual involved is not born into isolation, nor is he a totally unique individual in the sense that his characteristics and attributes have no connection with those of people who have gone before. For one thing, he is born into a family and into family relations. For another, he possesses at least some of the characteristics of the one who has engendered him. Spiritually, this means that the child of God exhibits those characteristics about which the letter has been teaching.

Love

The first characteristic is love, both for the parent and for the other children. Earlier John has said that it is a characteristic of the child of God to love, since God is love (4:7, 8). Now he shows equally that it is a characteristic of the child of God to be loved by those who are also members of God's family.

Verse 2 is not altogether unambiguous, however, as Dodd notes; for it can have two meanings. If the opening words, "this is how," refer to what follows, as is generally the case in John's writings, the meaning would be that if we are uncertain whether or not we love other Christians, we may reassure ourselves by determining whether or not we love God the Father. In other words, love of God becomes the fixed point from which we may determine our attitude to others. It may be said in support of this view that John undoubtedly held that love of God and love of man belong together, so that one may begin at either pole and arrive at the other. But the problem is that this form of reasoning is the opposite of what has been affirmed throughout the letter. It is by our love for one another that we are assured of our love for God; this is John's reasoning. Besides, just a few verses earlier John has argued that we cannot love God unless we love others.

The words of verse 2 are capable of another meaning, however, as Dodd shows in his careful discussion of the passage. In this reading the words "this is how" refer to what comes before. So the passage may be translated, "This is how [namely, the truth that if one loves the parent he inevitably loves the child] we know that, when we love God, we love the children of God and keep God's commandments." The logic would be: 1) Everyone who loves the parent loves the child; 2) Every Christian is a child of God; 3) Therefore, when we love God we love our fellow Christians.

Dodd concludes, "He [John] assumes the solidarity of the family as a fact of ordinary experience, and argues directly from it to the solidarity of the family of God. To be born of God is to be born into a family, with obligations, not only towards the Father of the family, but also (as part of our obligation to him) towards all his children."[2] Love for others is therefore a direct result as well as an obligation of having become one of God's children.

Obedience

Love divorced from obedience to the commands of God is not love, however. So John immediately passes from love to the matter of God's commandments, saying, "This is love for God, to obey his commands." Christians frequently attempt to turn love for God into a mushy emotional experience, but John does not allow this in his epistle. Love for the brethren means love that expresses itself "with actions and in truth" (3:18). Similarly, love for God means a love which expresses itself in obedience to His commandments.

At this point John says a striking and unexpected thing. He says that "his commands are not burdensome." This does not mean that total obedience to all the commands of God is an easy thing to achieve, for if that were so, Christians would not sin, and John says elsewhere that they do. John probably means two separate things by this statement. First, he may be thinking of the contrast which Jesus made between the commands of the scribes

---

[2]Dodd, *Johannine Epistles*, p. 125.

and Pharisees, which were "heavy loads," (Matt. 23:4; cf. Luke 11:46), and his own commands, which were easy—"For my yoke is easy and my burden is light" (Matt. 11:30). The Pharisees had created thousands of minute requirements by which the central commands of the law were to be guarded. But they were not God's commands, nor were they life-giving. They were burdensome. Jesus cut through these man-made rules to expose the central heart-attitudes which were required but which God would Himself supply in His regenerated people.

Later Paul argued for liberty from such burdensome rabbinical requirements: "It is for freedom that Christ has set us free. Stand firm, then, and do not let yourselves be burdened again by a yoke of slavery" (Gal. 5:1). Similarly, Peter at the Jerusalem council argued in nearly the same terms in order to secure liberty for Gentiles: "Now then, why do you try to test God by putting on the necks of the disciples a yoke that neither we nor our fathers have been able to bear? No! We believe it is through the grace of our Lord Jesus that we are saved, just as they are" (Acts 15:10, 11).

The second thing that John is probably thinking of is suggested by this passage. Here he is writing of the new life which Christians have from God and of the resulting love which they bear to Him. Without this life and love the commands of God, even in the form in which Christ gave them, could be burdensome. But now, the life of God within makes obedience to the commands possible, and the love which the Christian has for God and for other Christians makes this obedience desirable. The principle is seen in many areas of life, as Barclay argues. "For love no duty is too hard and no task is too great. That which we would never do for a stranger we will willingly attempt for a loved one. That which we would never give to a stranger we will gladly give to a loved one. That which would be an impossible sacrifice, if a stranger demanded it, becomes a willing gift when love needs it. . . . Difficult the commandments of Christ are; burdensome they are not; for Christ never laid a commandment on a man without giving him the strength to carry it; and every commandment that is laid upon us provides another chance to show our love."[3]

In all fairness, however, we must admit that there are times

[3]Barclay, *Letters of John and Jude,* pp. 123, 124.

when Christians find the commandments of God to be grievous. For who has not heard some Christian complain at some time that God is unfair in expecting him or her to live up to some conditions, particularly when it runs counter to what the individual wishes to do? And what Christian has not done it himself, at least mentally? The last phrase is the clue to understanding the problem, however, for the commands of God become burdensome only when we desire to do something else. In that case, love for our own will dominates our love for God, and fellowship is broken; and what was intended for our good seems cruel and restrictive. The solution is to return to that position in which we love God with all our hearts and souls and minds.

Faith

The third of John's tests is expressed in these verses as belief. Indeed, it is with this concept that the section both begins and ends (vv. 1, 5). Between belief that "Jesus is the Christ" and belief that "Jesus is the Son of God" is found John's discussion of both love and obedience. The implication is that, just as it is impossible to have love without obedience or obedience without love, so also is it impossible to have either love or obedience without belief in Jesus as the Christ and the Son of God. It was to lead men and women to this twofold confession that John's Gospel was written (John 20:30, 31).

John has talked about the content of the Christian's faith several times before. The new element in these verses is that of victory, expressed as an overcoming of the world. This is found three times: once, in the first half of verse 4, in the statement that whatever is born of God overcomes the world; once, in the second half of verse 4, in the statement that the active ingredient in this victory is faith; and once, finally, in verse 5, in the rhetorical question: "Who is it that overcomes the world? Only he who believes that Jesus is the Son of God."

These three statements express three important principles. First, that which is victorious over the world is that which has its origins in God. Indeed, if it were not for the reality of that new life which springs from God and which is implanted within the Christian, no victory would be possible. John has already spoken of the world and its assaults on God's people. There is the world without. John has spoken of this in chapter 2, verses 15-17, re-

157

ferring to the lure of the world as "the cravings of sinful man, the lust of his eyes and the boasting of what he has and does." There is also the world within, which John has discussed in terms of those false teachers who pretended to be among God's people but who were actually of the world, which they revealed by leaving the Christian assembly (2:19). How can any Christian resist such diverse and insidious evils? He could not were it not for the fact of the new birth and for the truth that he that is within the Christian is greater than he that is within the world.

The second principle involved in the Christian's victory is faith, which John defines as faith in Jesus as the Christ and as the Son of God. The importance of this confession is seen in contrast to the denial of these truths by the Gnostics. But the confession is equally important for our age. No one would deny that other points of doctrine are important. But since Jesus is the center of Christianity, obviously the truth about Him is most important and, in fact, determines what is to be believed in other areas.

The third principle of victory is faithfulness, which is, indeed, always involved in the idea of "faith" as the Bible defines it. It is not just a past overcoming that John is thinking of therefore [one of the occurrences of this word is in the aorist tense], but also a present overcoming [the other two occurrences are present] through a continuing and persevering faith in Jesus Christ. This is the same sense in which the word is used in Christ's messages to the seven churches of Asia Minor in Revelation, where the phrase "to him who overcomes" occurs seven times. There, as in John, it is not a superior class of Christians that is involved, nor those who do some great work as the world might evaluate it. It is rather those who remain faithful to the truth concerning Jesus as the Christ and who continue to serve Him.

This the Christians to whom John is writing have done through their faithfulness in view of the Gnostic threat, and this all who truly know the Lord will do also. Indeed, in the broadest view the faithfulness is not theirs, but rather his who has brought them to spiritual life and who, as a result, has also led them to faith in Christ, a pursuit of righteousness, and love for other Christians.

1 John 5:6-13
God's Own Testimony:
The Final Word

This is the one who came by water and blood—Jesus Christ. He did not come by water only, but by water and blood. And it is the Spirit who testifies, because the Spirit is the truth. For there are three that testify: the Spirit, the water, and the blood; and the three are in agreement. We accept man's testimony, but God's testimony is greater because it is the testimony of God, which he has given about his Son. Anyone who believes in the Son of God has this testimony in his heart. Anyone who does not believe God has made him out to be a liar, because he has not believed the testimony God has given about his Son. And this is the testimony: God has given us eternal life, and this life is in his Son. He who has the Son has life; he who does not have the Son of God does not have life.

I write these things to you who believe in the name of the Son of God so that you may know that you have eternal life.

The introduction to 1 John pointed out that three distinct purposes lie behind the writing of this letter: the need to encourage Christians in the assurance of their salvation, a desire to stress the historical groundings of the Christian faith, and a wish to reiterate and expound upon Christ's new commandment. Most of the letter has been given over to the theme of Christian assurance, as we have seen. But the practice of Christ's new commandment is one means by which assurance may be cultivated and established. Consequently, in the last of the preceding sections the need to love has been combined with both of the other tests to make up one comprehensive whole. With this behind him John seems now to take up the remaining theme once again—it has not been handled in and by itself since the preface—and join it to the others, thereby indicating that the historical data concerning Christ's life and ministry are also the basis (perhaps even the ultimate basis) for the Christian's assurance regarding salvation. To this God the Father bears a solemn witness.

There is a verbal connection with what precedes, for, since John has just spoken of belief in Jesus as the Christ and Son of God, it might well be asked at this point, Upon what basis is such a momentous confession founded? Or, to put it in other terms, How does one arrive at such a conviction? John's answer is that belief in Jesus as the Christ is based upon evidence embodied in testimony that is borne to him, to which he adds that ultimately such testimony is God's.

John does three things in this passage. First, he marshalls three witnesses to Jesus in which the testimony of the Father is found. Second, he contrasts the testimony of men with God's testimony, stressing that God's testimony is to be believed and trusted. Third, he sums up God's testimony and joins it to a final statement of his purpose in writing the letter.

THE THREE WITNESSES (vv. 6-8)

"This is the most perplexing passage in the Epistle and one of the most perplexing in the New Testament," writes Plummer at the beginning of his discussion of these verses.[1] The difficulties exist for two reasons: first, the text itself and, second, the meaning of the phrases involving "water" and "blood." Of the two, the first is the lesser problem. The second has produced a variety of interpretations even among the best of scholars.

The textual problem

The textual problem exists in the fact that from the KJV the whole of verse 7 and the words "in earth" from verse 8 should be deleted. Indeed, this has been done in the texts of the RSV, NASB, NEB, NIV, and other modern versions. The idea of the three heavenly witnesses—the Father, the Word, and the Holy Spirit—occurs first in a treatise written by a Spanish Christian named Priscillian,

---

[1]Plummer, *Epistles of S. John,* p. 157.

some time before his execution on a charge of heresy in A.D. 385. It was written into the margin of some old Latin manuscript and from thence passed into the text, being added to the Vulgate about A.D. 800. At this point the balancing words "in earth" were added to the authentic listing of the witnesses which followed.

But how did the error, present only in Latin manuscripts, get into our English texts which are based upon Greek? It is an interesting story. At the time of the late Renaissance and Reformation, when classical texts were first being edited critically, Erasmus of Rotterdam produced a Greek text in which the words in question were missing. At this time most of Europe was using the Latin Vulgate as its Bible version, so Erasmus was quickly criticized for omitting the passage. He replied that the words were not in any of the Greek manuscripts. Somewhat rashly, however, he added that if a Greek manuscript containing the passage could be produced, he would include it. Unfortunately, in time such a manuscript was found. It was not an old one; it was written about 1520. Erasmus knew that this was not valid evidence at all, since the manuscript probably included the passsage because of the Latin texts. Nevertheless, he had given his word. So he included the words in the third edition of his text, published in 1522. However, he also added a note in which he expressed his belief that the new Greek manuscript had been written on purpose just to embarrass him.

From Erasmus' text the passage was taken over into German by Luther and into English by Tyndale. Erasmus' text became the basis of the great edition of the Greek text by Stephanus in 1550, which in turn became the *Textus Receptus* or "Received Text" from which most subsequent translations, including the KJV, were made. Bruce, who tells this story in some detail, points out that the manuscript which proved to be such an embarrassment to Erasmus is now in the library of Trinity College, Dublin. He adds that there are only three more Greek manuscripts known to contain the passage: one from the fifteenth century, one from the sixteenth, and one in a seventeenth-century hand added to the margin of a twelfth-century text.[2]

There is nothing wrong with the three heavenly witnesses in themselves, of course; the point is simply that they were not in

[2]Bruce, *Epistles of John,* pp. 129, 130. The fullest discussion of the text and its variants is found in Westcott, *Epistles of John,* pp. 202-209.

the text as John wrote it, nor did they appear in any text of the passage at all for several centuries thereafter. What John wrote is what the modern versions give to us.

The Spirit, the water, and the blood

The second and much more difficult problem is the meaning to be given to John's enigmatic reference to the "water and blood" in verse 6 and to the threefold "Spirit . . . water . . . and blood" in verse 8. What is certain from the passage is that John is here attempting firmly to establish the historical factualness of the incarnation and earthly life of Christ and further to cite the testimony of God in regard to it. But certainty about what the phrase means seems to be beyond reach for those of us who, unlike John's readers, no longer know the significance of this part of his theological vocabulary.

There are three main interpretations to these phrases, to which a fourth may possibly be added.

1. The reference to water and blood most naturally reminds the student of the similar reference in John's Gospel in which attention is called to that "blood and water" which flowed from Christ's side after it had been pierced with a spear by a soldier at the time of the Crucifixion. In fact, if the Gospel of John is to be allowed to interpret the Epistles of John, as it has on other occasions, this would even be the logical place to start. Moreover, when this is done it is at once seen that there are important similarities. For one thing, in both passages John seems to put special evidence on the blood and water. For another, in both passages the idea of testimony is prominent (cf. John 19:35).

Unfortunately, the similarities are not as great under examination as they seem to be on the surface. For example, in regard to the matter of testimony, in the Gospel John bears witness to the blood and water, while in the letter it is the water and blood which are themselves the testimony. Similarly, in the letter John says that Jesus came *through* water and blood, while in the Gospel these come *from* Him. Indeed, even the order of the two words is different—blood and water versus water and blood— though this may not be of any great significance. The problem seems to be that the more the passages are studied the less the similarities appear and the less light the one passage throws on the other.

2. The second major approach to 1 John 5:6-8 is that of the Reformers, as well as of some moderns. It is to take the two key words, water and blood, as referring to the two sacraments. Calvin pursues this line of thought in some detail, linking the two elements not only to the two Christian sacraments of baptism and the Lord's Supper but also to the procedures of purification and sacrifice which existed under the Old Testament system. The difficulty with this view is that the symbols are not entirely appropriate; for while water obviously may signify baptism, blood does not signify the Lord's Supper. Rather, it is itself one (and even then only *one*) of the elements.[3]

3. The third and probably most satisfactory solution is to take "water" as a reference to the baptism of Jesus and "blood" as a reference to His death. It is true, as Stott acknowledges, that "water" and "blood" remain "strange and surprizing word symbols" for these events.[4] But just because they are strange to us does not mean that they were necessarily strange to John's readers. Indeed, from his use of them it appears that they were not.

If this is the meaning of these words, then two circumstances arising out of the context support it. First, John is obviously stressing the historical groundings of the faith in this passage. And if that is so, then an emphasis upon the earthly ministry of Christ bounded in one sense and on one side by His baptism and on the other by His death is understandable. Moreover, at each of these God intervened in a miraculous way to bear a testimony to Him: by a voice at the baptism ("This is my Son, whom I love; with him I am well pleased," Matt. 3:17), and by various miracles at the time of the Crucifixion. The second supporting circumstance is that throughout the letter John has been opposing

---

[3]Cullmann argues that it is a characteristic of John's writings to give a secondary and symbolic interpretation to otherwise perfectly factual events and, on this basis, sees the sacraments suggested to John by the flow of blood and water from Christ's side (*Early Christian Worship,* "Studies in Biblical Theology, No. 10" [London: SCM Press 1962], pp. 37-119). But if this is so, it is clearly a secondary meaning and must be secondary in reference to 1 John as well. That the author of 1 John is thinking of something different is evident from the fact that he uses the past tense—"This is the one who *came* by water and blood"—rather than the present tense which would be natural if the sacraments were uppermost in his mind.

[4]Stott, *Epistles of John,* p. 178.

163

the Gnostics, who, significantly enough, are known to have taught that the historical Jesus was not the Christ but rather only a man on whom the Christ descended at the baptism but who was deserted by Him before His crucifixion. If this is in view, then John would be emphasizing that there is only one Jesus, the Christ, who was then present on earth not only in and through the baptism but in and through the Crucifixion as well.

4. In spite of the fact that the third of these explanations fits the context well and is otherwise commendable, it is possible that still another view is involved. It must be remembered that in this context John is talking about the witness of the Father to Jesus, much as Jesus Himself does in the discourse recorded in John 5, and that it is hard to see how this can be adequately done without reference to the Scriptures in which that testimony is given most completely. Indeed, in John 5 the greatest place is given to a discussion of God's witness through the Scriptures (vv. 37-47), even though other witnesses are mentioned. If this is so, however, we ask ourselves at what place such a witness is involved and answer that the only place at which it can be involved is in the word "water," which is, in fact, used as a symbol for the Word of God elsewhere (Ps. 119:9; Eph. 5:26; John 15:3).

Can "water" symbolize the Scriptures at this point? It is not impossible. Besides, if this is the case, then the threefold witness of the Father to Jesus in verse 8 becomes a witness which involves each member of the Trinity. "Spirit" refers to the Holy Spirit's witness within the individual, "blood" to the historical witness of Christ's death as the focal point of His ministry, and "water" to God's unique witness to Christ through the inspired Scriptures. To reject these three would be therefore truly to reject God's witness and to call the only true and triune God a liar (v. 10).

John's emphasis upon the fact that there are three witnesses and that the witnesses agree recalls the important Old Testament principle: "A matter must be established by the testimony of two or three witnesses," (Deut. 19:15; cf. Num. 35:30; Deut. 17:6, 7).

DIVINE AND HUMAN TESTIMONY (vv. 9, 10)

John has outlined the nature of the testimony of God the Father to Jesus and is about to go on to summarize that testimony in order to provide a proper ending to the letter. But before he goes on he pauses to show why the divine testimony should be believed. There are two reasons: first, it is greater than human testimony, which all people accept, at least at times, and, second, willful unbelief is sin.

Verse 8 has introduced one important legal maxim into John's argument: the principle that a point of fact is to be established by the agreeing testimony of two or three witnesses. Here he introduces another: the principle of character in a witness. This is obviously an important principle in any system of law, but it was particularly important in Judaism where it took the form of a listing of those who were by reason of their professions or questionable actions unqualified to bear testimony. In this list are found thieves, shepherds (because they seem to have let their sheep graze on other people's land), violent persons, and everyone suspected of financial dishonesty including tax collectors and customs officials. The Pesachim 49b contains a passage indicating that the people of the land, the *'am hā āres* or common folk, were also excluded.

This principle is illustrated in John 8:14, in which Jesus says, "Even if I testify on my own behalf, my testimony is valid, for I know where I came from and where I am going." Earlier, on the basis of the principle requiring two or three witnesses, Jesus had said that if He should bear witness to Himself His witness would not be acceptable (John 5:31). But here in John 8 He argues on the basis of the principle of character to say that if the witness of mere men is accepted, if corroborated by others, why should not His testimony be accepted for itself alone in that He is much more than a man? The rabbis rejected the testimony of unreliable men. They accepted the testimony of an upright man when substantiated by that of other upright men. Clearly they should accept the testimony of Jesus, who knows both His origins and His destiny, judges according to the truth and not after the flesh, as His opponents do, and works in perfect unity with God the Father.

This same approach is applied in 1 John 5, as John argues from our willingness to accept human testimony (which we all know is fallible) to our obligation to accept the testimony of God. Men and women accept the witness of other human beings every day of their lives. Otherwise they would not be able to sign a contract, write a check, pay a bill, buy a ticket, ride a bus, or do any of the other thousands of things that constitute daily living. Well, then, says John, why should they not believe God, whose word alone is absolutely trustworthy?

If a person does believe God, he has an internal assurance that what he has believed is trustworthy. This is the work of God's Spirit, the *testimonium Spiritus Sancti internum,* as the Reformers termed it. It is in addition to the assurance provided on other grounds. On the other hand, if a person does not believe God, he makes Him out to be a liar; for in this way he eloquently testifies to his belief that God cannot be trusted. Here the heinous nature of unbelief is evident, for, as Stott writes, "Unbelief is not a misfortune to be pitied; it is a sin to be deplored. Its sinfulness lies in the fact that it contradicts the word of the one true God and thus attributes falsehood to him."[5]

GOD'S OWN TESTIMONY (vv. 11-13)

Talk about the testimony of God and its reliability might lead one to ask, But just what is it that is testified to? What is the essential content of this divine revelation? In one sense, this is an unnecessary question, for John has been answering it in one form or another all along. On the other hand, this is a point at which a short summary of God's testimony would be valuable. So John supplies it saying, "And this is the testimony: God has given us eternal life, and this life is in his Son. He who has the Son has life; he who does not have the Son of God does not have life." The testimony concerns salvation, John says. And the heart of it lies in the fact that salvation is to be found in Jesus as the Son of God, and in Jesus only.

John's reference to "eternal life" as the essence of salvation carries us back to the opening verses of the letter, in which he wrote that this life was revealed in Jesus, who is Himself the life. Eternal life is not merely unending life, therefore. It is the very life of God. What we are promised in Christ is a participation in the life of the One who bears this testimony. This life is not to be enjoyed by everyone, however. This life is in Christ. Consequently, it is as impossible to have life without having Christ as it is impossible to have Christ without at the same time possessing eternal life.

[5]Stott, *Epistles of John,* p. 182.

Toward the end of the Gospel, John gave his purpose in writing that book by saying he had written these things "that you may believe that Jesus is the Christ, the Son of God, and that by believing you may have life in his name" (John 20:31). That is, the Gospel was written primarily to those who were not yet Christians to lead them to become Christians. In a parallel way John now gives his purpose for writing the first Epistle, saying, "I write these things to you who believe in the name of the Son of God so that you may know that you have eternal life" (v. 13). Here, those to whom John is writing are Christians; and the purpose, as he notes, is to lead these to full assurance regarding their salvation. This has now been done, at least to the best of John's ability. Consequently, the body of the letter properly ends here. What follows is postscript.

Today many persons dismiss a claim to possess certain knowledge in spiritual things as presumptuous, but this is not correct, according to John's teaching. God has ordered His revelation in Christ so that the one believing in Christ may know that he possesses an eternal salvation. The real presumption is in questioning such assurances and thus casting doubt on God's word.

1 John 5:14-17
Confidence in Prayer and Intercession

> This is the assurance we have in approaching God: that if we
> ask anything according to his will, he hears us. And if we
> know that he hears us—whatever we ask—we know that we
> have what we asked of him.
>
> If anyone sees his brother commit a sin that does not
> lead to death, he should pray and God will give him life. I
> refer to those whose sin does not lead to death. There is a
> sin that leads to death. I am not saying that he should pray
> about that. All wrongdoing is sin, and there is sin that does
> not lead to death.

There are few subjects in the Christian life more puzzling to more
of God's people than prayer. On the surface we might think that
prayer should be the most natural and uncomplicated part of
Christian living, for what should be more natural than to speak
out of one's heart to one's heavenly Father? Nevertheless, in
practice Christians often are confused by prayer and ask: What is
prayer? Does prayer change things or does prayer merely change
the one who is praying? How should we pray? What should we
pray for? Can we be sure that God always hears prayer? Can we
be confident that He will answer it? Most of these questions are
answered in the verses which form the first half of the postscript
to 1 John.

Strictly speaking, the letter has ended with 5:13. In that
verse John has summed up his letter by saying that he has written
to those who have already believed on Jesus in order that they
might be assured of their salvation. But once again John seems

reluctant to leave the matter. So he adds a postscript in which he first returns to the subject of prayer (vv. 14-17) and then lists three final affirmations about which the Christian may have confidence (vv. 18-21). He has already discussed prayer once in chapter 3.

The outline for his discussion of prayer is striking. The verses contain two subjects: confidence in prayer (vv. 14, 15) and prayer for others (vv. 16, 17). Each of these contains a promise followed by a qualification.

CONFIDENCE IN PRAYER (vv. 14, 15)

Verse 14 contains the word "assurance" *(parrēsia)* which is translated three other times in John's letter as "confidence." Twice it has been used of the Christian's confidence before God in view of the final judgment (2:28; 4:17). On one other occasion, as here, it refers to the Christian's confidence in regard to prayer (3:21, 22). The Christian need not fear that for some unknown reason God will refuse to hear him when he prays or turn from him, says John. Indeed, such confidence is actually a product of knowing that one is a true child of God and of having no doubts on the matter, as he says in chapter 3.

The promise

In this verse John phrases the content of the Christian's confidence as being "that if we ask anything according to his will, he hears us. And if we know that he hears us—whatever we ask—we know that we have what we asked of him." In English this promise seems to fall into two parts, the two parts being 1) that God hears us, and 2) that He answers when He hears. This is not quite the point, however. To begin with, whenever the Bible speaks of God hearing prayer, this means, at least in the great majority of cases, that God answers. So in this case the first part of the promise is actually that God hears in the sense that He answers. But, then, what does the second part mean? Is it mere repetition? Actually it introduces an entirely new idea, for the promise is not just that God answers, but rather that because He answers we have the items we requested of Him *now*. In Greek the verb "have" is in the present tense. Consequently, the promise is not even that we will have them, but that we have them even as we pray.

How did the author of this letter arrive at such confidence? It is hard to miss the fact that he probably did so on the basis of Jesus' own teaching about prayer, much of which is recorded in John's Gospel. Jesus said, "I will do whatever you ask in my name, so that the Son may bring glory to the Father. You may ask me for anything in my name, and I will do it" (John 14:13, 14). He said, "If you remain in me and my words remain in you, ask whatever you wish, and it will be given you. . . . The Father will give you whatever you ask in my name" (John 15:7, 16). "Until now you have not asked for anything in my name. Ask and you will receive" (John 16:24).

Certainly these were new and bold teachings, and they were remembered as such by John. They are the basis of his extraordinary confidence.

The qualification

But the Christian is not to suppose that God will grant just anything he might happen to pray for, however foolish or sinful it may be, just because he prays for it. He must pray according to God's will. In prayer the Christian can be absolutely certain that God hears and answers his requests so that whatever he asks he obtains, but with this qualification: that he prays not according to his own sinful wishes but rather according to what an all-wise, infinite, and holy God desires.

This, interestingly enough, is found in all the verses that speak so firmly about the Christian's right to be confident in prayer. Earlier, in the third chapter, John said nearly the same thing as he does in this closing passage—"We have confidence before God and receive from him anything we ask" (3:21, 22). But there is a qualification there also, for the verses immediately go on to add, "because we obey his commands and do what pleases him" (v. 22). Similarly, in Jesus' statements about prayer, qualifications are also added to the effect that we must pray "in my [that is, Christ's] name," "remain in me [that is, in Christ]," and that Christ's "words" must "remain" in the believer.

This says a great deal about the nature of prayer, of course. Probably in most people's minds prayer is thought of primarily as that means by which God's will is changed or at least enlarged to include the concerns of the one praying. According to these verses prayer is not so much getting God to pay attention to our requests as it is getting our requests in line with His perfect and desirable will for us. It is learning to think God's thoughts after Him and to desire His desires. Dodd writes on this point, "Prayer rightly considered is not a device for employing the resources of omnipotence to fulfill our own desires, but a means by which our desires may be redirected according to the mind of God, and made into channels for the forces of his will."[1] In the same vein Barclay notes that prayer, even more than "talking to God," is "listening" to Him.[2]

PRAYER FOR OTHERS (vv. 16, 17)

Having indicated the nature of true prayer and having stated the confidence in prayer which every Christian should possess, John now moves on to the content of prayer in answer to the question: What requests should the believer bring before God? A first response to that question is nearly always personal, which indicates no doubt our own limited understanding of this privilege. We think of our needs for food and clothing, a good job (or a better one), our desire for a husband or a wife, the elimination of a vexing problem, and other things. In other words, we think of ourselves. It is somewhat of a surprise, therefore, to find that, first of all, John thinks not of himself but of others and that, as a result, his first specific example of prayer is intercession.

This, too, says much about prayer, for it tells us that the privilege of prayer should not lead us into a preoccupation with our own affairs, as though prayer were a blank check drawn on the bank of heaven given to us so that heaven's resources can be spent purely on our own needs or pleasure. Prayer implies responsibility, and part of that responsibility is in intercession for others. Do others have needs? Then we should pray for them. The one who truly understands prayer and who prays according to the will of God will pray for others, just as in material ways he will strive to show love practically (3:17, 18).

The promise

The encouragement to pray for others is based on a great promise; namely, the promise that God will hear and "give . . . life . . . [for] those whose sin does not lead to death" (v. 16). John has

---

[1]Dodd, *Johannine Epistles*, p. 134.
[2]Barclay, *Letters of John and Jude*, p. 137.

171

spoken often in this letter of the need to pursue righteousness as one evidence that the individual involved is truly a child of God. But in spite of the fact that the individual Christian must and, in fact, will pursue righteousness, he will, nevertheless, also sin and even from time to time become entangled in it. What then? Obviously, the Christian should confess sin and turn from it, knowing that he has an advocate in Jesus Christ and that the Father is faithful and just to forgive him on the basis of Christ's sacrifice and continuing intercession (1:9–2:2). But it is often the case, when he is in this state, that this is what the Christian least wants to do. So what then? Should he be left to himself to suffer the consequences of his sinning? Not at all, says John. Rather, those who are spiritual should pray in his behalf, knowing that God will hear and respond when they thus pray for others.

In all honesty it must be acknowledged that in this area Christians often fail grievously, for sin in a brother becomes all too often a cause for gossip rather than a cause for prayer. What is wrong in this case? The answer is in these verses, for they suggest that it is when a believer is himself in the will of God and is therefore praying according to the will of God that he will pray for others. John does not even use the imperative ("Pray!"). He uses the future indicative, saying that the spiritual person will intercede for the sinning brother.

The qualification

It is hard to imagine anything more obviously in accord with the will of God than the restoration of a Christian who has become entrapped in some sin. Yet, surprisingly, John seems to hesitate. His desire is obviously to encourage his readers to be bold in their prayers. He stresses confidence. But is it right, after all, that it is always God's will to restore the sinner? Always? In verse 16 John seems to recognize that it is not always the case and therefore introduces an exception based upon a distinction between sin which "leads to [literally, toward] death" and sin which does not. "There is a sin that leads to death," he says. "I am not saying that he should pray about that."

What is this sin that is "to death"? Apparently, in John's day and with his readers the phrase was a common one and was well understood, for John does not bother to explain it. But today the key has been lost, and opinion is widely divided in regard to John's meaning. Four views are prominent.

1. The first view is that John is referring to some particularly heinous sin, which God, so we are told, will not pardon. At first glance this seems to be suggested by a long history of divisions between various types of sin, beginning with the Old Testament Scriptures. In the law codes of the Old Testament several distinctions are fundamental: a distinction between capital offenses and those that are not capital offenses, for example; or a distinction between sins of neglect or ignorance and sins of presumption or premeditation. This latter is the same kind of distinction that is made in modern American law between murder in the first (that is, premeditated) and murder in the second (that is, unpremeditated) degrees. Rabbinical law further elaborated such distinctions, and in time the classification of sins as forgivable and unforgivable entered the church. At this time it was spelled out as the difference between "mortal" and "venial" sin so common in Catholic theology.

The difficulty with this interpretation is that it is somewhat of an anachronism to apply the distinction between mortal and venial sins here. Moreover, it may also be said that such a distinction is simply not supportable from the pages of the New Testament and that John, even in this very letter, seems to contradict it (see the discussion on 3:6, 9).

2. A second view, supported in part by the concerns of this letter, is that John is thinking of what we would call apostasy, namely a deliberate repudiation of the Christian faith by one who once was a Christian. Those who take this view find support for it both in 1 John, in regard to the Gnostics who had professed faith in Jesus as the Christ but who had later repudiated Him, and in other select New Testament passages which speak of falling away from Christianity. Hebrews provides the best examples of such texts, for it speaks of those who, like Esau, are "rejected," finding "no change of mind" though they seek it "with tears" (Heb. 12:17; cf. Heb. 6:4-6; 10:26, 27).

But is it really possible for one who is truly a Christian to apostatize? Or, laying aside the whole of biblical teaching which is clearly against this conclusion, is such a view even consistent with the theology that we find in this letter? Here Stott writes, "Surely John has taught clearly in the Epistle that the true Christian cannot sin, that is, persist in sin (3:9), let alone fall away altogether. He is about to repeat it: 'we know that anyone born of God does not sin, but He who was born of God keeps him, and the evil one does not touch him' (v. 18). Can he who does not sin, 'sin unto death'?"[3] In these verses John is teaching the doctrine of eternal security or perseverance; but if this is so, then there is no such thing as apostasy by a genuine believer. The Gnostics, for example, were just not Christians to begin with (2:19). Similarly, those touched upon in the problem texts in Hebrews are best understood as being merely external adherents to Christianity.

3. A third view is that John is speaking of that "blasphemy against the Spirit," about which Jesus warned His disciples. He warns of it in Matthew 12, defining it as that extreme form of rejection of truth seen in ascribing God's works to Satan. On this occasion the Pharisees had claimed that Jesus did his works of healing by Satan's power. He countered by saying, "Every sin and blasphemy will be forgiven men, but the blasphemy against the Spirit will not be forgiven. . . . anyone who speaks against the Holy Spirit will not be forgiven, either in this age or in the age to come" (Matt. 12:31, 32).

The major objection to this view is that it is hard to see how John could call such a hardened sinner a brother, as he seems to do. Stott, who holds to this interpretation, argues correctly that strictly speaking John does not call such a person a brother. He uses the word only for that one who does not thus sin, saying, "If anyone sees his brother commit a sin that does not lead to death, he should pray, and God will give him life. I refer to those whose sin does not lead to death." However, says Stott, in actual fact neither one can be thought of as a brother in the sense of being a true child of God, for the prayer is that even the brother might be given "life," and if this is so, then he must have been dead in sin originally.[4] In this case the prayer that John has in mind is a prayer for the salvation of unbelievers, with the promise that God will save such, as the Christian prays.

But is John using the word "brother" in a way which does not mean another "child of God"? Stott points out that the word can be used in a broader sense to designate one whom we might

---

[3]Stott, *Epistles of John,* p. 188.
[4]Stott, *Epistles of John,* pp. 189, 190.

call a "neighbor," citing 2:9, 11 and 3:16, 17 as examples. But it is not so clear that these cases do support a broader use of the word. Nor is it easy to feel that John can be departing from the more precise usage at this point of his letter.

4. The fact that none of the other explanations is entirely satisfactory leads one to wonder whether John may not be speaking just of physical death inflicted on a Christian by God as a result of a Christian's persisting in some deliberate sin. Certainly there are examples of such judgments. Ananias and Sapphira are two (Acts 5:1-11). A number of references in 1 Corinthians suggest others (5:5; 11:30). In speaking of the ministry of intercession John may therefore be saying that in some cases God will not turn back a physical judgment upon one of His disobedient children, no matter how much another Christian prays. So he does not say that prayer must be made in such a situation, although, we note, he does not forbid it.

The objection to this view is that "life" must mean spiritual life and that, therefore, "death" must mean spiritual death. But John is not necessarily making that distinction. For example, if the brother is a true Christian brother, then he is already alive spiritually; and the prayer would be, not so much that God would give him spiritual life, but that he might have life in abundance, as we might say.

A further qualification

The difficulty with a discussion such as this is that it becomes strangely fascinating to certain Christians, so much so that they tend to spend all their time on the exception (the sin unto death) and not on the central message of the passage. Whatever the interpretation we give to the exception, therefore, we must always bear in mind that it is the *exception* and that the burden laid upon us by John is to pray for any believer whom we see falling into sin.

Moreover, we must not even be quick to note the exceptional case even assuming that we have been able to decide what the nature of such a case is. Here the example of Jesus' prayer for Peter should make us cautious. Peter had spent three years with Jesus; but at the time of Christ's arrest, when asked by a servant girl and others if he knew Christ and was His disciple, Peter denied the Lord with oaths and cursings. We might say, if we did not know the end of the story, that if anyone had ever sinned unto death, certainly Peter had. Yet Peter did not die, either physically or spiritually. He had a lifetime of useful service. Moreover, far from refusing to pray for him, Jesus, we are told, actually interceded for him: "Simon, Simon, Satan has asked to sift you as wheat. But I have prayed for you, Simon, that your faith may not fail. And when you have turned back, strengthen your brothers" (Luke 22:31, 32).

We do not need encouragements not to pray. That comes naturally. We need encouragements to pray, particularly for others. In this responsibility we are greatly encouraged by John's teaching and by the example of the Lord Jesus Christ in His prayer for Peter.

1 John 5:18-21
Three Final Affirmations

> We know that anyone born of God does not continue to sin;
> the one who was born of God keeps him safe, and the evil
> one does not touch him. We know that we are children of
> God, and that the whole world is under the control of the
> evil one. We know also that the Son of God has come and
> has given us understanding, so that we may know him who
> is true. And we are in him who is true—even in his Son
> Jesus Christ. He is the true God and eternal life.
> Dear children, keep yourselves from idols.

It is entirely appropriate that a book dealing with the subject of
Christian assurance should end with three final affirmations, introduced by the repetitive phrase "we know" in verses 18, 19,
and 20. In some ways these statements are a summary of much
of what John has been teaching. In another sense they are a
reminder of how important affirmations are to Christianity.

Not everyone believes this, of course. In fact, some would
even try to eliminate affirmations in the interests of a greater,
though less meaningful, harmony among Christians. Erasmus of
Rotterdam was one. At the beginning of the Reformation Erasmus was a partial supporter of Martin Luther, whom he regarded
as being right in many things. But Erasmus, the humanist, did not
have Luther's spiritual undergirding. Consequently, as the Reformation developed Erasmus became increasingly distressed by
thoughts of a rupture within Christendom and became horrified
at what he regarded as Luther's excessive dogmatism. At last,
encouraged by friends, he wrote a book defending the free-

177

dom of the human will in spiritual matters and attacking Luther for his convictions. Luther might have admitted humbly that he could be wrong. He might have qualified his teaching in view of Erasmus' attack. But Luther did neither. Instead, he replied in *The Bondage of the Will* with an able defense of Christian certainty and with a reaffirmation of the Bible's teaching on the will's depravity in spiritual things. Luther declared, "Nothing is more familiar or characteristic among Christians than assertion. Take away assertions, and you take away Christianity. . . . Why then do you—you!—*assert* that *you find no satisfaction in assertions* and that you *prefer an undogmatic temper to any other?*"[1]

It is hard to doubt that the apostle John would have been pleased with Luther's argument, had he been there to hear it, for John too believed in assertions and would have maintained that it is impossible to have Christianity without them. Moreover, just as assertions were important and necessary in John's time and in Luther's time, so are they important and necessary in our time.

We therefore properly conclude a study of John's book with a study of these three certainties. We should know: 1) that the one born of God does not sin, 2) that we are of God, and 3) that the Son of God has come and has given us knowledge of the true God.

THE FIRST AFFIRMATION (v. 18)

John's first affirmation is that the one who is truly born of God does not sin. At first glance this statement seems to be contradictory to John's repeated declaration in chapter 1 that anyone who says that he does not sin or has never sinned is either self-deceived or a liar, just as 3:4-10 seemed to be contradictory to those same statements. But the contradiction is only an apparent one, and our discussion of the earlier passage indicates how we should deal with this one. Here, as in 3:4-10, the verbs are in the present tense, indicating habitual or continuous action. So the statement is not that the Christian cannot fall into sin; indeed, he can and does. Rather it is that, while he may fall into sin, he cannot continue in it indefinitely. In other words, if

---

[1]Martin Luther, *The Bondage of the Will*, trans. by J. I. Packer and O. R. Johnston (Westwood, N.J.: Revell, 1957), p. 67.

178

the individual is truly born of God, the new birth will result in new behavior.

Earlier, when John had talked of the fact that the one who is born of God does not sin, he explained it by saying that such a person "abides" in God and that "God's nature abides in him." Here he traces his assurance to the fact that Jesus keeps the Christian.

Problems with the Greek text underlying the sentence "the one who was born of God keeps him safe" (NIV) make the words capable of two different meanings. On the one hand, they may refer to the work of Jesus in keeping the Christian, as the NIV suggests by its translation (so also the NASB, NEB, RSV and *Phillips*). Or, on the other hand, they may refer to the responsibility of the Christian to keep himself, as the KJV indicates. In spite of the fact that the idea of the Christian keeping himself occurs just three verses later as well as in other passages (1 Tim. 5:22; James 1:27; Jude 21) and is certainly valid, it would seem nevertheless that the first view is better. To begin with, this is probably the best manuscript reading, *auton* ("him") rather than *heauton* ("himself"). The manuscript evidence for this is not overwhelming, but it is good and is that adopted by the American Bible Society's Greek New Testament. Again, the first view fits best in this passage, for while it is true that the Christian is to keep himself, it is nevertheless not true that his confidence should rest on that ability. Rather, it is to rest on the efforts of the Lord Jesus Christ on the Christian's behalf. No doubt John emphasized the birth of Jesus Christ for two reasons: first, to stress our kinship with Christ and, second, to remind us that the One who is to keep us from temptation was Himself also tempted.

But why should we need such a one to keep us? The answer is seen in John's mention of that one who would do us harm. He is "the evil one," the devil, who holds the entire world in his power (v. 19). Such a one could certainly destroy us were it not for God's faithful defense of His people.

The story of Job is an illustration of this point. Satan wished to destroy Job but was unable to do so due to the fact that God had placed a hedge about Job and about all that he had. Satan admitted this indirectly by arguing, "Does Job fear God for nothing? Have you not put a hedge around him and his household and everything he has? You have blessed the work of his hands, so that his flocks and herds are spread throughout the land. But stretch out your hand and strike everything he has, and he will surely curse you to your face" (Job 1:9-11). In this latter statement Satan was proved wrong, for when God agreed to lower the hedge a bit so that Satan could afflict Job, Job did not retaliate by cursing God. In fact, he blessed God saying, "Naked I came from my mother's womb, and naked I will depart. The LORD gave and the LORD has taken away; may the name of the LORD be praised" (v. 21). The point is that God had been keeping Job from Satan's clutches, and continued to do so even though, in this case, He allowed Satan to attack His servant to a limited degree and for a limited time. He had a triumphal ending in view. So Jesus keeps us from the one who would do us injury.

THE SECOND AFFIRMATION (v. 19)

The second of John's affirmations is that "we are children of God." He joins himself to his readers in this certainty. But where does the certainty come from? In the first instance the certainty that the one born of God does not sin comes from the ability of Jesus (or God) to keep the Christian. In this case the certainty that "we are children of God" comes from the fact that the tests of righteousness, love, and sound doctrine have been applied and the results discovered to be positive.

This has been John's overall purpose in writing, of course, for while he wishes to guard against presumption, he nevertheless does not wish to discourage those to whom he is writing. He wants them to know that they truly are God's children. Here his switch from the third person singular in the preceding verse ("anyone born of God") to the first person plural ("we") is most encouraging, for he wishes to show that in this point even the most normal Christian can have an assurance that differs neither in nature nor in degree from that assurance possessed by the apostles. Indeed, we no less than they can know that we are truly God's children.

This same truth and its corresponding assurance does not extend to everyone, however. True, the Christian is born of God and is kept by the power of God. But the one who is not a Christian is not born of God, nor is he kept by Him. On the contrary, he is in great danger; for, far from being free of Satan's power, he actually lies obliviously in Satan's arms. It is important to note that John does not say that the world is "of" Satan in a way parallel to his saying that we are "of God," for that is not true. Some persons are the devil's children, according to Jesus' teaching as recorded in John 8:44. But those to whom he referred there were an exceptional case, having become children of Satan by a deliberate commitment to him similar to (but in opposition of) that commitment through which a Christian becomes a child of God. Most persons are rather what we might call free agents. This does not mean that they are well off, however, for in their imagined freedom they choose to ignore their danger and thereby fall into the sphere of Satan's power. Nothing but the voice of the risen Christ can wake them and call them to God's service.

Once again John leaves no room for a third alternative, for either a person is of God or is in the power of the evil one. From our perspective the issues are often blurred, and we find it hard to tell whether one is of God or not. For us good and evil, love and hate, truth and falsehood seem mixed. But that is no comfort; nor is it an accurate portrait of the true state of things. In God's sight there are only those who are His true children and those who are of the world, whatever conception of themselves may be possessed by the latter. Consequently, the Christian should know that he is truly of God. The one who does not have this certainty should by the grace of God awake out of his sleep, turn from known sin, and embrace the Lord Jesus as both God and Savior.

THE THIRD AFFIRMATION (v. 20)

This leads to the third of John's affirmations, which is, as Stott notes, "the most fundamental of the three."[2] This strikes at the very root of the heretical Gnostic theology, for it is the affirmation that the Son of God, even Jesus, has come into this world to give us both knowledge of God and salvation. In other words, it is the assurance that He and nothing else is at the heart of Christianity; He and only He provides what all men desperately need. The need is not for philosophical enlightenment, as valuable as that may be in some areas. The need is first, to know God, and second, for a Savior.

---

[2]Stott, *Epistles of John,* p. 194.

Knowledge of God

The first gift that Jesus has brought us is the capacity of knowing God. This suggests not only that Jesus is God and that we see God in Him, as He said to Philip (John 14:9), but also that we are incapable of spiritual sight until He gives it to us. Indeed, we are like the blind man of John 9 who could not see Christ and did not even seek Him until Jesus first of all sought him out and healed him. After that we grow in knowledge, as the blind man grew (cf. John 9:11, 17, 33, 36, 38).

Moreover, the knowledge of God which Christ gives is knowledge, not just of any God, but of the true or genuine God. The word translated "true" in this verse is the word *alēthinos,* which is a popular one with John. In the Gospel he uses it of true or genuine worshipers (4:23), the true or genuine bread (6:32) and the true vine (15:1). In this first letter he has already used it of the true light which is dispersing the darkness (2:8). "True" refers to that which is authentic as opposed to that which is false, the ultimate reality as opposed to that which is merely its shadow. In John's day the Gnostic teachers had made much of their supposed knowledge of God, but it is John's contention that apart from the work of the Christ of history, who reveals God, such knowledge is not knowledge at all. At least it is not knowledge of the real God. Only through the real Son of God is the real God known.

Salvation

The second gift of Jesus is salvation, which John suggests by one of his favorite terms: "eternal life." Elsewhere he has indicated that the basis upon which we enjoy such life is the atoning death of Jesus Christ through which God's just wrath against sin is turned away and a new relationship is established between God and the sinner. He has also indicated that the channel through which this life is received is faith, that is, believing in what God has said concerning the work of His Son and committing oneself to Him as Savior. Here, however, John dwells once more on the idea of "eternal life," indicating that the knowledge of God and union with Him is life, in the sense of a complete salvation.

When John writes, "He is the true God and eternal life," it is possible that the word "He" refers to an antecedent immediately preceding, namely Jesus Christ. If this is so, then this is an exceptionally clear statement of the deity of Christ. Indeed, many of the Church fathers took the text in this manner. On the other hand, we must also say in all honesty that "He" can also refer to "him who is true," in which case all three uses of the word "true" refer to the same person, even the Father. This seems preferable. In view of the scope of biblical theology there is little difference, however, for Jesus is said to be the "true" One elsewhere, and we are also said to abide in Him as we are said to abide in the Father.

CONCLUSION

The proper contrast to the true or genuine God is that which is a false god or idol. Consequently, John concludes with the otherwise unexpected warning, "Dear children, keep yourselves from idols." In the context of this book we are probably not to think of the various carved idols of antiquity, though the admonition must include these as well. Rather, we are to think of the false god of the schismatics, who, though he was presented under the name of the Christian God, was not the true God, just as his apostles were not true teachers.

The application of this truth to today is in the fact that the mere names of Jesus Christ or God or Christianity do not authenticate the message or religion of the one proclaiming them. On the contrary, the profession must be tested by the basic doctrines of apostolic Christianity. What does the one speaking really believe about Jesus? Is He God incarnate or just a teacher? Did He die a real, atoning, vicarious death for sinners? Or is His death merely exemplary? Did He rise from the dead? Is the teaching of Jesus true, complete, and authoritative? Or is His teaching partial, thereby needing the teaching of others to bring us to a higher and indeed needed form of "Christianity"? According to John's book, and indeed to the entire Word of God, anything that detracts from Christ is idolatrous, for He is the true God, the true revelation of the Father, the true atonement for sin, the true bread, the true vine. He is the beginning and end of all true religion. Consequently, to know Him is to know the true God and eternal life.

Once we know Him, what then? Then we must keep ourselves from idols. In verse 18 John has written that the Son of God will keep the Christian, but this does not relieve the Christian from his own responsibility to persevere in God's service. Rather than drifting, he must draw near to God and grow in the knowledge of Him. For only then will he be truly kept from idols. An anonymous Keswick hymn puts it like this:

> Draw and win and fill completely,
>   'Till the cup o'erflow the brim;
> What have we to do with idols
>   Who have companied with Him?

Introduction to 2 and 3 John

The letters of 2 and 3 John are the shortest books of the New Testament, shorter even than Jude or Philemon which each have only one chapter. But this does not mean that either 2 or 3 John is insignificant. To be sure, in some ways each merely repeats the general message of 1 John, which is longer. But the repetitions are made in two distinct contexts which in turn give a unique direction to the letters and call forth new emphases.

The immediate problem in each book is that of traveling teachers or missionaries. According to Christian ethics all who thus traveled about were to be shown hospitality by Christians in the town to which they came. In this, Christians were doing what the best of non-Christians would also do. But in Christian circles this extension of hospitality was open to obvious abuse and raised moral questions as well. For example, suppose the visiting teacher claimed to be a Christian missionary or even a prophet but taught what was clearly false doctrine. Hospitality would demand that he be provided for, but to do so would seem to be participation in the spread of his false teachings. Should he be received or not? Or again, suppose the teacher overstayed his welcome or asked for money, thereby giving evidence of being motivated more by greed than by a desire for Christian service. How long should such a one be tolerated? Should money be given? The extent of this problem in the early church age is seen in the fact that the *Didache,* another early document, deals with the problem at length and even invents the term "Christmonger"

185

(Christemporos) to describe those who attempted thus to profit by Christianity.[1] Behind these questions lay the even greater problems of discerning truth from error and of distinguishing false teachers from true servants of the Lord.

The letters of 2 and 3 John deal with these problems and also share other Christian teaching incidentally. In 2 John the author seems to be writing to a local church. So here the issues are discussed in the broadest terms. First, the author reminds his readers of the tests of true Christianity which have already been developed in the earlier and longer letter. Second, he warns them to be on guard against false teachers. In this case, the test of truth and error is the test of Christian doctrine, particularly as it relates to Jesus as the Christ come in the flesh.

In 3 John the negative approach ("do not take into your house" the false teacher) gives way to a positive encouragement to receive those who really are the Lord's servants. In this letter several distinct personalities are in view. The letter is written to a Christian named Gaius. He is commended for having shown hospitality to teachers who had visited his area and is encouraged to continue showing it. Diotrephes is the second person mentioned. He is rebuked indirectly for his refusal to welcome the same teachers and for trying to keep other Christians, such as Gaius, from doing so. Finally, mention is also made of a third

---

[1]The *Didache* says, "About apostles and prophets, follow the rule of the Gospel, which is this: Let every apostle who comes to you be welcomed as the Lord. But he shall not stay more than one day, and if it is necessary, the next day also. But if he stays three days, he is a false prophet. And when an apostle leaves, let him take nothing except bread to last until he finds his next lodging. But if he ask for money, he is a false prophet. You shall not test or examine any prophet who speaks in the spirit. For every sin will be forgiven, but this sin will not be forgiven. But not everyone who speaks in the spirit is a prophet, but only if he has the ways of the Lord. So the false prophet and the prophet will be known by their ways. . . . Let everyone who comes in the name of the Lord be welcomed, and afterward when you have tested him you will know him, for you will have understanding of true and false. If the one who comes is a traveler, help him all you can. But he must not stay with you more than two or if necessary three days. If he wants to settle among you and has a trade, let him work for his living. But if he has no trade, see to it in your understanding that no one lives among you in idleness because he is a Christian. If he will not do this, he is trading on Christ *(Christemporos esti)*. Beware of such men" *(The Apostolic Fathers,* trans. by Edgar J. Goodspeed. New York: Harper & Brothers, 1950, pp. 16, 17).

186

personality, Demetrius, whose example in such matters is said to be a good one. These two letters, the one warning against receiving and encouraging false teachers and the other encouraging a genuine hospitality toward true teachers, belong together.

THE ELDER

One similarity between the two letters is that each begins by the author's introduction of himself as "the elder." In the one case he writes, "The elder, to the chosen lady and her children, whom I love in the truth" (2 John 1). In the other letter he writes, "The elder, to my dear friend Gaius, whom I love in the truth" (3 John 1). On the surface one would think that this designation is hardly worthy of special attention, but throughout much of the history of the church the term has been important in attempting to determine who the author of the books might be and whether or not that author, whoever he might be, is the same as the author of 1 John and/or the Gospel.

The word itself was a title used to designate a certain class of officers within the local church. In Greek it is the word *presbuteros* from which we get our terms "presbyter" and "presbytery." Apparently it was normal for each local congregation to have several elders, for Paul clearly appointed elders in each place where he had conducted a ministry and entrusted them with the work in that place before he moved on. In the case of 2 John 1 and 3 John 1 the word probably means more than this, however, for the author calls himself "*the* elder," as opposed to being just *an* elder, and assumes a special authority over the affairs of these two churches. An elder in the traditional sense would have an authoritative voice only in the affairs of his own local congregation.

John the elder

Traditionally the identification of "the elder" plus the unnamed author of 1 John and of the fourth Gospel has been fixed as John, the son of Zebedee, who became an apostle. The captions of the books themselves indicate this. But from time to time, particularly in recent years, it has become popular for scholars to say that there were two Johns who lived in Asia Minor, the apostle John and John the elder, and that it was John the elder rather than the disciple of Christ who wrote the three letters. Some feel that he is the author of the Gospel also.

There are several points from which this line of thinking originates, but the most important is a brief paragraph from the *Expositions of Oracles of the Lord* by Papais, a bishop of Hierapolis. His words are quoted by the early church historian Eusebius. Papias writes thus: "I shall not hesitate also to put down for you along with my interpretations whatsoever things I have at any time learned carefully from the elders and carefully remembered, guaranteeing their truth. For I did not, like the multitude, take pleasure in those that speak much, but in those that teach the truth; not in those that relate strange commandments, but in those that deliver the commandments given by the Lord to faith, and springing from the truth itself. If, then, any one came, who had been a follower of the elders, I questioned him in regard to the words of the elders,—what Andrew or what Peter said, or what was said by Philip, or by Thomas, or by James, or by John, or by Matthew, or by any other of the disciples of the Lord, and what things Aristion and the presbyter John, the disciples of the Lord, say. For I did not think that what was to be gotten from the books would profit me as much as what came from the living and abiding voice."[2]

In this quotation the twofold repetition of the name John suggests that there may have been two Johns known to Papias. And, in fact, this is the way Eusebius takes it. He writes, "It is worth observing here that the name John is twice enumerated by him. The first one he mentions in connection with Peter and James and Matthew and the rest of the apostles, clearly meaning the evangelist; but the other John he mentioned after an interval, and places him among others outside of the number of the apostles, putting Aristion before him, and he distinctly calls him a presbyter. This shows that the statement of those is true, who say that there were two persons in Asia that bore the same name, and that there were two tombs in Ephesus, each of which, even to the present day, is called John's. It is important to notice this. For it is probable that it was the second, if one is not willing to admit that it was the first that saw the Revelation, which is ascribed by name to John."[3]

---

[2]"The Church History of Eusebius," translated with prolegomena and notes by Arthur Cushman McGiffert, *The Nicene and Post-Nicent Fathers*, Series Two, Vol. 1 (Grand Rapids: Eerdmans, 1961), pp. 170, 171.

[3]Eusebius, p. 171.

Eusebius makes a good case for two Johns on the basis of Papias' words. But having acknowledged this, it is right to ask whether Eusebius is correct in his interpretation. There are reasons for questioning it.

First, the passage from Papias is at best ambiguous. Indeed, Eusebius himself seems to admit this in general when he later refers to his source as appearing "to have been of very limited understanding, as one can see from his discourses."[4] But whether or not Eusebius would say so explicitly, the truth of the statement is proved by the diversities of scholarly opinion today. Thus, Barclay speaks of the elder John as being "clearly distinguished from John the apostle,"[5] while others, such as Ross, deny that there were two Johns at all.

Second, in his discussion of Papias it may be Eusebius himself who is of limited intelligence in discerning what his source has to say. True, the language of Papias is ambiguous and may even be clumsy. But this may be due to the fact that Papias is actually trying to distinguish in a compressed fashion among three types of witnesses. In the first class are the apostles, all of whom saw the Lord and who testified with unique authority. Papias refers to these as "elders." These were the prime source of information naturally, and Papias had received knowledge of Jesus through the remembered teaching of seven of them: Andrew, Peter, Philip, Thomas, James, John, and Matthew. The second class of witnesses contains those who were disciples of the Lord only (not apostles) but who possessed special importance for Papias in that they were still living and could therefore be consulted. Papias mentions only one of these, Aristion. In the third and final category are those who were apostles but who, unlike most of the apostles, were living. Again, Papias has but one example, John. But John is mentioned twice in that, on the one hand, he was an apostle and belongs with the other apostles whom Papias mentions and, on the other hand, was living and so belongs with those individuals, either apostles or disciples, who were continuing to bear testimony to the Lord.

In support of this interpretation there is the fact that Papias speaks in the past tense of the witness of the seven apostles but

---

[4]Eusebius, p. 172.
[5]Barclay, *Letters of John and Jude*, p. 150.

changes to the present tense in drawing attention to what "Aristion and the presbyter John . . . say." It is also important to notice that while, in the second reference to John, John is termed "the elder" to distinguish him from Aristion, who was only a disciple, nevertheless in the earlier reference to the seven apostles all are called "elders," meaning apostles. So the phrase "the elder John" is not as unique or significant in reference to John as is often implied. Finally, it cannot even escape notice that while Eusebius argues for the existence of two Johns, he does not even then argue that the epistles of John (or only 2 and 3 John) were written by this second, shadowy figure. Instead, he suggests merely that the Revelation may have been written by him, thus indicating that in his view the letters as well as the Gospel should be assigned the traditional authorship.

Obviously, in view of Papias' language it cannot be demonstrated wtih certainty that the existence of one John at Ephesus rather than two is factual. Nevertheless, it is at least equally unproved that there existed a second John at Ephesus, known as "the elder," to whom the authorship of 2 and 3 John as well as the possibility of authorship of the other books in the traditional Johannine corpus must be referred.

It is sometimes mentioned that the tradition concerning the two tombs for John at Ephesus tends to support Eusebius' interpretation of Papias, but this is even less substantial than Papias' own words. To begin with, Eusebius has no personal knowledge of two tombs. He is only quoting information which he had received from Dionysius of Alexandria, who lived a century and a half after the death of John and who wrote from Egypt rather than from Asia Minor. Besides, even the existence of the two tombs, assuming that there were two, proves little; for it is more likely that they were rival tombs of the one John the apostle than tombs of two individuals about whom we know next to nothing.

On the other side of the argument, it may be noted that Polycrates, who lived in Ephesus and who was a bishop there, mentions the tomb of "John who rested on the Lord's bosom" and that of the martyred Polycarp. This is unusual if Polycrates had known of the tomb of another John who was distinguished as the author of the Book of Revelation and of the three Epistles. Polycrates wrote more than fifty years before Dionysius.

John the apostle

It is also possible to approach the question of the identity of "the elder" of 2 and 3 John from an entirely different point of view. Let us assume, for the sake of argument, that there were two Johns in Asia Minor, John the apostle and John the elder. Can it be, assuming the existence of this second person, that he is adequate to account for the books as we have them?

The author of 2 and 3 John identifies himself as "the elder," and this favors the hypothesis somewhat. But does what we know of him correspond with our theory? We notice that the author of these books is unnamed except for the title. But if this is so, then the author must have identified himself without using his name because, as Stott argues, "his identity was so well known and his authority so well recognized that he could use the title without needing to qualify or amplify it. Moreover, since the two Epistles were written to different churches, he was evidently known and acknowledged in a wide area of the province of Asia." The author obviously knows a great deal about these churches. He follows their affairs. He accepts responsibility for what happens to them. Obviously he also loves these people, cares for them, and takes time to instruct and warn them. "Is it possible," Stott continues, "that a man of such prominence, who exercised such authority and wrote three Epistles which are included in the New Testament canon, should have left no more trace of himself in history than one dubious reference by Papias?"[6]

We may wish to answer that such may indeed be possible, as an outside though highly unlikely chance. But it is not probable. Consequently, we rest on sound ground when we perceive the important and widespread authority of the author to be that of none other than John, the son of Zebedee, whom we understand from other sources to have lived in Ephesus and to have died there at a great age. Moreover, we may even understand his unusual employment of the title "elder." For if, as Papias would indicate, he outlasted all the other apostles, then he could properly have designated himself as "the elder" in a unique sense, thereby indicating that he was the last of those apostles who had

[6]Stott, *Epistles of John*, p. 39.

seen the Lord and had been commissioned by Him to bear an authoritative testimony.

THE OTHER BOOKS

When the question of authorship is approached in this manner, that is, from the perspective of the authorship of the two smallest books, it is evident that light is thrown upon the question of the authorship of the other books as well. In this matter the four books (not to mention the Revelation) are tied together. If one begins with the authorship of the Gospel and 1 John and defends those books as being by John the Apostle, it is possible nevertheless to argue that the shorter and less original books are by another writer (perhaps "the elder John" as distinguished from "the apostle John") who merely imitated the style of his master. However, if one begins with the smaller books and argues that they are Johannine, as has been attempted here, then the theory of a diverse authorship is hardly credible.

Brooke, who however argues only for a common authorship and not necessarily for the authorship of the books by John the apostle, puts the matter well: "The longer and the more carefully the Johannine literature is studied, the more clearly one point seems to stand out. The most obviously 'genuine' of the writings are the two shorter Epistles, and they are the least original. To believe that an author, or authors, capable of producing the Gospel, or even the First Epistle, modeled their style and teaching on the two smaller Epistles is a strain upon credulity which is *almost* past bearing. Are we not moving along lines of greater probability if we venture to suppose that a leader who had spent his life in teaching the contents of the Gospel, at last wrote it down that those whom he had taught, and others, 'might believe, and believing might have life in His name'; that after some years he felt that the message of the Gospel had not produced the effect on their lives and creed which he had expected, and that he therefore made the appeal of the First Epistle. . . . At the same time or at a later period he may have had to deal with the special circumstances of a particular Church or particular individuals, and again the special circumstances of his hearers and their intellectual and spiritual capacity have determined the form and the substance of his appeal."[7] If to this is added the view that the most

---

[7]A. E. Brooke, p. lxxviii.

likely person to have done all this is John the apostle, it seems to this writer that this is an excellent argument from which a conclusion can be reached.

It is only fair to note that in the view of some considerable scholars, among them C. H. Dodd, there are differences between the Gospel and the letters of such magnitude that (in their view) a common authorship is improbable. They speak of ideas in the first letter that do not appear in the Gospel, of peculiarities in the Gospel that do not appear in the letters, and of small but important differences in theology that exist between the Gospel and the first letter. Are there differences? Do they make the hypothesis of a common authorship impossible? This is a complex matter, of course, and one on which students of the books will differ. But my opinion, as well as that of many others, is that many of the alleged differences are either nonexistent or exaggerated, and none are sufficient to overthrow the conclusions reached earlier. A full discussion may be found in Dodd, Brooke, Stott, and other writers.[8]

THE MESSAGE FOR TODAY

The messages of 2 and 3 John are not just for an earlier age, despite the unique and particular problems to which the letters are addressed. Like all Scripture they have a message for our own time also.

There are always problems

The first message of 2 and 3 John is that we will always have problems in the Christian church. If we did not know better, we might think that certain earlier ages of church history were unlike our own in that they were relatively free of the plagues that trouble us. We might even argue that, if ever there was an age that would have been free of problems, it would be the apostolic age and that, if ever there were churches that would have been free of such things, it would have been those churches over which the apostle John presided. But in point of fact there were problems there too; and therefore we should not be surprised when we

---

[8]Cf. Dodd, *Johannine Epistles*, pp. xlvii-lxvi; Brooke, *Johannine Epistles*, pp. i-xxvii, lxxiii-lxxix; Stott, *Epistles of John*, pp. 16-41; Plummer, *Epistles of S. John*, pp. 34-41, Westcott, *Epistles of John*, pp. xxxix-xlvi.

have them. John had great problems. There were problems of schism and heresy in the churches to which he first writes. Moreover, these were compounded by a deep confusion on the part of those who really were believers. In the second and third letters John is obviously dealing with the problems of false teaching, both without and within. Finally, in 3 John we also detect an entire range of personality conflicts, precipitated by the arrogance and desire for power of a man named Diotrephes.

We can be encouraged by these facts, not that we rejoice in other people having problems, but rather that this at least helps to put our own problems in perspective. Moreover, we can refuse to be overwhelmed by our problems. Knowing that they are already known to God, we can begin to deal with them on the basis of the appropriate biblical principles and in the power of the Holy Spirit.

Our responsibility

The second message of these letters is of our own responsibility as Christians to deal with such problems. It is true that the churches of John's day had problems, much as we do, but this was not to be an excuse for them to do nothing. On the contrary, the fact that the letters are written to these churches by John and contain specific instructions indicates that there were actions that they were to take in order to cope with their problems. And so should we. We are not called to throw up our hands and thus abandon work that we consider to be unspiritual, without direction, or faltering. We are to assume responsibility for it and, where it is possible, reclaim it in the name of Christ.

The tests of life in life

Third, there is the application of the "tests of life," which we studied in connection with 1 John, to the whole of life. In the earlier book the tests of life occurred in the context of determining whether or not one is a true child of God. These obviously apply to the whole of life even there. But it is conceivable that a person could use them to determine whether or not he is a true Christian and then forget about them, believing that they no longer have any important bearing on his conduct. The letters of 2 and 3 John make clear that this is not possible. Here there is no question of those addressed doubting that they are Christians.

Yet the tests of life are still prominent. Indeed, they are the areas in which Christians are encouraged to remain strong and to grow.

In 2 John the tests are found in the first six verses. "Truth" is in verses 1, 2, 3, 4. "Love" is in verses 1, 3, 5, 6. "Command" occurs in verses 4, 5, 6. In 3 John "truth" is discussed in verses 3 and 4, "love" in verse 6, and "goodness" or "righteousness" in verse 11. The three words also occur in an incidental way several more times throughout the letter.

Faithfulness in small things.

The final message of 2 and 3 John is the need to be faithful in our responsibility, particularly in little things. Neither letter is dealing with particularly important things, as we might wish to evaluate them. There are no great campaigns to be conducted, no books to be written, no confrontations with the secular world to be launched. Rather, Christians are to be faithful merely in that which they have already learned and to express those convictions consistently in regard to whom they entertain and how they conduct themselves with one another. In a certain sense these are little things. In another sense they are terribly important, for it is here that most of the battles are won.

Moreover, lest we fail to notice it, we should observe that John himself is faithful even to the point of writing letters to encourage and direct those whom he loves. He is going to visit them shortly; at least he says that he hopes to see them. But he still writes, trusting that even so small a thing as a letter will do good. Are we equally faithful? Then we must take care of the little things, for it is in these rather than in the big things that we are most clearly revealed for what we are and whose we are.

OUTLINES

The letters of 2 and 3 John may be outlined in various ways, but in any form the major divisions are obvious. The following outlines may be helpful in studying the books.

Outline of 2 John
I.   Introduction (1-3)
II. The Double Message (4-11)
     A.   The life within (4-6)
     B.   The danger without (7-11)

195

III. Conclusion (12, 13)

2 John 1-13
Walking in the Truth

The elder,

To the chosen lady and her children, whom I love in truth—and not I only, but also all who know the truth—because of the truth, which lives in us and will be with us forever:

Grace, mercy and peace from God the Father and from Jesus Christ, the Father's Son, will be with us in truth and love.

It has given me great joy to find some of your children walking in the truth, just as the Father commanded us. And now, dear lady, I am not writing you a new command but one we have had from the beginning. I ask that we love one another. And this is love: that we walk in obedience to his commands. As you have heard from the beginning, his command is that you walk in love.

Many deceivers, who do not acknowledge Jesus Christ as coming in the flesh, have gone out into the world. Any such person is the deceiver and the antichrist. Watch out that you do not lose what you have worked for, but that you may be rewarded fully. Anyone who runs ahead and does not continue in the teaching of Christ does not have God; whoever continues in the teaching has both the Father and the Son. If anyone comes to you and does not bring this teaching, do not take him into your house or welcome him. Anyone who welcomes him shares in his wicked work.

I have much to write to you, but I do not want to use paper and ink. Instead, I hope to visit you and talk with you face to face, so that our joy may be complete.

The children of your chosen sister send their greetings.

No other books of the New Testament more clearly reflect the current letter-writing style of the first century than do 2 and 3 John. There is an opening greeting, in which the author identifies himself and names those to whom he is writing. There is an opening salutation. This is followed by the body of the letter, containing the message. Then there is a closing salutation in which the author expresses his hopes of seeing the one to whom he is writing soon and sends final greeting. The letters of 2 and 3 John follow this format. But, like the other New Testament books which also follow it, particularly the Epistles of Paul, these books introduce distinctly Christian ideas by which the conventional forms are both elevated and transformed.

In the case of 2 John, there is an opening introduction which is filled with Christian greetings. This is followed by a two-pronged message dealing with the life within the local Christian congregation and the danger without. Finally, there is a conclusion in which the members of one Christian congregation greet those in another.

THE INTRODUCTION (vv. 1-3)

It is strange that a letter which is apparently so straightforward should present deep problems regarding both its author and its recipients, but such is the case. There is disagreement as to the identity of the elder. This question has been discussed in the introduction to 2 and 3 John. And there is disagreement as to the identity of the recipient, "the chosen lady and her children."

There are two general viewpoints as to who "the chosen lady" might be. The first is that by this term John refers to an individual person. She may be unnamed, in which case "the chosen lady" is a good translation. Or, which is less likely, she may be named, in which case the Greek words *eklektē Kuria* could conceivably be translated "to the elect Kuria" or "to the lady Eklektē." In support of this approach there is the fact that a personal address of this kind is what would be expected in so short and straightforward a letter. Moreover, if the recipient is not an individual, then the address must be symbolic of something else; and it hardly seems necessary to read a symbolic message or meaning into so short a text. This view is presented well by Ross and others.[1]

---

[1]Ross, *Epistles of James and John,* pp. 129, 130.

The second viewpoint is that John is addressing an individual church which he thus stylizes by the phrase "the chosen lady." At first glance this seems unlikely for the reasons given above. But there are good arguments in its favor. First, there is a strange absence of clear personal references, which is made all the more strange by the marked contrast with 3 John, which is quite personal. Second, there is an apparently unconscious and repeated transition from the second person singular pronoun (vv. 4, 5, 12) to the second person plural pronoun (vv. 6, 8, 10, 13), which indicates that the author may have been thinking of a complete congregation rather than just of one individual. Third, there are expressions which are highly appropriate to the corporate view. These involve the expressions of love which John has for the chosen lady and her children, the revelation that some of her children abide in the truth while some apparently do not, and above all that the closing verse conveys greetings from the chosen lady's sister and the children who are with her. If this view is objected to because such a stylization is unnatural and unnecessary, it must be remembered that while that may be true for our age it was not necessarily true for John. In fact, a similar greeting from "she who is in Babylon, chosen" (also a feminine singular ending) occurs just a few pages earlier in the New Testament, in 1 Peter 5:13.

While the matter is probably incapable of a final solution within the limits of our present knowledge, the balance of probability seems to be on the side of the corporate interpretation.

The more standard part of John's greeting to the elect lady and her children is found in verse 3 in the phrase "grace, mercy and peace from God the Father and from Jesus Christ, the Father's Son." In 1 and 2 Timothy we have the threefold "grace, mercy and peace from God the Father and Christ Jesus our Lord." In most of the other Pauline books "grace and peace" are the norm. These phrases indicate that all spiritual blessings come from above and come jointly from God the Father and from Jesus Christ, God's Son.

The unique feature of this opening salutation is John's surprising emphasis upon truth and his linking of the truth he thus emphasizes to love. Indeed, the word "truth" occurs four times in these first three verses and one more time in verse 4. In these verses John claims to love the elect lady and her children "in the truth," that these are also loved by all others who "know the truth," that this is true precisely "because of the truth," and that in this they are all following the way of the Father and Son, who indeed dispense the great blessings of grace, mercy, and peace "in truth and love." These phrases are of importance, for they are expressions of the fact that Christians are bound to other Christians primarily by the special bond of truth and that this is the foundation of genuine Christian love. Why do Christians love one another after all? It is not on the ground of some special but imagined compatibility, for they are often highly incompatible. It is not merely on the ground of some deeply shared goals or programs, as would be true, for example, of some voluntary social service agency, though Christians do have many goals in common. What binds the Christian community together is a common commitment to the truth, out of which love rises. This means that Christians will differ fundamentally from the false teachers in their midst or from outright heretics. For a time false teachers and Christians may share common goals. For a time the false teachers may even be indistinguishable from those who are truly born again. But the false teachers will leave and go out into the world, as John said earlier, while on the other hand, the Christians will demonstrate that they are true Christians by remaining with one another in truth and by walking in love.

So the truth must endure. It must be held high. John Stott writes, "So long as the truth endures, in us and with us, so long shall our reciprocal love also endure. If this is so, and Christian love is founded upon Christian truth, we shall never increase the love which exists between us by diminishing the truth which we hold in common. In the contemporary movement towards Church unity we must beware of compromising the very truth on which alone true love and unity depend."[2]

THE DOUBLE MESSAGE (vv. 4-11)

Verse 4 brings the reader to the body of the letter, from which also we learn the occasion of its having been written. Apparently members of the church to which John is writing had crossed the apostle's path recently, and these had brought great joy to him

---

[2]Stott, *Epistles of John*, p. 203.

because of their apparent and continuing growth in the truth. He wishes to share this joy and have more of it. Consequently, he writes to the church from which these Christians came, first, to praise it and encourage it in its life and witness and, second, to warn it against a danger which John out of his wider experience perceives to be approaching from without.

The life within

There is much in the life of the local church to give John cause for rejoicing, but this does not mean that there is no more room for growth. These to whom he writes are Christians. Their lives meet the three tests: the moral test (which is righteousness or obedience to God's commands), the social test (which is love), and the doctrinal test (which is the test of truth or sound doctrine). But this does not mean that their lives are as marked by righteousness as they might be, that they love each other fully, or that they have totally assimilated the whole of Christian doctrine. So John writes to encourage them in what they are already doing and particularly to encourage them in a life marked out by mutual love.

In the first three verses of the letter it was the word "truth" that tied the thoughts together. Here the word is "commands" or "command," which also (like truth) occurs four times, once each in verses 4 and 5 and twice in verse 6. In the first instance, he indicates that we are commanded to follow the truth. In the second and fourth instances the command is the command to love. In the third occurrence the word "commands" is plural, thereby indicating all the commands which, if the Christian obeys them, will lead to righteousness.

And what is to be the Christian's obligation in each of these areas? John says that he is obliged to "follow along" in them or "walk" in them. In other words, by a deliberate and disciplined choice he is to pursue that path upon which he has been set by the very God of grace who saved him. Moreover, it is explicitly said that this is to be true in each area. The Christian is to walk "in the truth" (v. 4). He is to "walk in obedience to his commands" (v. 6). He is to "walk in love" (v. 6). It may be objected by some that this is not possible, that a person cannot be *commanded* to love, to follow truth, and to pursue righteousness. But that is precisely what we are commanded to do. Moreover, if we

201

do not understand this or like it, the fact only reveals how little we know of these great qualities.

Belief in God's truth is not optional, then. It is commanded. Besides, a failure to believe is therefore not an intellectual inability but rather a sin, as John has already indicated in the Gospel (John 3:18-21). Similarly, love is the expression of a self-sacrificing service to others which can be deliberately undertaken. And righteousness is that into which, by the grace of God but, nonetheless, by conscientious choice and deliberate action, a believer may grow.

The danger without

John has laid some stress upon the need for growth within the life of the local congregation, but now he lays even greater stress upon the danger which he perceives to be arising from a widespread movement of heretical "Christian" propaganda. As one reads these verses the movement seems to be similar to if not identical to that Gnostic threat alluded to in the first letter. But, unlike the situation in 1 John, in this case the danger has not yet reached the congregation.

The first thing that John says about this movement is that its adherents are numerous and that they are actively going out into the world for propaganda purposes. When John says that the deceivers "have gone out into the world," he may mean that they have left the Christian congregation in which they originated in order to found their own movement. This was apparently true of the situation reflected in 1 John, for the apostle wrote that "they went out from us, but . . . their going showed that none of them belonged to us" (2:19). On the other hand, the sentence may also indicate that these have gone out into the world in the sense of embarking upon a parallel program of evangelism. Because of the situation reflected in the letter (they had not come yet to the local church), this seems to be the preferable interpretation.

From their own perspective and in their own eyes these men were probably Christian missionaries. Undoubtedly they made significant Christian confessions. Yet from the viewpoint of the apostle they were dangerous heretics and imposters because they did not hold to the essential doctrines of the Christian faith. In particular, they did not hold to the truth that Jesus is the Christ come in the flesh. John says that a teacher who is in error at this point is both a deceiver and the antichrist.

Having told of the threat without and having warned against it, John now gives instructions by which the danger itself may be countered. His instructions have two parts. First, he challenges the believers to be on their guard, particularly where their own thoughts and attitudes are concerned. "Watch out" is what he says, for (as an immediate problem) they may be deceived and (as a result of that) they may well lose all they have worked for.

The nature of the deceit is suggested by the term translated "runs ahead" in verse 9. In Greek it is the word *proagōn,* from the two words "forward" and "to lead." The only truly idiomatic translation of the word in English is "progressive," but we must understand that the word is used both in irony and in one sense only. John is not saying, we must note, that there is never to be any form of progress in Christian circles. Clearly much of the Bible is written precisely to that end, and even this letter is written to encourage such progress. On the other hand, there is a type of "progress" which is not progress at all. It is movement which is actually a movement away from the basic truths of the faith and which is therefore devilishly detrimental. It is this against which John warns. Moreover, this is precisely the reason why he expresses the warning so strongly. For the movement presents itself as a great step forward and may, therefore, entrap the very people who most want to go ahead spiritually.

There is a true progress in the Christian life, but it is progress based upon a deeper knowledge of the historical, biblical Christ. Progress on any other ground may be called progress, but it is a progress that leaves God behind and is, therefore, not progress at all. This truth is extremely relevant to today's religious scene, for the danger today is in precisely this area. The danger is not so much in secularism, still less in communism or any other obviously anti-Christian system. The danger is in that which goes by the name of Christianity but which excludes the true Christ. It is in religion without the true God and that one mediator between God and man, even the God-man, Christ Jesus.

The second part of John's instructions to the local church reveals how strongly he feels about the danger. For here the Christians are not only warned; they are also instructed to have no part in encouraging either the false teachers or their false doctrines. In fact, says John, do not even greet them, for in so doing you may be sharing in their wicked work.

The very vehemence of this warning has caused some commentators to object, arguing that it is hardly necessary or right for a Christian to refuse even to speak to someone whom he regards as being a false teacher. Dodd, for instance, while he recognizes that the letter may be reflecting what can only be called an emergency situation within the church, nevertheless declines "to accept the Presbyter's ruling."[3] Barclay, who follows Dodd, argues that it is not satisfactory merely to refuse to have anything to do with false teachers. "We can never compromise with mistaken teachers, but we are never freed from the obligation of seeking to lead them into the truth." He adds, "Love must find a way."[4]

But this is not what John says. Here we are helped by a careful analysis of John's teaching.

First, we must note that John is not talking of all error but only of that which comes under the guise of Christianity. In other words, his expressions here cannot be used as the basis of a refusal to talk to non-Christians or to hold dialogue with adherents to another religion or philosophical system. Second, he is not even referring to all those who are in error within Christianity, but only to those who are teachers of such errors in the name of Christianity. All others should presumably be loved and instructed. Finally, he is not even referring to all teachers who err but only to those who are in error on the most fundamental truths and who are actively proclaiming their heresies. Obviously, there is no teacher who is 100 percent free of error. Yet we encourage them and learn from them. It is only when professing Christians teach the most anti-Christian doctrines that we are to deal so harshly.

It may even be, as Stott argues, that John's instructions "may well relate not only to an 'official' visit of false teachers but to the extending to them of an 'official' welcome, rather than merely private hospitality."[5] If at this point, however, the words still seem harsh, it can only be that John's concern for Christ and

---

[3]Dodd, *Johannine Epistles*, p. 152.
[4]Barclay, *Letters of John and Jude*, p. 169.
[5]Stott, *Epistles of John*, p. 213.

His glory is greater than ours and that our so-called tolerance is in reality just an indifference to truth and a misunderstanding of true love.

THE CONCLUSION (vv. 12, 13)

John has many more things which he could write. The first letter will give an idea of what some of them might be. But John has come to the end of his sheet of papyrus and will stop. Besides, it is not important, for he is hoping to visit his readers soon and so talk "face to face." In 1 Corinthians 13:12 Paul writes this phrase literally *(prosōpon pros prosōpon)*, but here the words are literally "mouth to mouth" *(stoma pros stoma)*. Today we might say "eyeball to eyeball." But whatever the phrase, the meaning is the same. It refers to a face-to-face encounter. Moreover, John states the relatively greater value of this as over against the mere writing of a letter. A letter is good, but it can be terribly misunderstood, particularly when hard things are being said. Far better is the personal visit and the personal word. As Barclay points out, there was a time when Oliver Cromwell greatly disliked John Fox, the Quaker. But then he met him and after a short while declared, "If you and I had but an hour together, we would be better friends."

The last words are a greeting from the members of the congregation where John is staying to their friends.

3 John 1-14
Imitating the Truth

The elder,

    To my dear friend Gaius, whom I love in the truth.

    Dear friend, I pray that you may enjoy good health and that all may go well with you, even as your soul is getting along well. It gave me great joy to have some brothers come and tell about your faithfulness to the truth and how you continue to walk in the truth. I have no greater joy than to hear that my children are walking in the truth.

    Dear friend, you are faithful in what you are doing for the brothers, even though they are strangers to you. They have told the church about your love. You will do well to send them on their way in a manner worthy of God. It was for the sake of the Name that they went out, receiving no help from the pagans. We ought therefore to show hospitality to such men so that we may work together for the truth.

    I wrote to the church, but Diotrephes, who loves to be first, will have nothing to do with us. So if I come, I will call attention to what he is doing, gossiping maliciously about us. Not satisfied with that, he refuses to welcome the brothers. He also stops those who want to do so and puts them out of the church.

    Dear friend, do not imitate what is evil but what is good. Anyone who does what is good is from God. Anyone who does what is evil has not seen God. Demetrius is well spoken of by everyone—and even by the truth itself. We also speak well of him, and you know that our testimony is true.

    I have much to write you, but I do not want to do so

with pen and ink. I hope to see you soon, and we will talk
face to face.
    Peace to you. The friends here send their greetings.
Greet the friends there by name.

Nothing is known of the Gaius to whom 3 John is written save
what the letter itself tells us. But this is no great loss, for all that
we need to know is apparent from the text. To be sure, the New
Testament knows of a number of other men named Gaius. There
is a Gaius of Macedonia, who together with Aristarchus was
seized by the rioting mob at Ephesus (Acts 19:29). There was a
Gaius who accompanied Paul on his last trip to Jerusalem and
who formed part of the group of delegates which presented the
offering from the gentile churches to the church in Judea (Acts
20:4). This Gaius was from Derbe and presumably represented
that church and possibly the other churches of Galatia. Finally,
there was the Gaius of Corinth in whose house Paul lived while
dictating the letter to the Romans (Rom. 16:23). But Gaius was a
common name, and there is no reason to identify any of these
persons with the Gaius of 3 John. According to 3 John, this Gaius
was simply a faithful and spiritual Christian leader in a local
church over which the apostle John had oversight.
    But troubles had come into this church and, in spite of a
letter sent by John to the chief offender, the problems had apparently grown worse. To begin with, a man named Diotrephes
had assumed an unwarranted and pernicious authority in the
church, so much so that by the time of the writing of this letter
John's own authority had been challenged and those who had
been sympathetic to John had been excommunicated from the
local assembly. Moreover, due to this struggle, traveling missionaries had been rudely treated, including probably an offical
delegation from John. Gaius had received such persons and is
here commended for it. Diotrephes had not and is rebuked. Diotrephes is also promised further chastisement when the apostle
comes to him, which he hopes to do shortly. Toward the end of
the letter a third personality is mentioned, Demetrius, whom the
apostle holds up as an example of one who does good and is
therefore clearly of God.
    The messages to or about these three personalities give a
straightforward outline to the book. There is: 1) the message to
Gaius, who is termed a fellowworker, 2) the message about Dio-

trephes, who is causing the problem, and 3) the message about Demetrius, who is designated an example to all.

Gaius: a Fellow Worker (vv. 1-8)

John's opening words to Gaius are nearly a conventional greeting. They give the author's name and the name of the recipient of the letter. They contain a wish for the recipient's good health and prosperity, the latter being so common that in Latin letters of the period an abbreviation was often used to convey it (SVBEEV, meaning, "Si vales, bene est; ego valeo"—"If you are well, it is good; I am well"). However, as in 2 John, these conventional forms are altered in significant ways in order to give distinctly Christian greetings. Most striking is the word "truth," for this is both unexpected and prominent. As in 2 John, the author combines it with love. Also striking is the way in which John wishes Gaius good health, adding (in effect) that he is not wishing him health of soul for the simple reason that he knows from reports of his actions that his soul is already prospering.

The truth of Gaius

Two characteristics of Gaius stand out, his truth and his love. John deals with each in turn. Gaius had obviously heard the truth of the Gospel and had received it wholeheartedly with the result that the truth was now in him and was causing him to pursue vigorously that way of life which the truth indicated. Moreover, this was not some hidden or secret thing. On the contrary, Gaius lived the truth in such an open way that he was observed by others who in turn reported the uprightness of his conduct and character to John. He was "a light" in this world, as Jesus had instructed His disciples to be. He had fulfilled the Lord's injunction, "Let your light shine before men, that they may see your good deeds and praise your Father in heaven" (Matt. 5:16).

Today many regard truth as nonessential, so long as good deeds are done. But John does not favor this view, nor does he regard it as possible. According to the apostle, good deeds flow from truth, just as love flows from it. For it is only as one walks according to the doctrines of the Word, which he has been taught, that truly righteous acts become possible. In this John preserves the same type of connection between truth and righteousness as he has already shown to exist between truth and love in the previous letter.

Moreover, it is as his children in the faith exhibit such conduct that John himself experiences the greatest joy. John's joy is that of a father who exults in the upright and productive life of a child whom he has reared well. There is no greater joy than this, John says. This emphasis upon joy is quite impressive, occurring, as it does, in a letter which reveals so much else to cause sorrow.

The love of Gaius

Gaius is not only noteworthy for his truth or uprightness of conduct, however (v. 3). He is also characterized by love, which he has demonstrated by his hospitality to traveling Christian teachers, particularly strangers (v. 5). In reference to this service the author does two things. First, he commends Gaius for the service he has already rendered. Second, he encourages him to continue such service in the days ahead. In connection with the last point John gives several reasons why such service is both right and necessary.

It is interesting that in commending Gaius for past acts of hospitality John commends him not for some special feeling of benevolence toward strangers but rather for a work faithfully done. The reason for this is that hospitality was a frequently repeated command of the apostles based upon the more general teaching on the same subject by the Lord Jesus Christ (cf. Matt. 25:34-36). Paul had written of the need to show hospitality many times. To both Timothy and Titus he had declared that a bishop must be "hospitable" (1 Tim. 3:2; Titus 1:8). He wrote that a widow was to be honored if, among other things, she would "practice hospitality" (Rom. 12:13). Peter said that we are to "offer hospitality to one another without grumbling" (1 Peter 4:9). The author of Hebrews declared, "Do not forget to entertain strangers, for by so doing some people have entertained angels without knowing it" (Heb. 13:2).[1] These injunctions were apparently known to Gaius, and he was careful to fulfill them. Consequently, he is said to have been faithful in the performance of this important duty.

But would this service continue? John gives no indication of

---

[1]There is an excellent discussion of the Christian obligation to show hospitality in Barclay, *Letters of John and Jude,* pp. 173, 174.

really doubting it. Still, as the next verses reveal, Diotrephes was apparently applying great pressure to stop such acts of charity, and a word of encouragement was appropriate. So John continues, "You will do well to send them on their way in a manner worthy of God. It was for the sake of the Name that they went out, receiving no help from the pagans. We ought therefore to show hospitality to such men so that we may work together for the truth" (vv. 6-8).

These verses give three reasons why the support of such persons is necessary. First, these are not mere visitors or even mere Christian visitors; they are God's servants. They went out for "the sake of the Name." They "work together for the truth." In other words, these are Christian missionaries and should be welcomed for the sake of the one they serve. "He who receives you receives me, and he who receives me receives the one who sent me" (Matt. 10:40). Second, these missionaries had determined to accept nothing from the heathen and, therefore, the burden for support by Christians was even greater. In the Greek text this contrast is quite sharp, for the word "pagans" which ends verse 7 is followed immediately by the word "we" in verse 8. The heathen will not support Christian work, nor should they. We, however, who are Christians, must do it. Finally, John argues that we should continue support because in doing so we "work together" with such persons. This last argument is a direct opposite to the warning against supporting false teachers in 2 John 10, 11.

Here is a great word for those who would like to be engaged in front-line Christian work but who cannot be, owing to ill health, circumstances, or other pressing obligations. In God's sight those are fellow workers who merely support others by their gifts, interest and prayers. Barclay writes, "A man's circumstances may be such that he cannot become a missionary or a preacher. Life may have put him in a position where he must get on with a secular job, and where he must stay in the one place, and carry out the routine duties of life and living. But where he cannot go his money and his prayers and his practical support can go; and, if he gives that support, he has made himself an ally of the truth. It is not everyone who can be, so to speak, in the front line; but every man by supporting those who are in the front line can make himself an ally of the truth.''[2] Moreover, all should be allies, for all Christians should be fellow workers with all other Christians in the great task of disseminating the life-transforming truth of the Christian gospel.

DIOTREPHES: A MAJOR PROBLEM (vv. 9, 10)

Christians are frequently and rightly distressed at the enormous problems that seem to exist within the visible church. But there is some comfort in the fact that this has always been so, even in the church of the apostolic period. The next section of 3 John is a case in point. John has written of Gaius who, we are told, has been obedient to the truth as taught by the apostle, has entertained strangers, and has shown love and in turn been loved by all the brethren. But no sooner has John written of Gaius than the letter turns to a discussion of Diotrephes, who was apparently a contrast to Gaius at every point. Gaius had walked in the truth, but Diotrephes would not acknowledge John's authority. Gaius had entertained strangers; Diotrephes not only failed to entertain them but had even forbidden others to do so. Gaius loved the brethren; Diotrephes was attempting to lord it over them.

The problem

In referring to Diotrephes John lists four areas in which the conduct of this man was out of line.

First, John says that Diotrephes "will have nothing to do with us" (v. 9). This is a general statement, of course, and may be applied broadly. But it is also likely that it has a specific reference to the letter that John says he sent to the church earlier. Some have imagined that this was our 1 or 2 John, but there is no real reason to think so. In fact, it is actually unlikely, for neither gives the kind of instruction that Diotrephes is likely to have rejected. Apparently this last letter dealt with local problems, perhaps the reception of traveling teachers with which 3 John also deals. But Diotrephes had rejected the counsel, refused to receive the messengers who carried it, and may even have destroyed the letter. This rejection of the apostolic authority was wrong and unwarranted, but it is not rare. It is only an early example of the same rejection seen in those who today prefer the

---

[2]Barclay, *Letters of John and Jude*, pp. 175, 176.

opinions of the latest theologian or popular religious writer to the binding authority of the inerrant Word of God.

Second, John says that Diotrephes was "gossiping maliciously" (v. 10). That is, not content with a rejection of John's authority, Diotrephes went on to justify his rebellion by explaining falsely why the counsels of John should not be followed. The Greek verb which is here translated "gossiping" comes from a root which was used of the action of water in boiling up and throwing off bubbles. Since bubbles are empty and useless, the verb eventually came to mean indulgence in empty or useless talk. This was the nature of Diotrephes' slander, though, of course, the words were no less evil in that they were groundless.

Third, Diotrephes is said to have specifically defied John in regard to the duty to receive traveling missionaries. John says that "he refuses to welcome the brothers" (v. 10). This was uncharitable, the kind of action that one might expect from one "who loves to be first." But in addition to this, it was also a direct rejection of the unanimous instruction of the apostolic band.

Fourth, Diotrephes is also said to have insisted that others in the church follow his lead rather than that of the apostle and also to have exercised an unwarranted discipline over those who disobeyed him. He put them "out of the church" (v. 10). Diotrephes excommunicated loyal believers because they failed to side with him in his rejection of John's authority.

A problem of this magnitude has led many commentators to speculate on what great issues might lie behind it, and some have suggested a monumental struggle between two contrasting types of authority and leadership in the early church age. On the one hand, there is the apostolic authority, which by the death of the apostles was passing. Dodd thinks that the author of 3 John, being in his view a disciple of the apostle John, was attempting to carry it over into the second generation. On the other hand, there is the new and emerging order of the monarchical episcopate, which indeed came to be the prevailing pattern of authority in the next century. If this is the case, 3 John could be a record of one part of this struggle as it occurred in one area of Asia between two strong personalities. This may be true in part. At least it may be the background against which the general problem of the letter may be understood. But having said this, it must also be said that this is not the explanation of Diotrephes' conduct that the book itself communicates. We may grant that there was a struggle for power over the affairs of the local church. But John attributes this, not to a difference of opinion about who should have the final word, but to obvious sin; for John argues that the struggle came about because Diotrephes "loves to be first."

This is the original and greatest of all sins. It is the sin of Satan, who was unwilling to be what God had created him to be and who desired rather to be "like the Most High" (Isa. 14:14). It is the opposite of the nature of Christ "who, being in very nature God, did not consider equality with God something to be grasped, but made himself nothing, taking the very nature of a servant, being made in human likeness. And being found in appearance as a man, he humbled himself and became obedient to death—even death on a cross" (Phil. 2:6-8). For Satan's attempt to exalt himself, that one shall be made low (Isa. 14:15). For His humility and obedience, God "exalted [Christ] to the highest place and gave him the name that is above every name" (Phil. 2:9). It is Christ rather than Satan or his followers who is to be our example.

The solution

One might think that because of the abominable conduct of Diotrephes John might well have threatened him with excommunication, since he had excommunicated others. But significantly John does not say this. He says only that when he comes he will "call attention to what he is doing." That is, he will expose Diotrephes. No doubt, John has in mind to exercise some form of remedial discipline if such becomes necessary. But John does not threaten. Nor does he indicate that a severe penalty, such as excommunication, would be desirable. It may be that in this attitude he most shows his truly legitimate authority and reveals the character of Christ who desires, not that sinners be condemned, but that they come to repentance.

On the other hand, Diotrephes should take no comfort from John's restrained tone, for the time is coming when he will be faced with his arrogance and evil deeds, and will have to give an account of them. So will all Christ's servants when the Lord Himself, and not merely His apostle, returns. Paul wrote, "So then, each of us will give an account of himself to God" (Rom. 14:12). The Christian is therefore to build his life according to God's

213

pattern so that he or she will stand approved in that day. Paul also wrote that each man's "work will be shown for what it is, because the Day will bring it to light. . . . If what he has built survives, he will receive his reward. If it is burned up, he will suffer loss; he himself will be saved, but only as one escaping through the flames" (1 Cor. 3:13-15).

DEMETRIUS: A FINE EXAMPLE (vv. 11, 12)

In verse 11 we have what seems to be a general exhortation to do good and not evil. Bruce sets it apart as a separate section of the letter. But in the context of the letter the evil example is most obviously Diotrephes, and the good example, Demetrius. Consequently, the exhortation leads directly into what follows. The personal nature of the maxim is conveyed by the word "imitate."

The Greek word for "imitate" is *mimeomai,* which is always translated "follow" in the KJV. It occurs four times in the New Testament. It is closely related to the word *mimētēs* ("follower"), which occurs seven times. Once, in Ephesians 5:1, Christians are encouraged to be imitators of God. On another occasion, 1 Peter 3:13, they are encouraged to be imitators of that which is good. But apart from these two instances, the examples in each case are human. Thus, Paul speaks three times of the need of Christians to imitate "us," that is, the apostles (1 Thess. 1:6; 2 Thess. 3:7, 9). Twice he says "me" (1 Cor. 4:16; 11:1). Once he speaks of being "imitators of God's churches in Judea, which are in Christ Jesus" (1 Thess. 2:14). The author of Hebrews twice speaks of imitating those whose lives are characterized by faith (Heb. 6:12; 13:7). These tests convey a great lesson, for this is as much as to say that men and women will always imitate other men and women, and that this is all right. However, Christian people must be careful who it is they imitate. Even in Christian circles there are bad examples, like Diotrephes; and there are good examples, like Demetrius. So choose your example carefully, John seems to be saying. Moreover, he gives the reason. For in attempting to imitate the good we indicate that we are of God, just as by imitating the bad those who do so indicate that they are not God's children.

John is not calling Gaius to imitate himself, however. There is an example closer at hand: Demetrius. We do not know anything about this Demetrius save what is told us in verse 12. He may have been the bearer of the letter. He may have been another member of the local church to which John is writing. All we know is that Gaius was acquainted with him and that he was highly commended by everyone, by the truth itself, and by the apostle. Demetrius may not have had the prestige and authority of Diotrephes. He apparently did not. But Demetrius is important nonetheless; for it is he, rather than Diotrephes, who should be imitated.

Thus it is that the first are made last and the last first (Matt. 19:30). Thus are the humble exalted and the mighty made low (Luke 1:52). Thus has God chosen "the foolish things of the world to shame the wise." He has chosen "the lowly things of this world and the despised things—and the things that are not—to nullify the things that are, so that no one may boast before him" (1 Cor. 1:27-29).

CONCLUSION (vv. 13-15)

The conclusion to 3 John is similar to the verses which end 2 John, except that the author appends a far more personal greeting. "Peace to you. The friends here send their greetings. Greet the friends there by name." The greeting "peace to you" was adopted by Christians from Hebrew usage, though it was infused with new meaning by Jesus following His resurrection (John 20:19, 21, 26). It is strikingly appropriate at the close of a letter dealing with much strife and bitterness. Strife often bedevils the church. But in the midst of it there can always be that peace of the Lord Jesus Christ which passes all human understanding.

Bibliography

Alexander, Neil, *The Epistles of St. John,* Torch Bible Commentaries (London: S.C.M. Press, 1962).

Barclay, William, *The Letters of John and Jude* (Philadelphia: Westminster Press, 1958).

Brooke, A. E., *A Critical and Exegetical Commentary on the Johannine Epistles,* "The International Critical Commentary" (London: T. & T. Clark, 1912).

Bruce, F. F., *The Epistles of John* (Old Tappan, N.J.: Fleming H. Revell, 1970).

Burdick, Donald W., *The Epistles of John,* "Everyman's Bible Commentary" (Chicago: Moody Press, 1970).

Calvin, John, *The Gospel According to St. John 11-21 and The First Epistle of John,* translated by T. H. L. Parker (Grand Rapids: Eerdmans, 1961).

Candlish, Robert S., *A Commentary on 1 John* (Carlisle, Pa.: Banner of Truth Trust, 1973).

Dodd, C. H., *The Johannine Epistles* (London: Hodder and Stoughton, 1946).

Henry, Matthew, *Matthew Henry's Commentary on the Whole Bible, Vol. VI—Acts to Revelation* (Old Tappan, N.J.: Fleming H. Revell, n.d.).

Ironside, H. A., *Addresses on the Epistles of John* (Neptune, N.J.: Loizeaux Brothers, 1931).

Law, Robert, *The Tests of Life* (Grand Rapids: Baker, 1968).

Plummer, A., *The Epistles of S. John,* "Cambridge Bible for

Bibliography

Schools and Colleges" (New York: Cambridge University Press, 1954).

Ross, Alexander, *The Epistles of James and John,* "The New International Commentary on the New Testament" (Grand Rapids: Eerdmans, 1954).

Stott, John R. W., *The Epistles of John,* "Tyndale New Testament Commentaries" (Grand Rapids: Eerdmans, 1964).

Westcott, Brooke Foss, *The Epistles of John* (Grand Rapids: Eerdmans, 1960).

Wilder, Amos N. (Introduction and Exegesis), and Hoon, Paul W. (Exposition), *The First, Second, and Third Epistles of John* "The Interpreter's Bible" (Nashville: Abingdon Press, 1957).

Listed below are those Bible translations specifically referred to in this study:

KJV. The King James Version, 1611.
NASB. New American Standard Bible, 1960-71.
NEB. The New English Bible, 1970.
NIV. The New International Version, 1978.
RSV. The Revised Standard Version, 1952, 1972.

Subject Index

219

Subject Index

Christianity, an historical faith, 15-17; apostolic, 183; defined, 23-32; essence of, 24-26; evidences for, 26-29; heart of, 181; message of, 33-42

Christians, what they are, 98, 99; what they shall be, 99-101

Christ Jesus, advocate, our, 46, 47, 50; atoning sacrifice, the, 48-52; body of, 86; deity of, 183; example of, 116-118; gifts of, 182, 183; High Priest, our, 109; historical, the, 19, 20; message of, 33-42; resurrection of, 147, 148; return of, 95-98, 147; righteous, 47, 48; sacrifice of, 142; work of, 46-52, 106, 107

Christ of faith, 89

Christ of history, 101

Church, and the world, 70-81, 136, 137; visible and invisible, 86, 87

Churches of Asia Minor, 158

Commandment, new, 17-19, 64, 159

Commands, 201

Commitment, 29

Confession, 145

Confidence, 13, 59, 147, 148; before God, 126-128; in prayer, 169-171

Confusion, 14

Conscience, evil, 125

Council, Jerusalem, the, 156

Covetousness, 79

Cromwell, Oliver, 205

Cross, of Christ, 117

Crucifixion, the, 16, 148, 162, 163

Cullmann, Oscar, 163

Danger, 202-205

Daniel, 84

Darkness, 66-68, 100; none in God, 36, 37

Day of Atonement, 49, 50, 52

Death, 49; of Christ, 142, 163, 182, 183; punishment by physical, 175; sin's consequence, 104; spiritual, 141

Deceit, 203

Deceivers, 202

Defiance, 212

Demetrius, 187, 207, 214, 215

Demythologizing, 29

Derbe, 207

Devil, 106, 111, 132, 133, 150, 179; see Satan

Didache, 185, 186

Dionysius of Alexandria, 190

Diotrephes, 186, 194, 207, 210-215

Discipleship, active, personal and costly, 60, 61

Discipline, 213

Docetism, 135

Doctrine, 139, 144-146

Dodd, C. H., 48, 61, 62, 72, 95, 101, 104, 126, 127, 135, 136, 146, 154, 155, 171, 193, 204

Doubt, 54, 121-129

Elder, the, 187-192

Elisha, and his servant, 136, 137

Emotional experience, knowledge of God through, 56

Ephesus, 188, 190, 191, 207

Episcopate, monarchial, 212

Erasmus of Rotterdam, 161; and Luther, 177, 178

Error, and truth, 130-137

Esau, 173

Essence of Christianity, 24-26

Eternal life, 166, 167, 182

Eusebius, 16, 188-190

Evidences for Christianity, objective, 26-29; subjective, 29

Excommunication, 212

Eyewitnesses, 30

Faith, 106, 157, 158; and love, 128; historical groundings of, 159; or life, 153; see Belief

Faithfulness, 158; in small things, 195

False prophets, 132-134

False teachers, 186, 203, 204

False teaching, 194

Family, Christian, the, 154, 155

Fatherhood of God, 94

Fathers, spiritual, 74, 75

Fear, 148

Fellowship, 30, 31, 150, 157; with God and man, 38

First John, purpose of, 11-21

"Flesh," the, 79

Forgiveness, 69; assurance of, 44-46; basis for 40, 41; in advance, 46

Fox, John, 205

Free will, God's, 116

Freudian psychology, 39

Gaius, 186, 187, 207-211, 214, 215; fellow worker, a, 208-211; hospitality of, 209, 210; love of, 209-211; truth of, 208, 209

Galatia, 207

Gift, of God, 141-143

Gifts, of Jesus, 182, 183; of the Holy Spirit, 145, 146

220

Subject Index

Gnostics, the, 15, 16, 24, 26, 29, 37, 38, 40, 43, 55, 59, 67, 84, 86, 89, 91, 105, 108, 110, 111, 135, 136, 158, 164, 173, 174, 181, 182; challenge of the, 134; errors of the, 88, 89; heresies of the, 145

Gnosticism, 15, 16

God the Father, abides forever, 80; children of, 87, 88, 94-101, 153, 154, 180, 181; faithful and just, 40; fatherhood of, 94; gift of, 141-143; knowledge of, 182; light, 34; love, 140, 141; love of, 98-101; "Most High," the, 213; nature of, 33-35, 140, 141; present activity of, 143, 144; promise of, 44-46; testimony of, 159-167; verdict of, 124, 125; will of, 170, 171

Gospel, the old, 19

Gossip, 212

Grace, 199

Graveclothes, Jesus', 27, 28

Greed, 185

Greetings, Christian, 198

Hate, and darkness, 67; and love, 112-120

Hearing Jesus, 26

Heart, condemning, 122-125

Heaven, 31

Hellenism, 56

Henry, Matthew, 72, 115

Heresy, 93, 194; chief, 88-90; defense against, 90-92

Historical Christ, 89, 101

Holiness, call to, 43-53; movement, 108

Holy of Holies, the, 49

Holy Spirit, the, 18, 91, 92, 96, 131, 132, 164; blasphemy against, 174, 175; gift of, 144, 145; gifts of, 145, 146; internal witness of, 166; internal work of, 146; water and the blood, 162-164; witness of, 128, 129

Hospitality, 185; of Gaius, 209, 210

Hour, Christ's, 148

Humble, the, 215

Hymns, "Arise, my soul, arise," 50; "Draw and win and fill completely," 184; "Long my imprisoned spirit lay," 42

Hypocrisy, 59

Idols, 183

Illustrations, adultery, 81; "a great sinner," 42; Christian witness at a music camp, 130, 131; physical birth, 99, 153, 154; priest and the new morality, 59; "something to keep a man straight," 44-46

Imitation, 214

Immorality, 9

Incarnation, the, 29, 135, 137, 150; denied by Gnosticism, 16

Isaiah, 12, 40

James, 154, 188, 189

Jehoshaphat, 133

Jeremiah, 40, 57, 133

Jesus Christ; see Christ Jesus

Jews, 111

Job, story of, 179, 180

John the apostle, 27, 28, 191, 192; conversion of, 27, 28

John the Baptist, 31, 36

John the elder, 187-191

John, Gospel of, its purpose, 12

John, 1, introduction to, 11-22

John, 2 and 3, introduction to, 185-196

John's readers, 72-76; appeal to, 76-80

Joy, 31, 32, 54, 200, 201; John's, 209

Jude, 185

Judgment, 147, 148

Kewsick, 184

Knowledge, 55-58, 88, 129, 167; cure for doubt, 122; of God, 9, 182; of salvation, 12

Knox, John, 19

Lady, the chosen, 198, 199

Last Supper, the, 17, 18

Latham, Henry, 28

Law, of God, 104; of love, 64-66

Lawlessness, 104; man of, 85

Law, Robert, 50, 55, 71, 72, 78, 107, 140

Legalism, 10

Lewis, C. S., 117

Lie, the, 89

Life, abundant, 175; eternal, 166, 167, 182; ethical, the, 20; of love, 66-68; within, 201, 202

"Limited atonement," 51

Lord's Prayer, the, 69

Lord's return, the, 95-98

Lord's Supper, the, 163

Love, 9, 10, 15, 154, 155; and hate, 112-120; and light, 67; and sound doctrine, 144-146; costly, 69; exhortation to, 138-150; for others, 118-120; in action, 124; lack of, 150; law of, 64-66; life of, 66-68; need for, 20, 21, 139; new commandment, a, 65, 66; not the world, 76-80; of Gaius, 209-211; of God the

221

Subject Index

Father, 98-101; of self, 157; of the brethren, 148-150; old commandment, an, 64, 65; perfection of, 146-150; reasons to, 140-144; social test, the, 63-69; types of, 149

Luther, Martin, 161; and Erasmus, 177, 178

Man born blind, 182
Man, brotherhood of, 94
Man of lawlessness, 85
Marcion, 89
Mark of the Christian, 20, 63
Mary Magdalene, 27
Mary of Bethany, 69
Materialism, 78
Matthew, 188, 189
Men, two types of, 58-60
Menninger, Karl, 39
Mercy, 199
Message, of 2 John, 200-205; of 2 and 3 John, 193-195
Messiah, the, 88
Micaiah, 133
Missionaries, 185; hospitality to, 210
Monotheism, 135
Moral test, the, 54-62
Morris, Leon, 50
Moslems, 111
Muggeridge, Malcolm, 24
Mystery religions, 56
Mysticism, 101

Nature, of God, 140, 141; old and new, the, 108
Negations, 36
New birth, the, 99, 110, 111, 116, 152
New Christians, 73, 74
New Commandment; see Commandment, the new
New morality, the, 10

Obedience, 127, 155-157; flowing from love, 59, 60
Original sin, 115
Orthodoxy, bitter, 10, 93
Outline, of 1 John, 21; of 2 and 3 John, 195, 196

Papias, 188-191
Passover, 49
Paul, Saint, 12, 97
Peace, 199, 215
People, of the land, 165
Perfection, of love, 146-150

Perseverance, 86, 184
Personality conflicts, 194
Pesachim, 165
Peter, the apostle, 18, 27, 28, 61, 96, 97, 154, 156, 188, 189, 209; denial of Jesus, his, 175, 176
Pharisees, 156, 174
Philemon, 185
Philip, 36, 182, 188, 189
Pirke Aboth, 47
Plato, 56
Pleasing God, 127, 128
Plummer, A., 12, 67, 160, 193
Polycarp, 190
Polycrates, 190
Prayer, 168-176; answered, 127, 128; confidence in, 169-171; for others, 171-176; intercessory, 171-176; problems with, 168
Presbyter, the, 187
Presbyterians, 152
Presumption, 125, 167, 180; challenged, 15
Priscillian, 160
Problems, 193, 194
Proclamation, 30; the Christian, 29, 30
Profession, 111; without obedience, 58, 59
Progress, Christian, 203
Promises, regarding prayer, 169-172
Propaganda, heretical, 202
Prophet, pseudo, a, 85; test of a true, 134-136
Prophets, true and false, 132-134
Propitiation, 48-52, 77, 106
Pseudoprophet, 85
Purification, 163
Purity, 35

Qualifications, regarding prayer, 170-176

Readers of 1 John, 72-76
Reason, knowledge of God through, 56
Rebellion, 105, 106
Redemption, 17
Reformation, 161, 177
Reformation theologians, 107
Reformers, 166
Religion, without God, 203
Renaissance, 161
Responsibility, 92; Christian, 194; in prayer, 171
Resurrection, 147, 148
Revelation, 20; divine, 166
Righteousness, 9, 10, 57, 97; and sin, 102-111; and the Lord's return, 95-98; ap-

222

Scripture Index

224

Scripture Index

Scripture Index

226